Philip Kerr

Straightforward

Pre-intermediate Student's Book

MACMILLAN

		Reading & Listening	Speaking	Writing (in the Workbook)
1A	**R**	*Mother love*	Talking about your family & friends	A personal message for a website
	L	A description of a typical English family	Describing a typical family in your country	
1B	**L**	A dialogue about an old photo	Discussing friendship	
			Communication activity: Facebook™	
			Did you know? Facebook™ website	
1C	**R**	*Who would you like as a neighbour?*	Talking about your neighbours	
			Ranking famous people as good/bad neighbours	
1D	**R**	Newspaper advertisements	Talking about different ways of making contact	
	L	Four phone messages	Roleplay: phone messages	
2A	**L**	Three people talk about their school days	Talking about your school days	A story 1
			Describing a favourite teacher	
2B	**R**	*Schools in Europe: The Republic of Ireland*	Talking about schools in your town	
			Comparing schools now & in the past	
2C	**R**	Web page: an internet discussion group	Discussing embarrassing situations	
			Discussing ways parents & children can embarrass each other	
2D	**L**	Asking for information in a language school	Choosing a language school	
			Roleplay: asking for information	
			Did you know? The English language	
3A	**L**	A dialogue between two friends about where they live	Roleplay: solving problems in a shared flat	A description of your town
3B	**R**	*Scotland: the people*	Discussing emigration	
			Did you know? The United Kingdom	
3C	**R**	Web page: *www.livinginmontreal.com*	Describing & comparing towns	
3D	**L**	Asking for directions in Newcastle	Comparing Newcastle to towns in your country	
			Roleplay: directions	
4A	**R**	A relationship style quiz	Discussing relationship styles	An email to a friend
			Discussing quotes about love	
4B	**R**	*If you ask me ...*	Describing a wedding	
			Did you know? Wedding traditions	
4C	**L**	A description of a film (*The Holiday*)	Inventing a film dialogue	
			Communication activity: retelling film stories	
4D	**L**	Two phone calls: arranging to go out	Describing an imaginary evening out with a famous person	
			Discussing the social life of different age groups in your country	
5A	**R**	*The ruins of Machu Picchu*	Talking about tourism in your country	An email to arrange a trip
			Planning improvements in your town for tourists	
5B	**L**	A radio programme about the worst hotel in Britain	Describing the best/worst hotel you have stayed in	
			Did you know? Las Vegas hotels	
5C	**R**	Web page: *www.heavenholidays.com*	Planning a trip for visitors around your country	
5D	**L**	Three dialogues at the airport	Describing a journey	
			Roleplay: on a plane	
6A	**R**	*Eating the Elvis Presley way*	Planning a 'theme' restaurant	A review of a restaurant
6B	**R**	Quiz: *Are you a foodie?*	Discussing a quiz	
	L	An interview about 'slow food'		
6C	**R**	*Coffee break*	Talking about your favourite drinks	
			Did you know? Starbucks™	
6D	**L**	Making a restaurant reservation	Talking about restaurants in your town	
	L	A dialogue in a restaurant	Roleplay: in a restaurant	

	Reading & Listening	Speaking	Writing (in the Workbook)
7A	**L** A radio programme about people who have met celebrities	Describing & guessing jobs	A letter of application
7B	**R** *Life on the other side*	Talking about your experiences of work Describing an imaginary life ***Did you know?*** Salaries in the UK	
7C	**R** An article about horoscopes & work **R** Horoscopes	Deciding what qualities are needed for different jobs	
7D	**L** An interview in a recruitment agency	Talking about finding a job in your town Roleplay: careers advice	
8A	**R** A conference programme	Talking about science fiction films Giving a thirty-second talk	A note giving instructions
8B	**L** A description of *Star Quest*, a TV game show	Deciding who is the best candidate for *Star Quest*	
8C	**L** Descriptions of gadgets **R** *A great idea?*	Discussing & choosing gadgets on a website	
8D	**L** A dialogue about how to send an email	Talking about how you use computers ***Did you know?*** Computer games in the US	
9A	**L** A radio programme about entertainment in London	Talking about entertainment in London & your town ***Did you know?*** Leisure activities in the UK	A review of a film
9B	**R** *Reality TV – love it or leave it*	Planning a reality TV show	
9C	**R** *Oscars® night*	Talking about going to the cinema Acting a scene from *Avatar*	
9D	**L** Four people buy tickets on the phone	Roleplay: at the box office Describing a concert	
10A	**R** *The United States of animals*	Talking about pets & animals Communication activity: guessing animals	A story 2
10B	**R** An article about stress	Discussing stressful jobs Ranking stressful experiences	
10C	**L** A news report about the marathon runners, Ranulph Fiennes & Mike Stroud	Talking about how fit you are ***Did you know?*** Sport in Australia	
10D	**L** Two doctors' appointments	Roleplay: at the doctor's	
11A	**L** Two people talk about things they wanted when they were younger	Describing a favourite possession Communication activity: describing & guessing objects	A description of a favourite possession
11B	**R** *Office worker flip flops out of a job*	Discussing clothes & appearance	
11C	**R** *Home comforts*	Giving a presentation on shopping in your town ***Did you know?*** Shopping in London	
11D	**L** Dialogues in a clothes shop	Roleplay: in a clothes shop	
12A	**L** A news report about the American adventurer, Steve Fossett	Discussing famous explorers Planning a 'round the world' trip	An opinion composition
12B	**R** An email describing Trinidad carnival	Talking about festivals Describing a festival	
12C	**R** *English as an International Language – no problem, OK?*	Talking about the English language in your country	
12D	**L** Three dialogues at a party	Discussing global issues ***Did you know?*** Oxfam	

1A | Family life

Vocabulary & speaking: family & friends

1 Match the words in the box to the definitions.

aunt	best friend	classmate	
colleague	cousin	daughter	
grandfather	mother-in-law	pet	
~~neighbour~~	nephew	niece	
roommate	son	son-in-law	uncle

1 *neighbour*

1 a person who lives very near you
2 a person you work with
3 an animal that lives with the family
4 your male child
5 your aunt's (or your uncle's) child
6 your brother's (or your sister's) daughter
7 your closest friend
8 your daughter's husband
9 your mother's (or your father's) sister

2 Work in pairs. Write definitions for the other words in the box.

3 Think of four people who are important to you. Then, work in pairs. Tell your partner as much as possible about these people.

Tara is my niece. She is nineteen years old and she studies at university …

Reading

1 Read the article about two families. Match the photos A–D to the stories.

2 Read the article again and answer the questions.

1 Where was Vera born?
2 Where is her husband from?
3 What's her son's name?
4 Where is the Shona family's new home?
5 How many children are there in Judy's family?
6 What is the family home when they travel?
7 What is the youngest child's name?
8 Where was the family's first show?

Mother LOVE

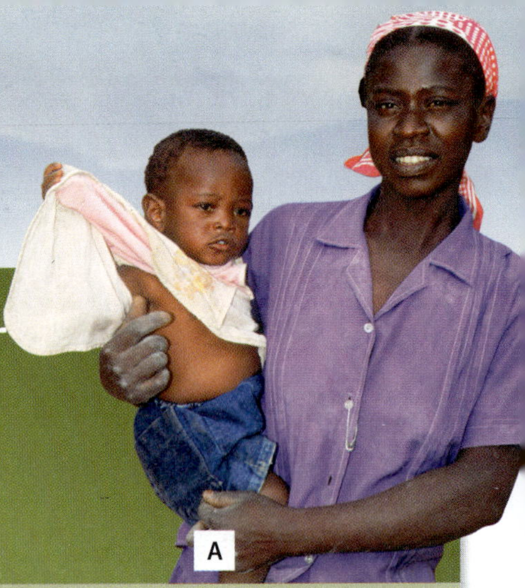
A

Vera Shona

Vera was born in Clapham, south London. Her parents were both originally from Zimbabwe, but came to England to work. After school, Vera studied nursing at South Bank University. At university, she met her future husband, Farai, who was born in Zimbabwe and who was also a nurse. The couple got married and two years later, they had a baby boy, Moyo. They then decided to go and live in Zimbabwe. 'Both Farai and I wanted to go back to our roots,' said Vera. They found jobs with a medical charity and left London to begin their new life in a small village in the north of the country. Vera and Farai run a health centre, but it is the only building in the village with electricity. Vera's son travels to a neighbouring village to go to school.

Judy Boehmer

Judy had her first child, Adam, 27 years ago. She now has four sons and seven daughters and a pet dog, Bosco, but she wants more boys. Judy and her husband, Larry, live in Atlanta, Georgia, but they also have a 10-metre-long motor home. The family sometimes travels more than 40,000 kilometres a year for their work. The children do not go to school, but they study at home with their parents.

The Boehmers are a circus family and all the children take part in the show. They do different kinds of juggling and Margaret, the youngest, stands on one leg in her mother's hand. The first show of the Boehmer Family Jugglers was at a theme park in Iowa, and they now perform all over America.

B

Glossary
juggle *vb* keep objects moving through the air by catching them and throwing them back in the air
roots *n* the place where you come from originally

3 Close your book. How much can you remember about the two families?

4 Do you think that the life of these two families is good for the children? Why or why not?

GRAMMAR: questions with *to be*

We make questions with the verb *to be* by putting the verb before the subject.

Yes/No questions

Is she *married?*
Were you *at school yesterday?*

Short answers

We can answer *yes/no* questions with short answers.

Yes, I am.	*No, I'm not.*
Yes, she is.	*No, she isn't.*
Yes, he was.	*No, he wasn't.*
Yes, they were.	*No, they weren't.*

Wh- questions

We can put question words before the verb.

Where were *you born?*
What is *her daughter's name?*

SEE LANGUAGE REFERENCE PAGE 14

C

D

1 Match the questions in column A with the short answers in column B.

A		B	
1	Are you married?	a	Yes, I was.
2	Is your family very large?	b	Yes, it is.
3	Were you born in this town?	c	Yes, there are.
4	Is your father a good cook?	d	No, I'm not.
5	Are your parents from this town?	e	No, he isn't.
6	Are there many people with the same name as you?	f	No, they aren't.

2 Change the answers to the questions in exercise 1 so that they are true for you.

3 Rearrange the words to make questions.

1 How many people are there in your family?

1 are family how in many people there your ?
2 are names their what ?
3 are how old they ?
4 are hobbies their what ?
5 born parents were where your ?
6 family in is person the who youngest your ?
7 family holiday last was when your ?

4 Work in pairs. Ask and answer the questions in exercise 3.

SPEAKING

1 1.1 Listen to a description of a typical English family. Put the topics in the order that you hear them.

☐ **Children**
How many children are there? What are their names? How old are they? What are their hobbies?

☐ **Family pet**
Is there a family pet? What is it? What is it called?

☐ **Food**
When does the family eat together? What is their favourite food?

☐ **Weekends and holidays**
What does the family do at the weekend? What do they do in the holidays?

1 **Parents**
What are the parents' names? How old are they? What are their jobs? What are their interests?

☐ **TV**
What are the family's favourite TV programmes?

2 Work in pairs. Think about a typical family in your country. Make notes using the questions in exercise 1.

3 Work in groups. Describe your typical family to each other.

1B | Where are they now?

SPEAKING

'A true friend is the best possession in the world.'

1 Translate the proverb above into your language. Are there any similar proverbs in your language?

2 Work in pairs. How many different ways can you complete the sentence below?

A true friend ...
always listens to you.
makes you laugh.
knows you well.

VOCABULARY: verb collocations (friendship)

1 Put the text in the correct order.

- ☐ each other very often, but we **keep**
- ☐ good friends. We come from similar
- ☐ David is one of my oldest
- ☐ backgrounds and we **have** a lot
- ☐ friends. We were at college together. We didn't **get**
- ☐ in common. He lives in Spain now, so we don't **see**
- ☐ in touch by phone and email.
- ☐ on well at first, but later we became

2 1.2 Listen to the recording to check your answers.

3 Complete the questions with a word in **bold** from exercise 1.

1 What sort of people do you ________ on well with?
2 How often do you and your best friend ________ each other?
3 Do you ________ a lot in common with your best friend? What?
4 How do you ________ in touch with friends in other towns or countries?

4 Work in pairs. Ask and answer the questions in exercise 3.

LISTENING

1 Work in pairs. Look at the photo. Choose one of the people in the photo and describe her/him to your partner. Your partner must decide who you are describing.

2 You are going to listen to a woman, Christine, talking to her husband about the photo. Before you listen, read the sentences and decide if they are true (T) or false (F).

1 The two girls on the left are sisters.
2 The girl with red shoes (Christine) was fourteen years old.
3 The photo was taken in 1973.
4 The boy with the guitar (Nicholas) was Christine's boyfriend.
5 Christine is now married to Nicholas.
6 The girl with blonde hair (Helga) was in love with Nicholas.
7 Helga was Christine's best friend.

3 1.3 Listen to the dialogue to check your answers. Correct the false sentences.

GRAMMAR: questions with auxiliary verbs

Present simple & past simple

We make questions in the present simple and past simple with an auxiliary verb (*do/does/did*) and the infinitive. We put the auxiliary verb before the subject and we put the infinitive after the subject.

question word	auxiliary	subject	infinitive
Where	do	you	live?
What	does	he	want?
When	did	they	arrive?

Other forms

All other verb forms (for example, present continuous, *can, will*) already have an auxiliary verb and a main verb. We put the auxiliary verb before the subject and we put the main verb after the subject.

question word	auxiliary	subject	infinitive
What	are	you	doing?
Where	can	we	meet?
When	will	we	know?

SEE LANGUAGE REFERENCE PAGE 14

1 Complete the questions with an auxiliary verb from the box.

does (x2)   did   is   was

1 What ______ your best friend's name?
2 Where ______ she/he live?
3 What ______ she/he do?
4 Where and when ______ you first meet?
5 When ______ the last time you met?

2 Work in pairs. Ask and answer the questions in exercise 1.

3 Look at the text below. Some of the text is missing. Prepare questions to ask about the missing information.

Christine Smith left school in 1976. She studied (1) ______ (*What?*) at Leeds University and then got a job (2) ______ (*Where?*). When she was in America, she met (3) ______ (*Who?*) at a party at the White House. He worked for (4) ______ (*Who?*). They started going out together and they got married (5) ______ (*When?*). They now have (6) ______ (*How many?*) children. Christine and her husband now live (7) ______ (*Where?*). She works for (8) ______ (*Who?*) and he is writing (9) ______ (*What?*). Christine wants to get in touch with (10) ______ (*Who?*) and promises to reply to all emails.

4 Work in pairs, A and B.

A: Turn to page 129. B: Turn to page 127.

Ask and answer the questions in exercise 3 to complete the missing information.

PRONUNCIATION: contractions 1

1 1.4 Listen to these contractions.

do not → don't
did not → didn't
what is → what's

2 Make contractions from these words.

1 does not 3 that is 5 were not
2 he has 4 was not 6 who is

3 1.5 Listen to the contractions and repeat.

SPEAKING

1 Correct the grammatical mistakes in the questions.

1 Who you did read about?
2 Is she/he be married?
3 How old she/he is?
4 How many children does she/he has?
5 Where she/he is living now?
6 What do she/he do?

2 Work in groups of four, A–D. You are going to read about the people in Christine's photo.

A: Turn to page 126. C: Turn to page 129.
B: Turn to page 127. D: Turn to page 131.

Use the questions in exercise 1 to find out about Christine's old friends. Who do you think Christine will get in touch with first?

DID YOU KNOW?

1 Work in pairs. Read the information about a social networking site and discuss the questions.

Facebook™ is one of the most popular websites in Britain with over twenty-five million users. Most of them are aged between 13 and 29 and it is slightly more popular with women than with men.

People use the social networking site to keep in touch with friends and to make new ones. They share photos, audio and video clips, and play online games.

Facebook™ began as a site just for Harvard University students, but is now so popular that it is a word in dictionaries.

- Have you got a similar website in your country?
- Are you still in touch with friends from your last school?

1c | Neighbours

Speaking

1 Work in pairs. Ask and answer these questions about your neighbours.

- What are their names?
- What do they do?
- Where do they come from?
- Are they good neighbours? Why or why not?

Reading

1 Read the magazine article. Put the information in the correct order.

☐ People do not want to live next door to politicians.
☐ Cheryl Cole was the most popular person in the poll.
☐ Jamie Oliver lives in a fashionable part of London.
☐ Many British people know a lot about the lives of TV celebrities.
☐ Cheryl Cole did not have any neighbours in her last house.
☐ Jamie Oliver lives with his family.

2 Read the article again and answer the questions.

1 How many people voted for Cheryl Cole?
2 What kind of house did Cheryl Cole live in?
3 How often does she travel between Britain and the US?
4 What part of London does Jamie Oliver live in?
5 How near is his house to a park?
6 What sort of neighbours does he have?

3 Which famous person in the article would you like as your neighbour?

Who would you like as … a neighbour?

Jamie Oliver

A recent opinion poll asked 1,000 people in Britain this question. The winner of the poll was the TV celebrity, model and pop singer, Cheryl Cole, with 31% of the vote.

Many people in Britain know very little about their neighbours, but they often know a lot about the lives of TV celebrities, especially those on reality TV shows. The British public obviously think they know a lot about Cheryl Cole, who has been a judge on the reality TV show, *The X Factor*. But Cheryl Cole does not, perhaps, want to live close to her fans. Her last home was a huge mansion in the country with no neighbours. Now, she travels many times a year between homes in London and the United States, and she tries to keep her address a secret.

The top man in the poll was the TV chef, Jamie Oliver. Oliver lives in the fashionable district of Primrose Hill, in north London, with his wife and children. It is a quiet and beautiful residential area, five minutes from one of London's best parks. His neighbours include film stars like Jude Law and Ewan McGregor, the supermodel Kate Moss, as well as politicians and bankers. Neighbours describe Oliver as a friendly, helpful neighbour … but no one asks him to help with the cooking!

The British like attractive TV personalities and cooking, but, it seems, they do not want to live next door to politicians. There was not a single politician in the top twenty names.

Glossary
celebrity *n* a famous sports or TV person
poll *n* a kind of vote where people are asked for their opinions
public *n* people in general

Cheryl Cole

GRAMMAR: *how* & *what* questions

We can combine *how* and *what* with other words to begin questions.

***How* + adjectives/adverbs/much/many**
How friendly *are your neighbours?*
How often *do you speak to your neighbours?*
How many *children do they have?*
How popular *is she?*

***What* + noun/kind of/sort of/type of**
What colour *is your car?*
What time *do you get up?*
What kind of *neighbour is he?*

SEE LANGUAGE REFERENCE PAGE 14

1 Complete the questions for the answers below.

1 How fast do you drive?
I usually drive quite fast, especially on the motorway.
2 What colour is your father's hair?
My father's hair is grey.
3 How well do you know your teacher?
I know my teacher very well.
4 What time do you have dinner?
I usually have dinner at about eight o'clock.
5 How many cousins do you have?
I have six cousins.
6 What kind of music do you like?
I don't like pop music very much, but I like everything else.

2 Work in pairs. Ask and answer the questions in exercise 1.

3 You have new neighbours and you want to know more about them. Write four questions that you would like to ask. Use the prompts below to help you.

- What time … ?
- What kind of … ?
- How much … ?
- How many … ?
- How often … ?
- How old … ?

4 Work in pairs and compare your questions. Which is the most interesting question?

PRONUNCIATION: the alphabet

1 Look at the three lists of letters. In each list, the letters use the same sound. Choose a letter from the box to complete each list.

G I J O Q R U W X Y

1 /eɪ/ A H ___ K
2 /iː/ B C D E ___ P T V
3 /e/ F L M N S ___ Z

2 1.6 Listen to the recording to check your answers.

3 1.7 Now listen to the other letters from the box and repeat after the recording.

4 1.8 Listen to a list of the six most common surnames in Britain and write them down.

5 1.9 Now listen to the recording to check your spelling.

SPEAKING

1 Make a list of five famous people from your country (film stars, musicians, politicians, sports stars, TV personalities, artists, business people).

Now put the people in your list in order (1 = best neighbour → 5 = worst neighbour).

2 Work in small groups. Talk about the people in your list and explain why you think they would be good or bad neighbours.

Useful language

X is probably a good/bad neighbour because …
I would/wouldn't like to live next door to Y because …
I imagine that Z is very …
It would be great to live near …

1D | Making contact

Speaking

1 Work in pairs. Discuss these questions.

- Which of the ways shown in the photos below do you use most often to contact other people?
- Which do you prefer? When and why?

2 Think of the last three phone calls that you made.

- Who did you call? (a friend/business call?)
- Why did you call her/him? (to give some news/ask a question?)

I phoned my brother because he is not well at the moment.
I phoned my friend, Karen, because I wanted to invite her for dinner.

Work in pairs and compare your answers.

Functional language 1: phone numbers

1 1.10 Listen to a phone message and choose the best ending, a, b or c.

1 To listen to the menu, press …
a) 4 b) # c) *.

2 For general enquiries, press …
a) 1 # b) 2 # c) 3 #.

3 Kate's home phone number is …
a) 0307 775 3046 b) 0307 755 3846 c) 0307 755 3046.

4 Kate's mobile number is …
a) 0477 320188 b) 0477 328118 c) 0477 321880.

2 Look at audioscript 1.10 on page 133 to check your answers.

3 Work in pairs, A and B. You are going to practise saying phone numbers.

A: Turn to page 126. B: Turn to page 128.

Listen to the phone numbers your partner says and write them down.

Reading

1 Read the advertisements on page 13 and put them into four groups.

- Accommodation
- English language lessons
- Jobs
- Making friends

2 Read the advertisements again and answer the questions.

1 What does Mary teach?
2 What is the name of the recruitment agency?
3 Where does Mike live?
4 When are the Kung Fu classes?
5 What does Patrick want?
6 How much does the room near London Bridge cost?
7 Where can you get free accommodation?
8 What languages can you practise on Thursday evenings?

3 Imagine that you are in London and you want to improve your English. Which advertisements would you choose and why?

A **Beautiful?** We have a beautiful room for a beautiful person in our flat near London Bridge. £750 per month.
Call David and Gavin on 0803 731886

B **Experienced teacher offers private English lessons.**
All levels (beginners – advanced).
Mary Sharp 0307 727 2377

C **Kung Fu classes.**
Monday 7.30–8.30.
Get fit and make friends at the same time.
Stuart.Tel: 0308 783 9494

D **New friends.** English gentleman would like to meet new people from all over the world.
Interests: cinema, concerts, pubs, learning languages.
Patrick Trotter 0906 641480

E **Notting Hill**, single room in house near Underground station. No pets.
£600 per month + bills.
0780 696 91134 Ask for Mike.

F Student needed for **general hotel work. Good pay** and **free accommodation.**
No experience necessary.
Regent Hotel 0308 845 6921

G Temporary work. We are urgently looking for temporary staff for shops, restaurants and offices in this area.
Call now. **Sayers Recruitment and Training** 0870 446091

H Thursday evening conversation classes in central London.
All languages! Come and talk!
Call 0278 846772 for more information.

Listening

1 1.11–1.14 Listen to four phone calls. Match the calls 1–4 to the advertisements A–H.

Which caller does **not** leave a message on an answering machine?

2 1.11–1.14 Listen to the messages again and answer the questions.

1 What is Davina's phone number?
2 What is a good time to call her?
3 What is Bella's phone number?
4 What is her family name?
5 What is Ruby's number?
6 Why does Sara want English lessons?

Functional language 2: phone messages

1 1.15 Listen and complete the phone messages.

This is 641480. I'm afraid there's no one to take your call right (1) ______. Please leave your (2) ______ and (3) ______ after the tone and I'll call you back.
Ah, yes, hello. Mr Trotter, my (4) ______ is Davina and I'm (5) ______ in your advertisement. Could you call me back, please? Any time before …

Stuart here. I'm not home at the (6) ______, so please leave a (7) ______ after the beep. Thanks.
Hello, good morning. (8) ______ is Bella Moor, that's Moor – M – double O – R. I'm (9) ______ about the Kung Fu classes. You can call me back on my (10) ______, that's 0447 …

2 Write your own answering machine message. Use the language in exercise 1 to help you.

3 Work in pairs, A and B.

A: You are going to telephone another student. First of all, decide why you want to call them. Use the language in exercise 1 and in the Useful language box below to prepare what you want to say. Listen to the message on their answering machine and then leave your own message.

B: Another student is going to telephone you. Read out the answering machine message that you have prepared and then listen to the message that your partner leaves. Write down their name, phone number and any other important information.

Useful language

Hi, this is … / Hello, it's … here.

I'm calling about … / I'm interested in …

Can/Could you call me back later?

My (mobile) number is … / I'm on …

4 When you have finished, change roles. Then change partners and repeat the task with other students in the class.

Self-assessment (tick ✔)

- ☐ I can understand and write down telephone numbers.
- ☐ I can understand answering machine messages.
- ☐ I can leave a message on an answering machine.
- ☐ I can find information in newspaper advertisements.

1 Language reference

Grammar

Yes/No questions

Questions with *to be*
We make questions with the verb *to be* by putting the verb before the subject.

verb	**subject**	
Is	*he*	*French?*
Are	*you*	*married?*

We can answer these questions with short answers.

Is he French? ***Yes, he is.***
Are they married? ***No they aren't.***

Present simple *to be*		
Am	I	married?
Is	she/he/it	
Are	you/we/they	
Past simple *to be*		
Was	I	at school yesterday?
	she/he/it	
Were	you/we/they	
Short answer		
Yes, No,	I	am/was. 'm not/wasn't.
	she/he/it	is/was. isn't/wasn't.
	you/we/they	are/were. aren't/weren't.

Questions with present simple & past simple
We make questions in the present simple and past simple with an auxiliary verb (*do/does/did*) and the infinitive without *to*. We put *do/does/did* before the subject and we put the infinitive after the subject.

auxiliary	**subject**	**infinitive**	
Do	*you*	*like*	*pop music?*
Does	*she*	*live*	*in London?*
Did	*she*	*enjoy*	*the party?*

We can answer these questions with short answers.
Do you like pop music? ***Yes, I do.***
Does she live in London? ***No, she doesn't.***

Present simple			
Do	I	like	pop music?
Does	she/he/it		
Do	you/we/they		
Past simple			
Did	I	go	to the cinema last night?
	she/he/it		
	you/we/they		

Short answer		
Yes, No,	I	do/did. don't/didn't.
	she/he/it	does/did. doesn't/didn't.
	you/we/they	do/did. don't/didn't.

Questions with other verb forms
All other verb forms (for example, present continuous, *can*, *will*) already have an auxiliary verb and a main verb. We put the auxiliary verb before the subject and we put the main verb after the subject.

auxiliary	**subject**	**main verb**
Are	*you*	*listening?*
Can	*we*	*start?*
Will	*she*	*phone?*

We can answer these questions with short answers.

Are you listening? ***Yes, I am.***
Can we start? ***No, we can't.***
Will she phone? ***No, she won't.***

Wh- questions

We can put question words before the verb. The most common question words are: *what, which, when, where, why, who* and *how*.

What *is her daughter's name?*
Who *was your first boyfriend?*
When *did they arrive?*

We can combine *how* and *what* with other words to begin questions.

How + | adjectives (*far, old, popular, tall*)
adverbs (*often, well*, etc)
much (*much money, much time*)
many (*many children, many cousins*)

How old *is Sarah?*
How often *do you travel by train?*
How many *CDs does he have?*

What + | noun (colour, time, etc)
kind of/sort of/type of

What colour *is their car?*
What time *is it?*
What kind *of pizza do you like?*

Functional language

Phone messages

This is 0307 775 3046.
This is Kate Woods.
You have reached the voicemail of …
Thank you for calling …

I'm afraid there is no one to take your call right now.
I'm not home/in the office at the moment.

Please leave	*your name and number a/your message*	*after*	*the beep. the tone.*

This is a message for …
I'm interested in …
I'm calling about …

I'll call you back.
Could you call me back, please?

Word list

Family

aunt *n C* ** /ɑːnt/
couple *n C* *** /ˈkʌp(ə)l/
cousin *n C* ** /ˈkʌz(ə)n/
daughter *n C* *** /ˈdɔːtə(r)/
grandfather *n C* * /ˈgræn(d)ˌfɑːðə(r)/
grandmother *n C* * /ˈgræn(d)ˌmʌðə(r)/
husband *n C* *** /ˈhʌzbənd/
mother-in-law *n C* /ˈmʌðə(r) ɪn lɔː/
nephew *n C* /ˈnefjuː/
niece *n C* /niːs/
parent *n C* *** /ˈpeərənt/
pet *n C* * /pet/
son *n C* *** /sʌn/
son-in-law *n C* /ˈsʌn ɪn lɔː/
uncle *n C* * /ˈʌŋk(ə)l/
wife n C *** /waɪf/

Friendship

best friend *n C* /best frend/
classmate *n C* /ˈklɑːsˌmeɪt/
colleague *n C* ** /ˈkɒliːg/
get on (well) with (sb) *phr* /get ɒn (wel) wɪð/
have a lot in common with (sb) *phr* /hæv ə lɒt ɪn ˈkɒmən wɪð/
keep in touch with (sb) *phr* /kiːp ɪn tʌtʃ wɪð/
neighbour *n C* ** /ˈneɪbə(r)/
roommate *n C* /ˈruːmˌmeɪt/

Other words & phrases

accommodation *n U* ** /əˌkɒməˈdeɪʃ(ə)n/
advert(isement) *n C* /ədˈvɜː(r)t[ɪsmənt]/
appointment *n C* *** /əˈpɔɪntmənt/
background *n C* ** /ˈbækˌgraʊnd/
beach *n C* ** /biːtʃ/
blonde *adj* /blɒnd/
box *n C* *** /bɒks/
building *n C* *** /ˈbɪldɪŋ/
busy *adj* *** /ˈbɪzi/
career *n C* ** /kəˈrɪə(r)/
celebrity *n C* * /səˈlebrəti/
charity *n C / U* ** /ˈtʃærəti/
circus *n C* /ˈsɜː(r)kəs/
clothes *n pl* *** /kləʊðz/
college *n C/U* *** /ˈkɒlɪdʒ/
concert *n C* ** /ˈkɒnsə(r)t/
contact *v* *** /ˈkɒntækt/
district *n C* *** /ˈdɪstrɪkt/
doll *n C* /dɒl/
dress *n C* ** /dres/
electricity *n U* ** /ɪˌlekˈtrɪsəti/
email *n C* *** /ˈiːmeɪl/
enquiry *n C* /ɪnˈkwaɪri/
experience *n U* ** /ɪkˈspɪəriəns/
expert *n C* ** /ˈekspɜː(r)t/
fan *n C* ** /fæn/
fashionable *adj* ** /ˈfæʃ(ə)nəb(ə)l/
fit *adj* * /fɪt/
flat *n C* ** /flæt/
flowery *adj* /ˈflaʊəri/
guitar *n C* ** /gɪˈtɑː(r)/
health *n U* ** /helθ/
hobby *n C* /ˈhɒbi/
housework *n U* /ˈhaʊsˌwɜː(r)k/
include *v* *** /ɪnˈkluːd/
judge *n C* ** /dʒʌdʒ/
juggle *v* /ˈdʒʌg(ə)l/
laugh *v* *** /lɑːf/
lovely *adj* /ˈlʌvli/
male *adj* *** /meɪl/
meat *n U* *** /miːt/
medical *adj* *** /ˈmedɪk(ə)l/
member *n C* *** /ˈmembə(r)/
message *n C* *** /ˈmesɪdʒ/
model *n C* *** /ˈmɒd(ə)l/
motor home *n C* /ˈməʊtə(r) həʊm/
nurse *n C* ** /nɜː(r)s/
obviously *adv* *** /ˈɒbviəsli/
opinion *n C* *** /əˈpɪnjən/
perform *v* *** /pə(r)ˈfɔː(r)m/
pink *adj* /pɪŋk/
politician *n C* ** /ˌpɒləˈtɪʃ(ə)n/
poll *n C* * /pəʊl/
popular *adj* *** /ˈpɒpjʊlə(r)/
practise *v* ** /ˈpræktɪs/
prefer *v* *** /prɪˈfɜː(r)/
press *v* *** /pres/
private *adj* *** /ˈpraɪvət/
pub *n C* ** /pʌb/
public *n U* *** /ˈpʌblɪk/
quiet *adj* *** /ˈkwaɪət/
recent *adj* *** /ˈriːs(ə)nt/
recruitment agency *n C* /rɪˈkruːtmənt ˈeɪdʒ(ə)nsi/
repair *v* * /rɪˈpeə(r)/
result *n C* *** /rɪˈzʌlt/
root *n C* *** /ruːt/
secret *n C / adj* ** /ˈsiːkrət/
secretary *n C* *** /ˈsekrətri/
share *v* *** /ʃeə(r)/
shirt *n C* *** /ʃɜː(r)t/
show *n C* *** /ʃəʊ/
similar *adj* *** /ˈsɪmɪlə(r)/
simple *adj* *** /ˈsɪmp(ə)l/
soap opera *n C* /səʊp ˈɒp(ə)rə/
staff *n U* *** /stɑːf/
surprise *n C/U* *** /sə(r)ˈpraɪz/
temporary *adj* *** /ˈtemp(ə)rəri/
terrible *adj* ** /ˈterəb(ə)l/
theme park *n C* /θiːm pɑː(r)k/
together *adv* *** /təˈgeðə(r)/
tone *n C* * /təʊn/
traditional *adj* *** /trəˈdɪʃ(ə)nəl/
typical *adj* *** /ˈtɪpɪk(ə)l/
university *n C/U* *** /ˌjuːnɪˈvɜː(r)səti/
urgently *adv* /ˈɜː(r)dʒ(ə)ntli/
user *n C* * /ˈjuːzə(r)/
village *n C* *** /ˈvɪlɪdʒ/
voicemail *n U* /ˈvɔɪsmeɪl/
vote *n C/v* *** /vəʊt/
website *n C* /ˈwebˌsaɪt/
wedding *n C* ** /ˈwedɪŋ/
winner *n C* ** /ˈwɪnə(r)/
wonder *v* *** /ˈwʌndə(r)/

Abbreviations

n	noun	*sth*	something
v	verb	*C*	countable
adj	adjective	*U*	uncountable
adv	adverb	*pl*	plural
sb	somebody	*s*	singular

*** the most common and basic words
** very common words
* fairly common words

2A | School days

Vocabulary & speaking: adjectives with prepositions

1 Which sentences have a positive (+) meaning and which have a negative (–) meaning?

1 I was **good at** mathematics.
2 I was **bored with** my school.
3 I was **afraid of** the older children.
4 I was **fond of** my science teacher.
5 I was **interested in** science and technology.
6 I was **terrible at** arriving on time.
7 I was **keen on** sports and swimming.
8 I was **worried about** my grades.

2 Think about your experience of school. Change the sentences in exercise 1 so that they are true for you.

3 Work in pairs. Compare your sentences. Were your experiences similar or different?

Listening

1 **1.16–1.18** Listen to three people talking about their school days. Match the speakers 1–3 to the topics a–c below.

a my favourite subject
b my favourite teacher
c my problems at school

2 **1.16–1.18** Listen to the recording again and complete column A with a phrase from column B.

A	B
1 I never missed	a good grades.
2 I always got	b my exams.
3 I was terrible at	c my homework.
4 I failed	d his lessons.
5 I never did	e that school.
6 I didn't want to leave	f most subjects.

3 Did you have any similar experiences at school?

Grammar: past simple

1 Complete the table. Look at audioscripts 1.16–1.18 on page 134 to check your answers.

infinitive	past simple	infinitive	past simple
hate	(1) ______	study	(5) ______
listen	(2) ______	talk	(6) ______
leave	(3) ______	teach	(7) ______
love	(4) ______	try	(8) ______

2 Now put the verbs in the table into four groups.

a Regular verbs: infinitive + *-ed*
b Regular verbs: infinitive + *-d*
c Regular verbs: infinitive ending in *-y* → *-i* + *ed*
d Irregular verbs:

We make negatives with *didn't (did not)* + infinitive.
*I **didn't want** to leave school.*

We make questions with *did* + subject + infinitive.
*Where **did you go** to school?*
***Did you like** school?*

SEE LANGUAGE REFERENCE PAGE 24

3 Complete the dialogue. Put the verbs in brackets into the past simple.

A: Where (1) *did you go* (*you / go*) to school?
B: My father (2) ______ (*work*) for a multinational company and we (3) ______ (*live*) in lots of different countries, so I (4) ______ (*go*) to five different schools.
A: (5) ______ (*you / enjoy*) your school days?
B: No, I didn't. Not really. I (6) ______ (*not have*) many friends because we (7) ______ (*not stay*) long in one place. I (8) ______ (*leave*) one school after six months!
A: (9) ______ (*you / do*) well in your exams?
B: Yes, I did. Because I (10) ______ (*not / go*) out with friends, I (11) ______ (*study*) a lot in the evenings and at the weekends. I (12) ______ (*not / get*) top grades, but I (13) ______ (*get*) a place at Cambridge University.
A: What was that like? (14) ______ (*you / like*) it?
B: Yes. I (15) ______ (*think*) it was great.

4 Work in pairs. Write a similar dialogue.

PRONUNCIATION: regular past simple verbs

1 1.19 When we say regular past simple forms, we usually add the sound /t/ or /d/ to the infinitive. We do **not** need an extra syllable. Listen to these examples.

open /'əʊpən/ → opened /'əʊpənd/
love /lʌv/ → loved /lʌvd/
try /traɪ/ → tried /traɪd/

But if the infinitive ends in /t/ or /d/, we **do** need to add an extra syllable (/ɪd/) when we say the regular past form. Listen to these examples.

want /wɒnt/ → wanted /'wɒntɪd/
decide /dɪ'saɪd/ → decided /dɪ'saɪdɪd/

2 Put the verbs in the box into two groups: no extra syllable (NS) and extra syllable (ES).

arrived *NS*	ended	hated	helped
needed	studied	waited	worked

3 1.20 Listen to the recording to check your answers.

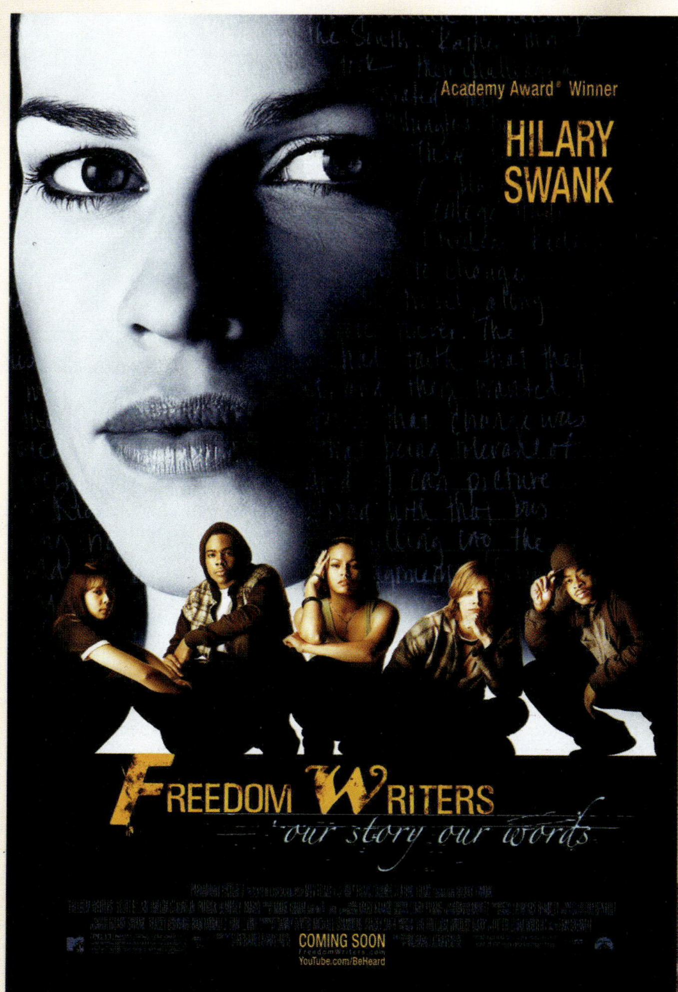

SPEAKING

1 Do you know any films or TV programmes about schools and teachers?

2 You are going to talk about a teacher that you really liked. Use these questions to help you.

- What was the teacher's name?
- What did she/he teach?
- Where did she/he teach?
- How often did you have lessons with her/him?
- What did she/he look like?
- Why did you like her/him?
- Do you remember a particular moment with this teacher?
- What happened?

3 Work in groups. Describe the teacher that you really liked to your group.

2B Irish schools

Speaking

1 Work in pairs. Discuss these questions.

- Are there any big differences between the schools in your town? Are some schools better than others? If so, why?
- What is your idea of a good school?

Vocabulary: education

1 Complete the sentences with a word from the box.

age	certificate	compulsory	punishment	results	sex	system

1 Some schools in England are for boys and girls and some are single ______.
2 In the English education ______, there are private schools and state schools.
3 Some subjects, like English and maths, are ______ until the age of sixteen in England.
4 English children must sometimes stay in class at break as a ______.
5 The minimum leaving ______ in England is sixteen, but most students continue for another two years.
6 There is no leaving ______ in England, but many students take 'A level' exams when they are eighteen.
7 School students in England get their exam ______ in the summer holidays after they leave school.

2 1.21 Listen to the recording to check your answers.

3 Change the sentences in exercise 1 so that they are true for your country.

Reading

1 Read a magazine article about education in Ireland. Match the paragraphs 1–4 to the headings a–d below.

1 = b

a Rich and poor, boys and girls
b A success story
c School subjects
d Traditional teaching

This month we take a look at schools in:

THE REPUBLIC OF IRELAND

(1) ______

Ireland now has one of the best education systems in the world. Class sizes are small, exam results are good and most children are happy to stay at school after the minimum leaving age of sixteen. It is easy to forget that the picture used to be very different.

(2) ______

For years, Ireland had one of the most complicated education systems in the world. There were many different kinds of school, but most of them had a lot in common. Classes were large and the teaching was very traditional. As in many countries, teachers used to hit the children if they made mistakes (the government banned corporal punishment in 1982).

(3) ______

Parents used to pay for their children's education and, as a result, there were schools for the rich and schools for the poor. Boys and girls went to different schools and studied different subjects. Nowadays, most schools are free and only about half the schools are single-sex. In many ways, education is now a woman's world. Girls do better than boys in their exams, more girls go to university and most teachers are women.

(4) ______

At the end of secondary school, students take their final exams (the 'Leaving Certificate'). Compulsory subjects are maths, Irish and English. In addition, they must choose two or three extra subjects. Some of these, like business organization, help to prepare them for the world of work. This is very different from the past when Latin, Greek and religion used to be the most important subjects.

2 Read the article again and find one piece of information to show that each statement is true.

1 The exam results are good.

1 Ireland has a good education system.
2 Teaching in Ireland used to be very traditional.
3 Irish boys and girls used to have very different experiences of school.
4 Education in Ireland is a woman's world.
5 Irish students study many different subjects.

3 Are there any similarities between education in Ireland and education in your country?

GRAMMAR: *used to*

We use *used to* + infinitive to talk about past states.
Latin and Greek ***used to be*** *important school subjects.*

We also use *used to* + infinitive to talk about past actions that happened many times.
Teachers ***used to hit*** *children.*

We can always use the past simple instead of *used to*.
Boys and girls ***used to go/went*** *to different schools.*

However, we cannot use *used to* for past actions that happened once.
The government ***banned*** *corporal punishment.* (**not**

2) As a child, he used to be called Jonny O' Keeffe.
3) he used to go to a famous school
4) he didn't used to like his school
5) he used to miss lessons
6) he didn't used to do well in his exams.
7) he used to spend a lot of time playing pool.

yers ... Farrell (the actor)? See page 128 for the answer.

2) —
5) his family didn't used to have much money
6) his father used to tell funny storys to frank
7) Frank used to loves listening to his father.

2

1
2
3
4 His family moved to Ireland.
5 His family didn't have much money.
6 His father told funny stories to Frank.
7 Frank loved listening to his father.
8 Frank won the Pulitzer Prize for this book about his childhood.

3 Write six sentences about yourself when you were at primary school. Begin three sentences with *I used to …* and three with *I didn't use to …* .

PRONUNCIATION: irregular past simple verbs

1 Underline the word in the groups 1–4 below which has a different sound from the other words in the group.

1	bought	caught	found	thought
2	came	gave	made	said
3	broke	drove	lost	spoke
4	felt	knew	met	went

2 1.22 Listen to the recording to check your answers.

SPEAKING

1 Think about schools in your country now and in the past. How are they different? Make notes, using your own ideas and the ideas in the box to help you.

computers/technology · class sizes · types of school · the school buildings · when you can leave school · school subjects · exams · behaviour · punishment

2 Work in pairs and compare your ideas. Are schools now better or worse than they used to be?

Schools in my country used to be very different. For example, …

2c | Red faces

Speaking & reading

1 Work in pairs. Which of the situations below is the most embarrassing? How many more situations can you add to the list?

Embarrassing situations

- You are wearing the wrong kind of clothes (eg to a party).
- You do really badly in a test and everyone knows.
- You fall asleep in a public place.
- In front of other people, your parents say something about you that you don't want the other people to know.
- Your telephone rings at the wrong moment, eg in an exam.
- Your stomach makes a strange noise.

2 Read the messages from an internet discussion group and match them to three of the situations in exercise 1.

File Edit View Favourites Tools Help Links

Teacher-talk

Doug 20 April
In October last year, I was working at a school in Cambridge and it was only my second month in the job.
At the end of the month the head teacher organized a party for all the new teachers.
It was a good chance to get to know my new colleagues and I was really looking forward to it. As the party was on 31st October, I thought it was a Hallowe'en party. So, the day before the party, I went to a costume hire shop and got a witch's costume. When I arrived at the head's house, he opened the door and looked at me as if I was completely mad. All the other teachers were wearing normal clothes! Doug

Tamsin 26 April
It was the end of term in June and the students were doing their exams. I was in charge that day and, as usual before the start of the exam, I told the students all the rules: no talking, no mobile phones and so on. I was walking up and down between the rows of desks when suddenly my own phone rang. That was bad enough, but the phone had a really silly ring tone. It took me ages to find the phone in my bag and my face went bright red. One of the students was laughing so much that she fell out of her chair. Tamsin

Kelly 3 May
Worst moment? It was one day last May. When I woke up in the morning, I wasn't feeling very well. But it was a beautiful day and I decided to go to school. In the first class I gave the students an exercise to do and sat down at my desk. It was hot and the sun was coming through the window and I fell asleep.
I probably slept for only two or three minutes. Then I heard a noise and I woke up. All the children were laughing and the headmaster was standing at the door of the class! Fortunately, he was very sympathetic later in the morning when I explained that I was feeling ill. Kelly

Glossary
witch *n* a woman with magic powers

3 Read the messages again and answer the questions.

1 Why did Doug's head teacher organize a party?
2 Why was Doug looking forward to the party?
3 Why did he wear witch's clothes?
4 Why was Tamsin in an examination room?
5 What was special about Tamsin's phone?
6 Why didn't she turn off her phone immediately?
7 Why did Kelly decide to go to work when she wasn't well?
8 Why did Kelly wake up?

4 Work in pairs. Describe an embarrassing experience that happened to you or someone you know.

GRAMMAR: past continuous

We use the past continuous to describe actions in progress at a particular time in the past.

*Where **were** you **working** in October last year?*
*I **was working** at a school in Cambridge.*
***Was** she **feeling** ill?* *Yes, she **was**. / No, she **wasn't**.*

We use the past simple for actions that interrupt the actions in the past continuous.

*I **was walking** up and down when my phone **rang**.*

SEE LANGUAGE REFERENCE PAGE 24

1 Complete the text. Put the verbs in brackets into the past simple or the past continuous.

A few days ago, I (1) ______ (*wait*) for the bus with my younger brother. We (2) ______ (*go*) home after an afternoon at the shops. A very large woman with a big shopping bag (3) ______ (*stand*) in front of us. After a few minutes, the bus (4) ______ (*arrive*). The woman (5) ______ (*get*) on the bus when she (6) ______ (*turn*) round. 'Can you help me with my bag?' she (7) ______ (*ask*) us. 'Yes, of course,' (8) ______ (*say*) my brother. 'Are you going to have a baby?'

2 Look at the pictures A–C on page 132 for one minute. Then work in pairs. Turn to page 127 and answer the questions.

3 Work in pairs. Ask and answer questions about what you were doing at the times below.

- fifteen minutes ago
- one hour ago
- at six o'clock this morning
- at eleven o'clock last night
- at three o'clock last Saturday
- at this time last week

What were you doing fifteen minutes ago?
I was having a cup of coffee.

SPEAKING

1 Work in groups and look at the two lists below. Read the sentences and decide which list they belong to.

1 Speak in front of their friends about funny things that they did when they were younger.
2 Don't say hello to their friends when they visit your home.
3 When their friends are visiting, speak with your mouth full of food.
4 Tell them (in front of their friends) to wear clothes that they do not like.

How to embarrass your parents

-
-
-
-
-

How to embarrass your children

-
-
-
-
-

2 Now discuss how parents can embarrass their children and how children can embarrass their parents. Add three more sentences to each list.

3 Present your lists to the rest of the class.

2D | Which school?

Speaking

1 Work in pairs. You and your partner win first prize in a competition. Read the information and decide which city you both want to study in.

Vocabulary: school facilities

1 Look at the advertisement for an English school. Match the words in **bold** to the definitions below.

1 = library

1 a place to borrow or read books
2 a restaurant/café in a place of work
3 money you pay for a professional service
4 place or position
5 teaching
6 that you can change
7 they have done this job a lot
8 they have professional exams/qualifications

2 List three important things for you in choosing a language school.

3 Work in pairs and compare your lists.

Victoria School of English
Sydney

The Victoria School has a central **location** near the Opera House. Our **qualified** and **experienced** teachers provide top quality **tuition** with **flexible** timetables. The school has an ultra-modern multi-media centre with 20 PCs, a language laboratory and a **library**. The school has its own **cafeteria** and an exciting social programme.

Special **fees** for international students.

Victoria School

Listening

1 1.23 A man is asking for information about a course in a French language school. Listen to the dialogue and underline the correct information.

CLASS SIZE	10 / 15 / 20 students per class
LEVEL	Beginner / Intermediate / Advanced
TIMETABLE	Mon & Wed / Tues & Thurs / Tues & Fri 7.30–9.00 / 8.00–9.30 / 8.30–9.30
COURSE LENGTH	10 / 12 / 15 weeks
FRENCH CLUB	Friday mornings / Friday evenings / Saturday evenings
PRICE	£120 / £150 / £180

2 Match the words in column A with the words from column B to make phrases.

A		B	
1	day-time	a	activities
2	native	b	class
3	registration	c	courses
4	social	d	form
5	ten-week	e	speakers

3 1.23 Listen to the dialogue again to check your answers.

Functional language: asking for information

1 Rearrange the words to make questions.

1 *Please could I have some information about your school?*

1 about could information have school I please some your ?
2 about could courses me tell you your ?
3 a are class how in many students ?
4 beginners classes do for have you ?
5 are classes the time what ?
6 course does how last long the ?
7 activities any are social there ?
8 fees course the much are how ?

Look at audioscript 1.23 on pages 134–135 to check your answers.

Speaking

1 Work in pairs. You are going to plan an evening school. Use these questions to help you.

- Where is your school?
- What is it called?
- What kinds of courses does the school offer?
- Who are the teachers?
- What facilities does the school have?
- How much do the courses cost?
- What is special about your school?

2 Find another pair and work in groups of four. Find out about each other's schools.

Did you know?

1 Work in pairs. Read the information about the English language and discuss the questions.

- About 375,000,000 people speak English as a first language.
- More than 500,000,000 people speak English as a second language.
- About 1,000,000,000 people study English around the world.
- About 500,000 people take examinations (British or American) in English as a foreign language every year.
- About 1,000,000 people go to Britain or America to study English every year.

- When and where do people use English in your country?
- Do many people in your country study English? Why do they study?
- What English language examinations do people take in your country?
- Do you know anyone who has studied English in an English-speaking country? Did they like it?

Self-assessment (tick ✔)

- ☐ I can understand specific information in a conversation.
- ☐ I can ask for information about courses in a school.
- ☐ I can discuss the use of English in my country.
- ☐ I can combine words to make collocations.

2 Language reference

GRAMMAR

Past simple

We use the past simple to talk about past actions and states. The actions and states are finished.

*I **left** school in 1999. Then I **went** to university.*
*I **liked** rock music when I **was** a teenager.*

We often use a time expression with the past simple, for example, *yesterday*, *last week*, *in 2003*.

*I saw John **yesterday**.*
*We lived in Brussels **in 2003**.*

Affirmative & Negative				
I He/She/It You/We/They	found didn't find	a job.		
Question				
When	did	I he/she/it you/we/they	find	a job?
Short answer				
Did you find a job?		Yes, I did. / No, I didn't.		

With regular verbs, we usually add *-ed* to the infinitive in the affirmative. There are three groups of exceptions.

1 When the verb ends in *-e*, we add *-d*.
like ➔ *like**d***   *love* ➔ *love**d***
2 When the verb ends in *-y* after a consonant, we change the *-y* to *-ied*.
study ➔ *stud**ied***   *try* ➔ *tr**ied***
3 With some verbs that end in a consonant, we double the consonant.
plan ➔ *pla**nned***   *stop* ➔ *sto**pped***
Other verbs in this group include: *admit, chat, control, drop, nod, occur, refer, regret, rob, transfer* and *trap*.

Many common verbs have irregular past forms.
eat ➔ *ate*   *go* ➔ *went*   *leave* ➔ *left*

Used to

We use *used to* to talk about past states and past actions that happened many times.

*My family **used to live** in Rome.*
*We **used to go out** for a meal every Saturday.*

We can always use the past simple instead of *used to*, but we cannot use *used to* for actions that happened only once.

*We **used to live** in Rome.* = *We **lived** in Rome.*
*My family **moved** back to London in 1995.*
Not ~~*My family **used to** move back to London in 1995.*~~

Affirmative & Negative			
I He/She/It You/We/They	used to didn't use to	like walk to	school.
Question				
Did	I he/she/it you/we/they	use to	like walk to	school?
Short answer				
Did you use to like school?	Yes, I did. / No, I didn't.			

Past continuous

We use the past continuous to describe actions in progress at a particular time in the past. We often use the past continuous to describe the background situation of a story.

*It was the end of term and the students **were doing** their exams.*

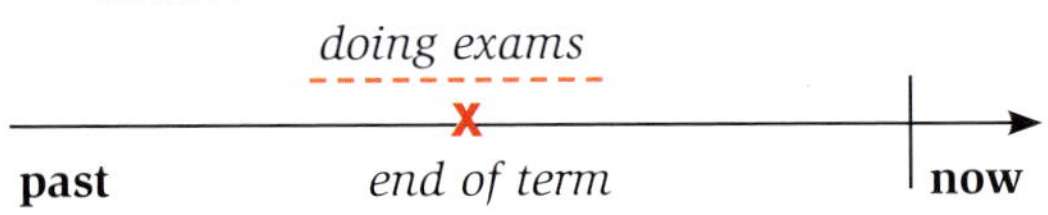

We often use the past simple and past continuous together. We use the past simple for actions that interrupt the actions in the past continuous.

*I **was walking** into class when my phone **rang**.*
(First, I walked into class. Second, my phone rang.)

We cannot normally use stative verbs in the continuous form. See page 44 for a list of common stative verbs.

*She **knew** that he was happy.*
Not ~~*She **was knowing** he was happy.*~~

Affirmative & Negative				
I He/She/It	was wasn't	talking	on the phone.	
You/We/They	were weren't			
Question				
When	was	I he/she/it	talking	on the phone?
	were	you/we/they		
Short answer				
Were you talking?	Yes, I was. / No, I wasn't.			
Were they working?	Yes, they were. / No, they weren't.			

We make the past continuous with *was/were* + infinitive + *-ing*. If the infinitive ends in a consonant + *-e*:

live ➔ *liv**ing***

With some verbs that end in a consonant, we double the consonant. See the list of verbs in group 3 in the past simple above.

Functional language

Asking for information

(Please) could I have some information about … ?
Could you tell me about …, (please)?
How much is/are … ?
What time is/are … ?
How long does/do the … last?
Do you have … ?
Is there a … ?
Are there any … ?
How many … are there?

Word list

Adjectives with prepositions

afraid **of** ***	/əˈfreɪd əv/
bored **with** **	/bɔː(r)d wɪð/
fond **of** *	/fɒnd əv/
good **at** ***	/gʊd ət/
interested **in** ***	/ˈɪntrəstɪd ɪn/
keen **on** **	/kiːn ɒn/
terrible **at** **	/ˈterəb(ə)l ət/
worried **about** *	/ˈwʌrid əˈbaʊt/

Education

break *n C* ***	/breɪk/
cafeteria *n C*	/ˌkæfəˈtɪəriə/
certificate *n C* **	/sə(r)ˈtɪfɪkət/
compulsory *adj* *	/kəmˈpʌlsəri/
computer *n C* ***	/kəmˈpjuːtə(r)/
course *n C* ***	/kɔː(r)s/
desk *n C* ***	/desk/
education system *n C*	/ˌedjʊˈkeɪʃ(ə)n ˈsɪstəm/
examination *n C* ***	/ɪgˌzæmɪˈneɪʃ(ə)n/
(exam) *n C* **	/ɪgˈzæm/
experienced *adj* *	/ɪkˈspɪəriənst/
fail (an exam) *v* ***	/feɪl/
fee *n C* ***	/fiː/
get a place (at university)	/get ə pleɪs/
grade *n C* *	/greɪd/
headmaster *n C*	/ˌhedˈmɑːstə(r)/
headmistress *n C*	/ˌhedˈmɪstrəs/
head teacher *n C*	/ˌhedˈ tiːtʃə(r)/
homework *n U* *	/ˈhəʊmˌwɜː(r)k/
language laboratory *n C*	/ˈlæŋgwɪdʒ ləˌbɒrət(ə)ri/
leaving age *n C*	/ˈliːvɪŋ eɪdʒ/
leaving certificate *n C*	/ˈliːvɪŋ sə(r)ˈtɪfɪkət/
lesson *n C* ***	/ˈles(ə)n/
location *n C* **	/ləʊˈkeɪʃ(ə)n/
mixed sex *adj*	/mɪkst seks/
multi-media centre *n C*	/ˌmʌltiˈmiːdiə ˌsentə(r)/
pass (an exam) *v* ***	/pɑːs/
private school *n C*	/ˈpraɪvət skuːl/
(corporal) punishment *n U* *	/(ˈkɔː(r)p(ə)rəl) ˈpʌnɪʃmənt/
pupil *n C* ***	/ˈpjuːp(ə)l/
qualification *n C* *	/ˌkwɒlɪfɪˈkeɪʃ(ə)n/
registration form *n C*	/ˌredʒɪˈstreɪʃ(ə)n fɔː(r)m/
result *n C* ***	/rɪˈzʌlt/
single sex *adj*	/ˈsɪŋg(ə)l seks/
social programme/ activity *n C*	/ˈsəʊʃ(ə)l ˈprəʊgræm/ /ækˈtɪvəti/
state school *n C*	/ˈsteɪt skuːl/
subject *n C* ***	/ˈsʌbdʒɪkt/
term *n C* ***	/tɜː(r)m/
timetable *n C*	/ˈtaɪmˌteɪb(ə)l/
tuition *n U*	/tjuːˈɪʃ(ə)n/
university *n C* ***	/ˌjuːnɪˈvɜː(r)səti/

School subjects

art *n U* ***	/ɑː(r)t/
biology *n U*	/baɪˈɒlədʒi/
Greek *n U*	/griːk/
history *n U* ***	/ˈhɪst(ə)ri/
Irish *n U*	/ˈaɪrɪʃ/
Latin *n U*	/ˈlætɪn/
mathematics (maths) *n U*	/ˌmæθəˈmætɪks/; /mæθs/
music *n U* ***	/ˈmjuːzɪk/
religion *n U* ***	/rɪˈlɪdʒ(ə)n/
science *n U* ***	/ˈsaɪəns/
technology *n U* ***	/tekˈnɒlədʒi/

Other words & phrases

accent *n C* *	/ˈæks(ə)nt/
actually *adv* ***	/ˈæktʃuəli/
and so on *phr*	/ænd səʊ ɒn/
anyway *adv* ***	/ˈeniˌweɪ/
as usual *phr*	/əz ˈjuːʒʊəl/
(fall) asleep *adj* **	/(fɔːl) əˈsliːp/
ban *v* **	/bæn/
behaviour *n U* ***	/bɪˈheɪvjə(r)/
borrow *v* **	/ˈbɒrəʊ/
care (about sb) *v* ***	/keə(r)/
club *n C* ***	/klʌb/
choose *v* ***	/tʃuːz/
(multinational) company *n C* ***	/(ˌmʌltiˈnæʃ(ə)nəl) ˈkʌmp(ə)ni/
competition *n C* ***	/ˌkɒmpəˈtɪʃ(ə)n/
complicated *adj* **	/ˈkɒmplɪˌkeɪtɪd/
cool *adj* ***	/kuːl/
costume *n C*	/ˈkɒstjuːm/
embarrass *v*	/ɪmˈbærəs/
enjoy *v* ***	/ɪnˈdʒɔɪ/
exciting *adj* **	/ɪkˈsaɪtɪŋ/
flexible *adj* *	/ˈfleksəb(ə)l/
flight *n C* ***	/flaɪt/
fun *adj* **	/fʌn/
funny *adj* ***	/ˈfʌni/
gig *n C*	/gɪg/
government *n C* ***	/ˈgʌvə(r)nmənt/
great *adj* ***	/greɪt/
hire *v* *	/ˈhaɪə(r)/
in addition *phr*	/ɪn əˈdɪʃ(ə)n/
in charge (of) *phr*	/ɪn tʃɑː(r)dʒ/
(all) inclusive *adj*	/ɔːl ɪnˈkluːsɪv/
jealous *adj* *	/ˈdʒeləs/
minimum *adj/n* **	/ˈmɪnɪməm/
miss (a lesson) *v* ***	/mɪs ə ˈles(ə)n/
mobile phone *n C*	/ˈməʊbaɪl fəʊn/
native *adj* *	/ˈneɪtɪv/
normal *adj* ***	/ˈnɔː(r)m(ə)l/
of course *adv* ***	/əv kɔː(r)s/
organize / organise *v* ***	/ˈɔː(r)gənaɪz/
painter *n C*	/ˈpeɪntə(r)/
pool *n U* **	/puːl/
provide *v* ***	/prəˈvaɪd/
row *n C* ***	/rəʊ/
rule *n C* ***	/ruːl/
shopping bag *n C*	/ˈʃɒpɪŋ bæg/
silly *adj* *	/ˈsɪli/
stupid *adj* **	/ˈstjuːpɪd/
sympathetic *adj*	/ˌsɪmpəˈθetɪk/
ultra-modern *adj*	/ʌltrəˈmɒdə(r)n/
witch *n C*	/wɪtʃ/
worry (about sb/sth) *v* ***	/ˈwʌri/

3A | Flatmates

VOCABULARY: *house* & *home*

1 Do you live in a house or a flat? What do you like most about your home? Discuss and compare your answers in pairs.

2 Complete the sentences with *house* or *home*.

1 What is your *home* town like?
2 At what age do people usually leave ______ in your country?
3 How do you feel when you are away from ______?
4 Is your mother a ______ wife or does she have another job?
5 How much ______ work does your teacher usually give you?
6 What time do you usually get ______ in the evenings?
7 Who does most of the cleaning and the other ______ work where you live?

3 Work in pairs. Ask and answer the questions in exercise 2.

PRONUNCIATION: /h/

1 Find two words in the box that do **not** begin with the sound /h/.

happy	holiday	honest	hotel	who
hospital	home	house	what	whole

2 1.24 Listen to the recording to check your answers.

3 How well can you say the sentence below?

> In Hertford, Hereford and Hampshire hurricanes hardly ever happen.
>
> (from the film *My Fair Lady*)

4 1.25 Listen and repeat.

LISTENING

1 1.26 Listen to two friends talking about their home life. Choose the correct alternative to complete the summary of the dialogue.

Ali lives with (1) *friends / his family*, but is unhappy there. Ali shares a room with (2) *his brothers / two friends*, and he also has two cousins staying with him. He finds it difficult to (3) *sleep / study* at home. He wants to move in with his friend, Charlie. Charlie shares a flat with (4) *his cousin / four other people*. Ali and Charlie agree to (5) *do some shopping / go to a café* and then to go to look at Charlie's flat.

2 1.26 Listen to the dialogue again. Choose the best definition for the phrases, a or b.

1 Tough.
a) That's difficult. b) That's easy.
2 It's driving me mad.
a) It makes me angry. b) It makes me sad.
3 I don't want to put you off.
a) I don't want to encourage you.
b) I don't want to discourage you.

3 Work in pairs. Discuss these questions.

- What do you think Ali should do?
- What are the advantages and disadvantages of living at home when you are a student?
- Do most students live at home in your country?

GRAMMAR: countable & uncountable nouns with *some, any* & *no*

Countable nouns
We can count countable nouns (for example, *one problem, two problems*). They have both a singular and plural form.
There's a new ***problem****.*
He's got ***problems*** *at home.*

Uncountable nouns
We cannot count uncountable nouns. (We cannot say *two* ~~*homeworks*~~.) They only have a singular form.
I have to do my ***homework****.*

Some, any* & *no
We can use *some, any* and *no* with both countable and uncountable nouns.
Some
We usually use *some* in positive sentences.
We've got ***some*** *cousins.* (countable)
I'm going to get ***some*** *food.* (uncountable)
Any
We usually use *any* in negative sentences and questions.
I can't have ***any*** *friends.* (countable)
I can't do ***any*** *work.* (uncountable)
Have you got ***any*** *better ideas?* (countable)
Do you have ***any*** *time at the weekend?* (uncountable)
No
A positive verb + *no* has the same meaning as a negative verb + *any*.
There are ***no*** *problems.*
= *There* ***aren't any*** *problems.* (countable)
I ***get no*** *independence.*
= *I* ***don't get any*** *independence.* (uncountable)

SEE LANGUAGE REFERENCE PAGE 34

1 Are the nouns in the box countable (C) or uncountable (U)?

bread U brother C cash U food U
friend C independence U money U
parent C peace U sofa C space U

Look at audioscript 1.26 on page 135 to check your answers.

2 Choose the correct words to complete the dialogue.

Mum: What's the (1) *problem / problems*, Ali? You look really unhappy at the moment.
Ali: There's (2) *any / no* problem, Mum.
Mum: Yes, there is. What's the matter? (3) *Is / Are* your teachers at college giving you a lot of (4) *homework / homeworks*?
Ali: No, it's not that. But you know I've got (5) *any / some* very important exams in two weeks …
Mum: Yes?
Ali: Well, I can't find the (6) *time / times* to study. I don't get (7) *any / no* peace in my room with the others there. It's really hard to work.
Mum: I'm sorry. I know what you mean. There really isn't (8) *any / some* space in the house when we have guests, is there?
Ali: Mum – I'm thinking of moving in with (9) *any / some* friends.
Mum: Oh, you can't do that! I know, I've got (10) *an / some* idea. Why don't you do your (11) *work / works* with me in the living room?

3 Work in pairs, A and B.

A: Turn to page 127. Look at the picture of Charlie's living room.
B: Turn to page 129. Look at the picture of Charlie's living room after a party.

How many differences can you find?

Are there ***any*** *plants in your picture?*
There are ***some*** *plates on the floor.*
There's ***no*** *rug in this picture.*

SPEAKING

1 Work in groups of three to five. You share a flat with the other students in your group. There are some problems and no one is really happy.

Read your role card and decide what you want to say to your flatmates. At the end of the discussion, make a list of four rules for the flat so that everyone is happy.

No smoking in the flat.

A: Turn to page 126. B: Turn to page 128.
C: Turn to page 129. D: Turn to page 130.
E: Turn to page 131.

You are sitting in the living room with your flatmates. Student C begins the discussion.

There are some things I want to talk about …

don't have any dirty
help with the house cleaning

3B | Migrants

READING

1 On a piece of paper, write everything that you know about Scotland. You have two minutes.

Now work in pairs and compare your ideas.

2 Match the words in the box to the definitions 1–6.

emigrants	immigrants	tribes
settlers	invaders	colonies

1 countries, or parts of a country, that are controlled by another country
2 large groups of related families
3 people who come to live in a country from another country
4 people who enter another country with an army
5 people who go to live in a place where not many people live
6 people who leave their country to live in another country

3 Read the article and put the sentences a–e in the gaps 1–5.

a We can still see the origins of many Scottish people in surnames like Macleod (from Norway) or Sinclair and Bruce (from France).
b This continues today and over 50,000 people in Scotland were born in Ireland.
c There are, for example, 75 places in the world called Hamilton (a common Scottish surname).
d Like most European countries, Scotland is a multicultural society.
e After this invasion, some of the Britons married Romans and began to adopt Roman customs.

Scotland: THE PEOPLE

The first people of Scotland belonged to two tribes called the *Picts* and the *Britons*. Most of the Picts lived in the north and east of the country. The Britons occupied the south and the area that is now called England. Both tribes spoke a Celtic language that is related to Irish and Welsh. Then the Romans invaded. (1) ____

In the 5th century, some Irish tribes began settling in the country. The Romans called these people the Scots, and later their new country was named after them. Two centuries later, Anglo-Saxons (many of them were from Germany and Holland, but some also came from Denmark) also settled in the south, and their language was an early form of English. A century later, Viking invaders from Norway also founded colonies. Most of these were in the north and the west. Much later, many people from France also arrived. (2) ____

Immigration to Scotland increased in the 19th century, especially from Ireland. (3) ____ In total, about 20% of the population probably have Irish origins. But in the 20th century, new immigrants began to arrive. Most of them come from Pakistan and India, but there are large communities from China and Poland. (4) ____

Scotland has a population of about five million, but there are about 30 million people of Scottish origin around the world – in north America, Australia and New Zealand. Most of these families left Scotland in the 19th century and some of them gave their names to the towns that they founded. (5) ____

Glossary
adopt *vb* start using a new or different way of doing something
found *vb* start an organization or institution

Speaking

1 Work in pairs. Discuss these questions.

- Did many people leave your country in the past? Why did they leave? Where did they go?
- Do many people from your country live abroad?
- Do you know anybody who lives abroad? If so, why did they go?
- What do people from your country miss when they are abroad?

Grammar: *some, many & most*

We can use *some, many* and *most* with or without *of*.

Some of *them gave their names to their home towns.*
Most of *these families left Scotland in the 19th century.*
Many *people from France also arrived.*
Some *Irish tribes began settling in the country.*

not many *some* *many* *most*	*of*	*the, my, his,* etc + plural noun *(people)* *them* *us*
not many *some* *many* *most*		+ plural noun *(Scots, days)*

See Language Reference page 34

1 In four of the sentences below the word *of* is missing. Insert *of* where necessary.

1 Many the passengers on the *Titanic* were leaving for a new life in America.
2 Most the Scots in America came in the 19th century.
3 Most Afro-Americans live in the southern states and the industrial cities.
4 Some US cities, like Boston, have big Irish communities.
5 There aren't many places in California that do not have a Spanish-speaking community.
6 Some the first immigrants to America were Dutch.
7 Not many the new immigrants to America come from Western Europe.
8 There are many Koreans and Japanese in LA.

2 Make true sentences using the phrases in the table.

Not many Some Many Most	people in this country people in this town students		are difficult to understand. are married. are very interesting. arrive late. don't have much money. drive a nice car. have a job. like their work. live near here. need English at work. speak two or three languages.
	of	the students in this class my friends my work colleagues our English lessons	
		us	

3 Work in pairs and compare your answers.

Did you know?

1 Work in pairs. Read the information about the United Kingdom and discuss the questions.

- Write the capital cities on the correct places on the map.
- What do you know about the different countries in the United Kingdom?

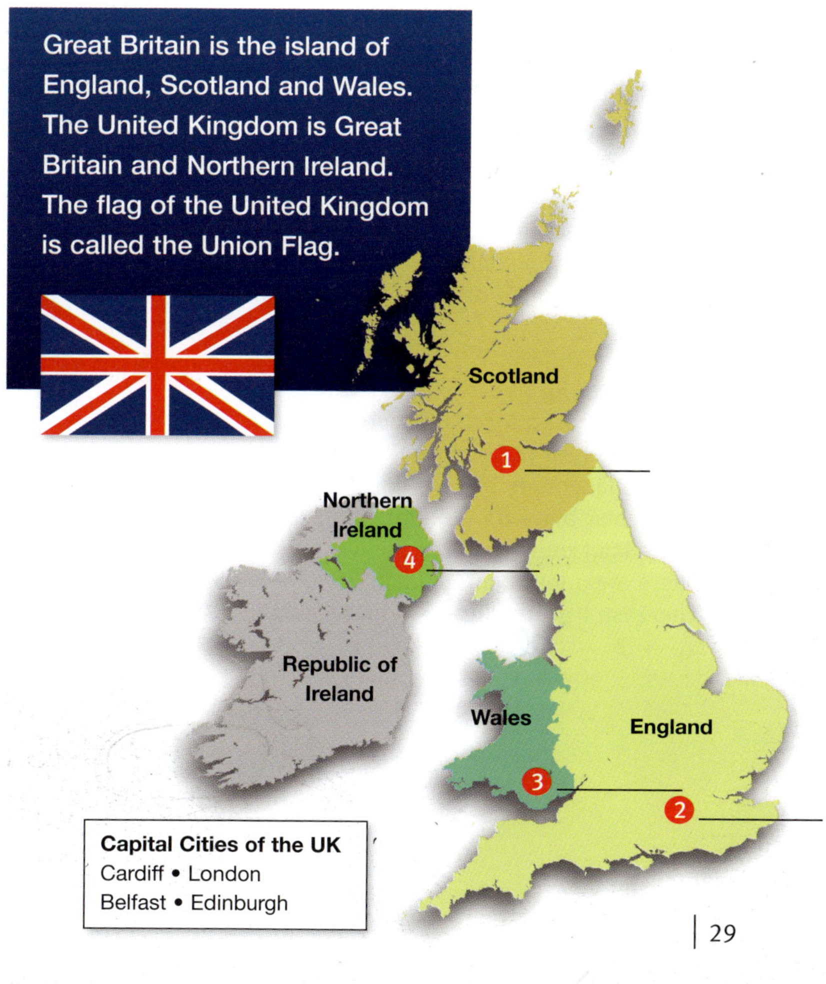

3c | Home town

VOCABULARY: towns

1 Look at the words in the box.

art gallery bar bus cinema
crime flat house library Metro
nightclub park pollution restaurant
studio theatre traffic tram

Put the words into these groups.

- public transport
- types of accommodation
- nightlife, culture
- other

Can you add any other words to the groups?

2 Imagine that you are going to live somewhere new. Which things are most important for you?

READING

1 Imagine that you are going to live in Montreal. Read the web page opposite. Choose which area (Verdun, Outremont or Old Montreal) you would prefer to live in. Why?

Work in pairs and compare your answers.

2 Read the web page again. Which part of Montreal do the sentences refer to: Verdun (V), Outremont (O) or Old Montreal (OM)?

1 = OM

1 There are a lot of cars.
2 It doesn't cost a lot to live here.
3 It has the best places to eat.
4 It isn't dangerous.
5 It's a good place for outdoor sport.
6 There isn't much to do in the evening.
7 There are a lot of cultural activities.
8 There isn't much cheap accommodation.

GRAMMAR: quantifiers

1 Look again at the text about Montreal. Find the expressions in the table below and complete the examples with nouns from the text.

quantifiers with plural countable nouns	quantifiers with uncountable nouns
too many tourists	*too much* traffic
a lot of ______	*a lot of* ______
many ______	*not much* ______
not many ______	*a little* ______
a few ______	*not enough* ______
not enough ______	

SEE LANGUAGE REFERENCE PAGE 34

2 Here is some more information about these places. Choose the correct expression to complete the sentences.

Verdun
1 There are *a lot of / much* cheap flats.
2 There are *not many / not much* hotels for tourists.
3 There are *a little / a few* big factories.
Outremont
4 There's *not many / not much* crime.
5 There are *a lot of / too much* French speakers.
6 There is *not many / not much* unemployment.
Old Montreal
7 There are *too many / too much* cars.
8 There are *many / too much* things to do for children.

3 Write six sentences about your town. Use a different quantifier in each sentence.

SPEAKING

1 Turn to page 127 and complete column A.

2 Work in pairs. Ask questions about your partner's town. Write the answers in column B on page 127.

Useful language

What is the name of your town?
How much … is there?
How many … are there?

3 Compare your answers.

If you described the same town as your partner, did you have the same answers?

If you described a different town, which town is the better place to live?

File Edit View Favourites Tools Help Links

Living in Montreal

Home | Mini guide | Choosing an area | Public transport | Eating | Health | Services

Harbor and waterfront

Verdun

We live down by the river. It's a poor area and there's a lot of crime, but the shops are good and there are a few good restaurants. The shopping area is not very attractive, but it is changing. Public transport is excellent and we're near the city centre. In the summer, Verdun is the place to be. The river here is really beautiful and you can have picnics in the park. There isn't enough nightlife for us, so we go to the area near the university for that. Accommodation is cheap!!

BRIGITTE GOFFIN & BERNARD YIP (students)

Want to know more? CLICK HERE

Outremont

Outremont has many advantages. The best restaurants in town, the most beautiful park and the biggest houses. You feel safe here. You meet interesting, important people and it's good for business. There are not many Japanese restaurants and we do very well. When we're not working, we like having a coffee outside one of the cafés. We don't have much time to enjoy the area, but we like going up to the park at Mount Royal sometimes. The only problem, really, is that you need to speak French in this part of town (and we don't!).

K.INAMOTO (restaurant owner)

Want to know more? CLICK HERE

Old Montreal

True, there are too many tourists and there's too much traffic. The Metro doesn't take you into the centre of Old Montreal. There is a little crime in the area, but not too much. But why am I being so negative? Old Montreal is the *only* place to be. There are a lot of good bars and restaurants. There are excellent museums (if you like that kind of thing), an IMAX® cinema, an interesting park to go rollerblading in the summer or ice-skating in the winter. What more do you want? Just one big problem: not enough cheap flats. I found the last one!

Mr. J. B. LAZARIDIS (computer programmer)

Want to know more? CLICK HERE

Marie Reine du Monde Cathedral

Old Montreal

3D | Lost!

Speaking

1 Read the information about the city of Newcastle.

2 Work in small groups.

Are there any towns or cities in your country that are similar to Newcastle? In what ways?

Bilbao is near the sea. It also has a famous football team …

Official name:	Newcastle-upon-Tyne.
Location:	North-east England. On the River Tyne, 13 kilometres from the North Sea.
Population:	Approximately 200,000.
History:	Old Roman town. 19th century industrial centre (ships, coal).

A lively city with good nightlife.
Centre for contemporary art.
Interesting place to visit.
Famous football team.
Beautiful countryside.

Vocabulary: places in a town

1 Label the map below with the words in the box.

bridge	art gallery	castle	bars and restaurants
bus station	cathedral	church	~~library~~
opera house	shopping centre	stadium	train station

2 Are the statements below true (T) or false (F)? Correct the false sentences.

1 The art gallery is opposite the library.
2 The bars and restaurants are near the river.
3 The cathedral is opposite the stadium.
4 The opera house is next to the castle.
5 The shopping centre is between the art gallery and the bus station.
6 There is a Metro station not far from the stadium.

3 Do you have these places in your town? Where are they?

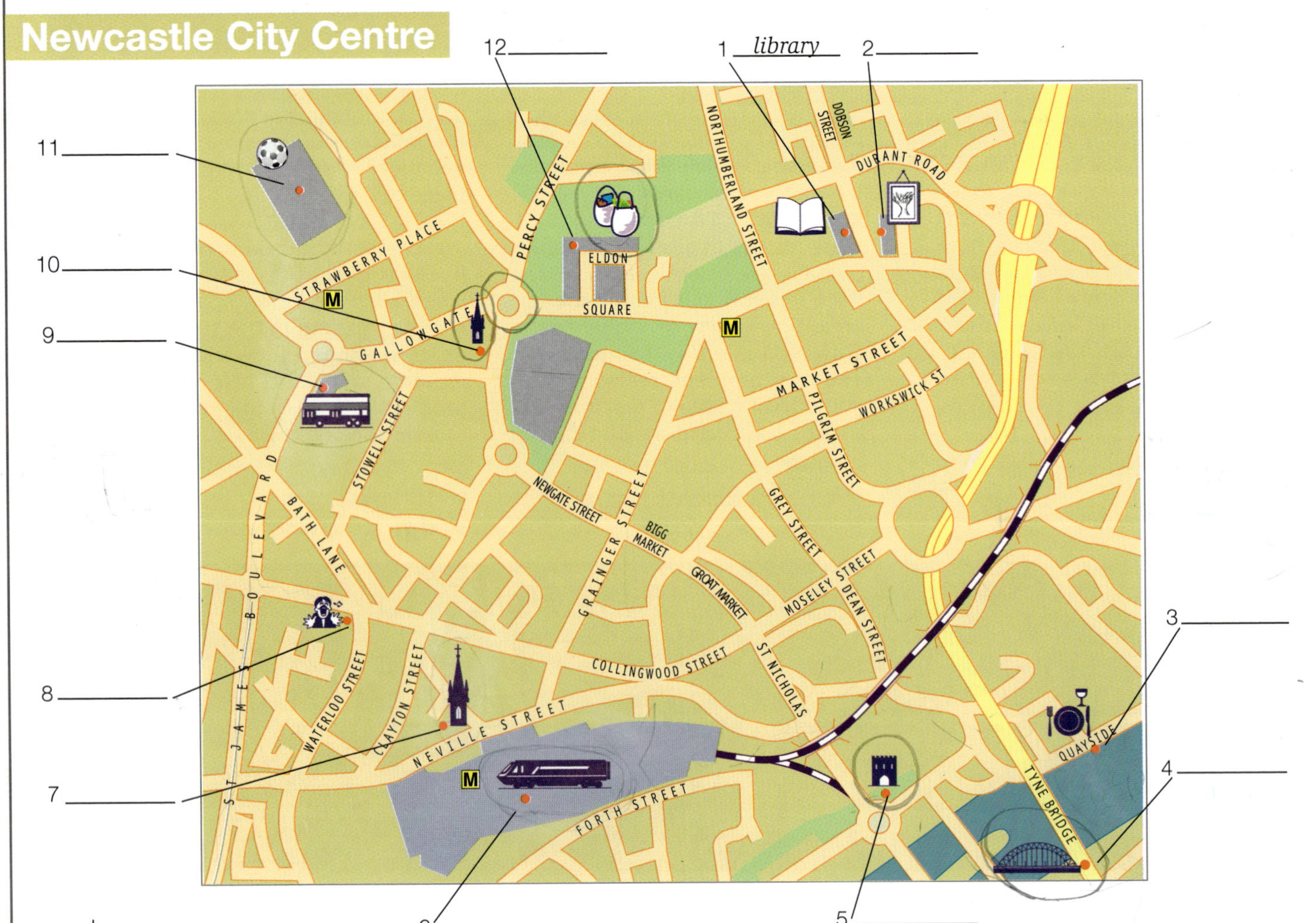

LISTENING & FUNCTIONAL LANGUAGE: directions

1 1.27–1.29 Listen to three dialogues. Two football supporters want to get from the football stadium in Newcastle to the train station. Answer the questions.

1. Circle on the map the places that they walk past.
2. Do Kate and Ali get to the station in the end?

2 1.27 Listen to the first dialogue again and complete the sentences.

1. ________ right.
2. ________ straight on.
3. ________ the first street on the right.
4. ________ the road.
5. ________ past the Metro station.
6. ________ to the end of the road.

3 Match the phrases in exercise 2 to the pictures A–F.

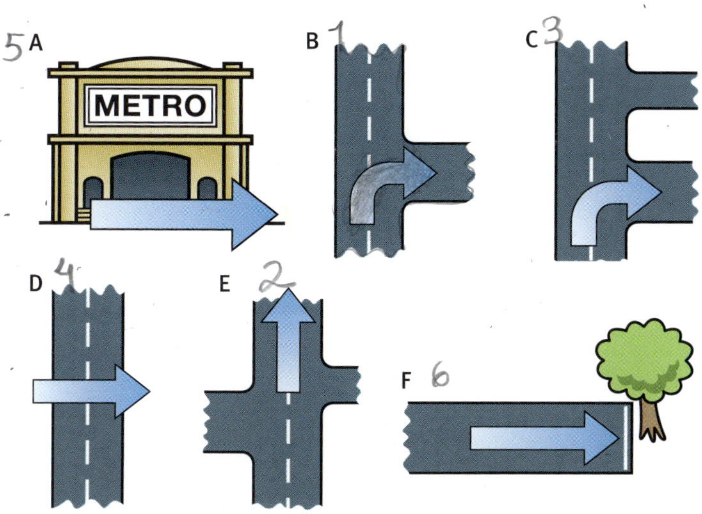

4 Work in pairs, A and B. You are at the train station in Newcastle.

A: Choose a place you want to go to. Ask B for directions.
B: Look at the map and give A directions.

Questions

Excuse me,	*where's the …* *can/could you tell me the way to …* *how do I get to …*	*please?*

Prepositions

behind *between* *near* *not far from*
in front of *opposite* *next to* *on the corner of*

PRONUNCIATION: *to*

1 1.30 Listen to the pronunciation of the word *to* (/tə/) in the middle of these phrases:

- interesting place to visit
- difficult to give directions
- next to the castle

2 Look at audioscript 1.27 on page 135. There are four examples of *to* in the middle of a phrase. Find them and underline them.

3 1.31 Listen to the recording to check your answers.

4 Practise saying the phrases with the short pronunciation of *to* (/tə/).

Self-assessment (tick ✔)

- ☐ I can describe a town in my country.
- ☐ I can understand and give directions.
- ☐ I can use prepositions when giving directions.

3 | Language reference

Grammar
Countable & uncountable nouns

Countable nouns
Most nouns in English are countable. We can count them. They have both a singular and plural form for example, *one house, two houses*.

It's a new house.
He's got two houses in London.

A small group of countable nouns has irregular plurals (*child/children, man/men, woman/women, foot/feet, tooth/teeth, mouse/mice*).

Uncountable nouns
Some nouns are uncountable. We cannot count them. For example, we cannot say *two ~~homeworks~~*. They only have a singular form.

I want to do my homework.

Some nouns can be both countable and uncountable. The uncountable noun refers to the thing in general; the countable noun refers to a particular example of it.

***Crime** is a problem in many cities.*
(uncountable: crime in general)

*Sherlock Holmes solved hundreds of **crimes**.*
(countable: particular crimes)

Determiners

Some & any
We use *some* and *any* to describe an indefinite quantity of something. We can use *some* and *any* with both countable and uncountable nouns.

We usually use *some* in positive sentences.

*I've got **some** biscuits.* (countable)
*He's going to buy **some** milk.* (uncountable)

We usually use *any* in negative sentences and questions.

*Mark doesn't like **any** vegetables.* (countable)
*I haven't got **any** money.* (uncountable)
*Have you got **any** apples?* (countable)
*Do you have **any** advice for me?* (uncountable)

No
We use *no* with both countable and uncountable nouns. A positive verb + *no* has the same meaning as a negative verb + *any*.

*There are **no** biscuits.* = There aren't any biscuits. (countable)

*I have **no** time.* = I don't have any time. (uncountable)

Quantifiers
We can use quantifiers before a noun to show how much of something there is.

quantifiers with plural countable nouns	quantifiers with uncountable nouns
too many	*too much*
a lot of	*a lot of*
many	*not much*
not many	*a little*
a few	*not enough*
not enough	

*There are **too many** tourists in this town.*
*I know **a few** good restaurants near here.*
*We do **not** have **much** time.*

We do not usually use *much* in affirmative sentences. We use *a lot of* instead.

*There's **a lot of** work to do.* Not *~~There's much work~~*.

Some, many & most
We can use *some, many* and *most* with or without *of*.

<table>
<tr><td>Not many
Some
Many</td><td>of</td><td>my friends
the students
them</td><td rowspan="2">live at home.</td></tr>
<tr><td>Most</td><td colspan="2">students</td></tr>
</table>

***Some of** my friends are working.*
***Most of** the people I know are very interesting.*
***Many** people spend their holidays abroad.*
***Most** days, I do some homework.*

Functional Language

Directions

Excuse me,	*where's the …*	*please?*
	can/could you tell me the way to …	
	how do I get to …	

behind
between
in front of
near
next to
not far from
on the corner of
opposite

Cross the bridge/road.
Go past the …
Go straight on.
Go to the end of the road/street.
Take the first/second street on the left/ right.

Word list

House & home

(be) away from home *phr*	/bi: ə'weɪ frəm həʊm/
get home *phr*	/get 'həʊm/
home town *n C*	/'həʊm taʊn/
homework *n U* *	/'həʊmˌwɜ:(r)k/
housewife *n C*	/'haʊsˌwaɪf/
housework *n U*	/'haʊsˌwɜ:(r)k/
leave home *phr*	/li:v 'həʊm/

Towns

accommodation *n U* **	/əˌkɒmə'deɪʃ(ə)n/
art gallery *n C*	/'ɑ:(r)t gæləri/
bar *n C* ***	/bɑ:(r)/
bridge *n C* **	/brɪdʒ/
bus station *n C*	/bʌs 'steɪʃ(ə)n/
castle *n C* **	/'kɑ:s(ə)l/
cathedral *n C*	/kə'θi:drəl/
church *n C* ***	/tʃɜ:(r)tʃ/
cinema *n C* **	/'sɪnəmə/
crime *n C/U* ***	/kraɪm/
culture *n U* ***	/'kʌltʃə(r)/
flat *n C* **	/flæt/
industrial *adj* ***	/ɪn'dʌstriəl/
library *n C* ***	/'laɪbrəri/
Metro *n C*	/'metrəʊ/
museum *n C* ***	/mju:'zi:əm/
nightclub *n C*	/'naɪtˌklʌb/
nightlife *n U*	/'naɪtˌlaɪf/
opera house *n C*	/'ɒp(ə)rə haʊs/
park *n C* **	/pɑ:(r)k/
pollution *n U* **	/pə'lu:ʃ(ə)n/
public transport *n U*	/'pʌblɪk trænspɔ:(r)t/
restaurant *n C* ***	/'rest(ə)rɒnt/
roundabout *n C*	/'raʊndəˌbaʊt/
shopping centre *n C*	/'ʃɒpɪŋ sentə(r)/
stadium *n C*	/'steɪdiəm/
studio *n C* **	/'stju:diəʊ/
theatre *n C* **	/'θɪətə(r)/
traffic *n U* ***	/'træfɪk/
tram *n C*	/træm/
train station *n C*	/treɪn 'steɪʃ(ə)n/

Other words & phrases

abroad *adv* ***	/ə'brɔ:d/
adopt *v* *	/ə'dɒpt/
area *n C* ***	/'eəriə/
cash *n U* ***	/kæʃ/
century *n C* ***	/'sentʃəri/
cheap *adj* ***	/tʃi:p/
coal *n U* *	/kəʊl/
colony *n C*	/'kɒləni/
community *n C* ***	/kə'mju:nəti/
countryside *n U* **	/'kʌntriˌsaɪd/
custom *n C* **	/'kʌstəm/
dirty *adj* ***	/'dɜ:(r)ti/
discourage *v*	/dɪs'kʌrɪdʒ/
drive (sb) mad *v*	/draɪv (sb) mæd/
emigrant *n C*	/'emɪgrənt/
encourage *v* ***	/ɪn'kʌrɪdʒ/
flatmate *n C*	/'flætˌmeɪt/
flag *n C*	/flæg/
found *v* *	/faʊnd/
guest *n C* **	/gest/
hang on *v*	/'hæŋ ɒn/
immigrant *n C*	/'ɪmɪgrənt/
immigration *n U*	/ˌɪmɪ'greɪʃ(ə)n/
independence *n U* **	/ˌɪndɪ'pendəns/
invade *v*	/ɪn'veɪd/
invasion *n C*	/ɪn'veɪʒ(ə)n/
migrant *n C*	/'maɪgrənt/
multicultural *adj*	/ˌmʌlti'kʌltʃərəl/
normal *adj* ***	/'nɔ:(r)m(ə)l/
occupy *v* ***	/'ɒkjʊpaɪ/
ordinary *adj* ***	/'ɔ:(r)d(ə)n(ə)ri/
origin *n C* **	/'ɒrɪdʒɪn/
outdoor *adj*	/ˌaʊt'dɔ:(r)/
owner *n C* ***	/'əʊnə(r)/
passenger *n C* **	/'pæsɪndʒə(r)/
peace *n U* ***	/pi:s/
picnic *n C*	/'pɪknɪk/
population *n C* ***	/ˌpɒpjʊ'leɪʃ(ə)n/
put (sb) off *v*	/pʊt (sb) ɒf/
rollerblading *n U*	/'rəʊlə(r)ˌbleɪdɪŋ/
settle *v* ***	/'set(ə)l/
skating *n U*	/'skeɪtɪŋ/
sofa *n C*	/'səʊfə/
space *n U* ***	/speɪs/
tough *adj* **	/tʌf/
tourist *n C* **	/'tʊərɪst/
tribe *n C*	/traɪb/
twin *n C* *	/twɪn/

4A | Relationships

Speaking & Reading

1 Work in pairs. Answer the questions.

- Do you agree or disagree with the quotations below? Explain your reasons.

> Love is a serious mental disease. (Plato)
> Love is life. Everything that I understand, I understand only because I love. (Tolstoy)
> Love is all you need. (John Lennon)
> Love makes time pass. Time makes love pass. (French proverb)
> Men love with their eyes; women love with their ears. (Zsa Zsa Gabor)

- What is your definition of love?

2 Do the quiz opposite. Then read the analysis of your relationship style.

3 Do you agree with the results of the quiz? Why or why not?

Grammar: present simple

We use the present simple to talk about habits and things that are generally/always true.
*I usually **try** to solve my problems myself.*
*They **want** to be close to other people.*

Remember to add *-s* to the third person singular.
*He quickly **forgets** about arguments with his friends.*

Frequency adverbs and phrases
We usually put words like *often, sometimes, never* before the main verb, or after the verb *to be*.
*I **never** tell my secrets to people I do not know well.*
*They **often** find it easy to make friends.*

We can put phrases like *from time to time, every day, once a week* at the beginning or end of the sentence.
*I check my emails **twice a day**.*

See Language Reference page 44

1 Rearrange the words to make questions.

1 do do friends with what you your ?
2 being like do other people with you
3 cities do friends have in other you
4 away do from how much home spend time you
5 daytime do in the do what you ?
6 day do every how many send texts you ?
7 do doing like on own what you your ?
8 do have kind of parents relationship what with you your ?

2 Work in pairs. Ask and answer the questions in exercise 1.

3 Make the sentences true for you using words and phrases from the boxes.

always usually often sometimes never

once twice three times	a	day week month year
every		
from time to time		

1 I get up late in the morning.
2 I go for a walk in the afternoon.
3 I am tired in the evenings.
4 I have dinner in a restaurant.
5 I read before I go to bed.
6 I visit friends at the weekend.

4 Make questions from the sentences in exercise 3. Begin: *How often do you ... ?*

Work in pairs. Ask and answer the questions.

Pronunciation: final -s

1 1.32 Listen to the pronunciation of the final *-s* in these words. There are two ways of pronouncing the letter *-s* at the end of singular verbs and plural nouns.

/z/ goes lives days friends
/s/ likes wants books streets

2 1.32 Listen and repeat.

3 How do you pronounce the final *-s* in these words?

knows learns maps spends talks writes
facts parties problems questions states things

4 1.33 Listen to the recording to check.

What is your **relationship style?**

Psychologists believe that there are three basic styles of relationship. Do the quiz to find out your style!

	True	False
It is usually easy for me to show my feelings to other people.		
I often worry that people don't like me very much.		
My work or my studies are more important than my social life.		
I sometimes prefer to spend my free time on my own.		
I always choose friends who are good fun to be with.		
From time to time, I invent excuses when I don't feel like going out.		
I have a good relationship with my parents.		
I do not often talk to my parents about my friends.		
I usually check my personal emails more than twice a day.		
I know that I can always rely on my friends.		
I have lots of friends, but I do not have many very close friends.		
It often takes me a long time to make new friends.		
I feel that my friends usually understand me.		
I do not fall in love very quickly.		
I do not worry when I do not see my friends for a long time.		
I do not usually like it when people stand too close to me.		
I never tell my secrets to people that I do not know well.		
I communicate with my friends by text, Twitter™ or Facebook™ more than three times a day.		
I usually try to solve problems myself before I ask my friends for help.		
I quickly forget about arguments with my friends.		
It is important to me to see my best friends at least once a week.		
I do not always understand why other people like me.		
I don't care too much if other people don't like me.		
I do not want other people to use me.		

Now calculate your score. Look ONLY at your 'true' responses. Are they mostly green, blue or red?

Mostly green – a secure relationship style
People with a secure relationship style usually feel confident and safe in their relationships. They think positively about their friends, their partners and themselves. They often find it easy to make friends, but they do not worry about being alone from time to time.

Mostly blue – an anxious relationship style
People with an anxious relationship style are often worried that something bad will happen in their relationships. They want to be close to other people – sometimes too close – but they find it difficult to trust others. They do not always have a positive opinion about themselves. Their relationships with other people can be very up and down.

Mostly red – an avoidant relationship style
People with an avoidant relationship style like to be independent. They do not always want or need to be close to other people. They have friends but they know that relationships do not always last for ever. They often prefer to hide their true feelings.

4B | Wedding bells

A

B

C

D

E

VOCABULARY & SPEAKING: weddings

1 Find these things in the photos.

bouquet	bride	church	groom
priest	ring	wedding cake	

2 Complete the description of English weddings with words from the box.

ceremony	guests	honeymoon
reception	registry office	speech

The (1) ______ usually takes place in a church or (2) ______. After the ceremony, the couple and their (3) ______ go to the (4) ______, where they drink champagne and eat the wedding cake. Later on, at the wedding meal, the best friend of the groom makes a (5) ______. The married couple often leave the party early to go on their (6) ______.

3 **1.34** Listen to the recording to check your answers.

4 Describe a wedding that you have been to. Use these questions to prepare what you are going to say.

- Who got married?
- Where and when were the ceremony and the reception?
- What did the bride and groom wear?
- Who did you go with?
- How many guests were there? Who were they?
- Was there any music at the wedding?
- What did you eat and drink?
- Did anyone make a speech? What did they say?
- Did anything interesting or unusual happen?

READING

1 *Marriage is a thing of the past.* Do you agree? Work in pairs. Explain why or why not.

2 Read the magazine article and find out if the writer agrees that marriage is a thing of the past.

COMMENT

IF YOU ASK ME . . .

Sue Carey disagrees with her university professor

(1) ______ More and more people are living together and having children without getting married, she told us. The number of divorces is increasing all the time. It doesn't matter if you are single or married, she said with a smile of victory. 'The prison of marriage belongs to an older generation!'

(2) ______ But now, twenty years later – is marriage dead? You do not need to think about it for long: go to any newsagent and look at the magazines on sale. On the cover of every popular magazine like *Hello!* someone is getting married. Or maybe someone is getting divorced. The stories sell the magazines and, in thousands of offices around the world, people are sitting around and looking at the wedding photos of the rich and famous.

(3) ______ In the UK, people are waiting until they are older to get married, but the number of weddings is actually increasing. True, divorces are also going up, but people are getting married again, for a second, third or fourth time.

(4) ______ In the year after university, I went to the weddings of four of my friends. My own (first) marriage was two years later. We want to read about marriage, look at films and photos, and do it ourselves. It appears that we can't get enough of it. Sorry professor, but the conclusion seems clear: marriage is very much alive and well.

3 Read the article again and put the sentences a–d in the gaps 1–4.

a Marriage is certainly changing.
b Marriage, said one of my professors at university, belongs to the past.
c She sounded sure of herself and we all agreed – or, at least, nobody disagreed.
d The simple fact is that most of us believe that marriage is good for us.

4 Work in pairs. Discuss these questions.

- Is marriage changing in your country? How?
- At what age do people usually get married?
- What are the advantages and disadvantages of getting married?

Grammar: present continuous

We use the present continuous to talk about things that are happening now or around now.
*What **are** you **doing**? I'**m preparing** my speech.*
*More and more people **are getting** married.*
*Why **is** the number of weddings **increasing**?*

We cannot normally use some verbs (stative verbs) in the continuous form.
agree belong cost know like love
matter mean need seem understand want

See Language Reference page 44

1 Complete the sentences. Put the verbs in brackets into the present continuous.

1 Hi. Yes. I'm on the train. We ____ (*come*) into Central Station.
2 Excuse me! I ____ (*try*) to work!
3 I ____ (*tell*) you the truth. I promise.
4 Let's stay here. It ____ (*rain*) outside.
5 And three players ____ (*speak*) to the referee, who ____ (*hold*) up a red card.

Imagine a situation for each sentence. Who is speaking? Where are they?

2 Choose the correct verb form to complete the sentences.

1 The average UK wedding usually *costs / is costing* about £13,000.
2 We can see the Princess now – she *wears / 's wearing* a beautiful white dress.
3 Every time I *get / am getting* divorced, I keep the house.
4 Look! She *doesn't wear / isn't wearing* her wedding ring.
5 More and more women in England *keep / are keeping* their own name when they get married.
6 *Do you ever talk / Are you ever talking* to your husband?
7 My girlfriend *doesn't love / isn't loving* me.
8 It *doesn't matter / is not mattering* if you're married or not.

3 Look at the picture of a wedding reception on page 130. Prepare five questions with the present continuous about the picture.

How many people are dancing?
What is the man with the white jacket doing?

4 Work in pairs. Close your books and ask your partner the questions you have prepared.

Did you know?

1 Work in groups. Read the information about wedding traditions in Britain and America and discuss the questions.

- Are they the same in your country?
- What wedding traditions do you have in your country?

The groom arrives at the wedding before his bride.

The bride wears a long white dress and a group of young girls (bridesmaids) follow her into the church.

The bride throws a bouquet of flowers in the air and other single women try to catch it. The woman who catches it will be the next to get married.

The bride and groom cut the wedding cake together.

After a wedding, the groom carries the bride into their new home.

A woman wears her wedding ring on the third finger of the left hand.

4c | At the movies

Speaking

1 Look at the photos from three films. What do you think is happening in each photo?

2 Work in pairs. Choose one of the photos and prepare a short dialogue (three or four lines long) to go with it.

3 Perform your dialogue in front of the class. The other students must decide which photo you have chosen.

Listening

1 1.35 Listen to a woman talking about the film in the poster. What kind of film is it?

2 1.35 Listen to the recording again. Answer the questions. Write A (Amanda), I (Iris), G (Graham) or M (Miles).

1 Who lives in England? _____ _____
2 Who lives in America? _____ _____
3 Who has split up with her boyfriend? _____
4 Who decides to swap homes? _____ _____
5 Who doesn't know that his partner is cheating on him? _____
6 Who does Jasper visit? _____
7 Who does Iris go to England with? _____

Look at audioscript 1.35 on page 136 to check your answers.

3 If you have seen this film, did you like it? If you have not seen this film, would you like to see it? Why or why not?

VOCABULARY: relationship verbs

1 Complete the phrases in columns A and B with a word from the box.

about (x2) in (x3) on out (x2) to up

A

1 He asked her ____ and
2 He was crazy ____ her and
3 They had a big argument ____ something and
4 They had a lot ____ common and
5 They went ____ together for a long time but

B

a she didn't want to get married ____ him.
b she was ____ love with him, too.
c then they split ____.
d they went ____ a date to the cinema.
e they fell ____ love very quickly.

2 Now complete the sentences in column A with a phrase from column B. Sometimes there is more than one possible answer.

3 Work in pairs. Use the expressions in exercise 1 to talk about people you know.

My brother, Lewis, asked my best friend, Stephanie, out.

FUNCTIONAL LANGUAGE: telling stories

> When we tell a story informally (for example, personal stories, or the story of a film), we often use the present simple.
>
> *Iris **meets** Miles and they **get** on very well, but Miles **is** also crazy about someone else.*

1 Work in groups of four: pair A and pair B.

Pair A: Turn to page 126.
Pair B: Turn to page 131.

Read the story of the film twice and then close your books.

2 Now practise telling your story together.

3 Swap partners and work with a student who read about a different film. Tell each other your stories.

PRONUNCIATION: /ɪ/ & /iː/

1 1.36 Listen to the recording and repeat the words in the table.

/ɪ/	/iː/
live	leave
think	teeth
still	street
rich	feel
hit	meet

2 Underline the sounds /ɪ/ and /iː/ in the film titles below.

Beauty and the Beast *The Big Sleep* *Mission Impossible*
Pretty Woman *ET* *Robin Hood: Prince of Thieves*
The Prince of Egypt

3 1.37 Listen to the recording to check your answers.

4D | Going out

Speaking

1 Work in pairs. Discuss these questions.

- Which famous person would you like to spend an evening with? Why?
- Where would you like to go?
- What would you like to do during the evening?

Listening

1 1.38–1.39 Listen to two dialogues. How well do the people know each other? Why are they telephoning?

2 1.38–1.39 Listen to the dialogues again and complete the information.

1 Nancy and Sebastian met at a friend's house on _____ of last week.
2 Sebastian is going to his parents' _____ anniversary on Saturday.
3 They agree to meet at a café on Sunday at half past _____.
4 Jason usually goes _____ on Sundays.
5 He agrees to join his friends for _____ after their meal.
6 Sebastian thinks it is going to _____ on Sunday.

Functional language: invitations & suggestions

1 Choose the correct verb form to complete the invitations and suggestions.

Invitations and suggestions

1	Would you like *go / to go / going*	to the cinema?
2	Shall we *go / to go / going*	
3	Why don't we *go / to go / going*	
4	How about *go / to go / going*	
5	What about *go / to go / going*	
6	Do you fancy *go / to go / going*	
7	Let's *go / to go / going*	to the cinema.

Responses

OK, *Yes,*	*that's a good idea.* *why not?*
I'd rather … (+ infinitive) *I'd rather not.* *I'd love to, but I'm afraid I'm busy.* *That's very kind of you, but …*	

Look at audioscripts 1.38–1.39 on page 136 to check your answers.

2 Complete the sentences. Put the verbs in brackets into the correct form.

Lucy: Hi, Dan, would you like (1) _____ (*go*) out somewhere on Monday?
Dan: _____
Lucy: What a pity! Why don't we (2) _____ (*do*) something on Tuesday, then?
Dan: All right. Let's (3) _____ (*do*) that. Where shall we (4) _____ (*go*)?
Lucy: How about (5) _____ (*go*) to a club?
Dan: _____
Lucy: Well, why don't we (6) _____ (*have*) a meal at the Hard Rock Café?
Dan: _____
Lucy: OK. That's a good idea. Where shall we (7) _____ (*meet*)?

3 Complete the dialogue in exercise 2 with the sentences a–c.

a I'd rather not. I'm not too keen on clubbing.
b I'd rather go for a pizza, if that's OK with you.
c That's very kind of you, Lucy. I'd love to, but I'm afraid I'm busy on Monday.

4 Work in pairs. Practise the dialogue.

5 Imagine you are a famous person (alive or dead). Decide what you like doing when you go out for the evening.

Work in pairs. Try to make arrangements to go out together.

GRAMMAR: prepositions of time

in +	month (***in*** *January*) year (***in*** *2004*) season (***in*** *the summer*) *the morning, the afternoon, the evening*
on +	day(s) (***on*** *Monday*, ***on*** *Mondays*) dates (***on*** *7th June*) *Monday morning, Tuesday evening*
at +	time (***at*** *3 o'clock*, ***at*** *dinner time*) *night* *the weekend*

SEE LANGUAGE REFERENCE PAGE 45

1 Complete the sentences with *in*, *on* or *at*.

1 We met ______ Friday February 14th.
2 He called me ______ Saturday morning.
3 We had our first date ______ the evening.
4 I saw him again ______ Monday and Wednesday.
5 I met his parents ______ the weekend.
6 I asked him to marry me ______ Sunday evening.
7 Our wedding is ______ March – on the 14th!

2 Complete the sentences with *in*, *on* or *at* and a time expression.

In my country/town …
1 the most popular time to get married is …
2 people usually have dinner …
3 most people go on holiday …
4 the best time to go shopping is …
5 the best programmes on TV are …
6 the roads are really busy …

3 Work in pairs. Compare your sentences.

SPEAKING

1 Work in groups. Describe the social life of the following groups of people in your town.

14–15 year-olds
18–21 year-olds
28–35 year-olds
65–75 year-olds

Now compare your ideas with the ideas of students from other groups.

Which age group has the most fun?

Useful language

It varies (= it's not always the same)
It depends (*on* …)
On the whole, … (= usually/generally)

2 What about you? Are you the same as most people in your country?

Self-assessment (tick ✔)

☐ I can invite someone to go out and respond to invitations.
☐ I can make and respond to suggestions.
☐ I can discuss social activities.

4 | Language reference

Grammar

Present simple

We use the present simple to talk about habits and things that are generally/always true.

*I **buy** a newspaper every day.*
*Mark **comes** from Australia.*

We can also use the present simple to tell a story informally, for example, personal stories, or the story of a film.

*She **doesn't know** his real name, but they **seem** to have a lot in common and they **get** on really well.*

Affirmative & Negative		
I	work don't work	in a bank.
He/She/It	works doesn't work	
You/We/They	work don't work	

Question			
Where	do	I	work?
	does	he/she/it	
	do	you/we/they	

Short answer	
Do you work in a bank?	Yes, I do. / No, I don't.
Does she live at home?	Yes, she does. / No, she doesn't.

The present simple with *I/you/we/they* has the same form as the infinitive. We usually add *-s* to the verb with the third person singular, (*he, she* and *it*). There are two groups of exceptions.

1 We add *-es* to verbs that end in *-o, -s, -sh, -ch, -x*.
*she watch**es*** *he go**es*** *it finish**es***
2 We change *-y* to *-ies* in verbs that end in *-y*.
*she stud**ies*** *he carr**ies*** *it fl**ies***

Frequency adverbs & phrases

We can use frequency expressions with the present simple to talk about how often something happens.

We usually put single words (*never, rarely, sometimes, often, usually, generally, always*) before the main verb.

*He **always** wakes up late.*
*Do you **usually** get up early?*

If the verb is *to be*, we put these words after the verb.

*She is **always** tired.*
*They were **never** late.*

We can put phrases (*once a week, twice a month, every year*) at the beginning or the end of the sentence.

*He studies **twice a week**.*
***Twice a week**, he goes to English classes.*

Present continuous

We use the present continuous to talk about things that are happening now or around now.

*What **are** you **doing**? I'**m cooking** a meal.*
*My husband'**s working** very hard at the moment.*

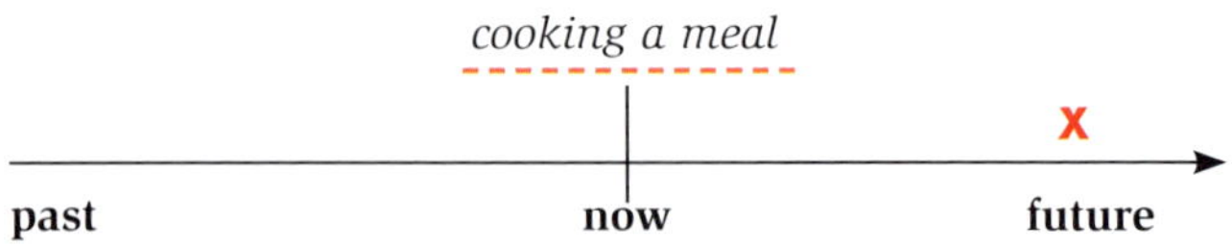

Affirmative & Negative		
I	'm 'm not	eating.
He/She/It	's isn't	
You/We/They	're aren't	

Question			
What	am	I	eating?
	is	he/she/it	
	are	you/we/they	

Short answer	
Are you going to the party?	Yes, I am. / No, I'm not.
Are they going to the party?	Yes, they are. / No, they aren't.

We make the present continuous with *is/are* + infinitive + *-ing*. There are some spelling exceptions. See the notes on past continuous on page 24.

See page 54 for more information about the present continuous.

Stative verbs

We cannot normally use stative verbs in the continuous form. Here are some common stative verbs.

agree appear believe belong cost dislike fit forget hate know like love matter mean need own prefer remember seem understand want

*Yes, I **agree** with you.* Not *~~I'm **agreeing** with you~~.*
*I **understand** Italian.* Not *~~I'm **understanding** Italian~~.*

Prepositions of time

in +	month (***in*** *January*) year (***in*** *2004*) season (***in*** *the summer*) periods of time (***in*** *the 1990s,* ***in*** *the 20th century,* ***in*** *the holidays*) *the morning, the afternoon, the evening*
on +	day(s) (***on*** *Monday,* ***on*** *Mondays,* ***on*** *my birthday,* ***on*** *Christmas Day*) dates (***on*** *7th June,* ***on*** *Friday 13th*) *Monday morning, Tuesday evening*

We use *on Mondays* (plural) to talk about Mondays in general – something we do every Monday. We use *on Monday* (singular) to talk about either Mondays in general, or one particular Monday.

On Mondays/Monday*, I usually go out with my best friend.*
On Monday*, I'm seeing the doctor.*

at +	time (***at*** *3 o'clock,* ***at*** *dinner time*) *night* *the weekend* holiday periods (***at*** *Easter,* ***at*** *Christmas*)

We can make the time more approximate by putting an adverb between *at* and the time.

at	***about, almost, around, just after, just before nearly***	*two o'clock*

FUNCTIONAL LANGUAGE

Invitations & suggestions

Would you like to + infinitive … ?
Shall we + infinitive … ?
Let's + infinitive … .
Why don't we + infinitive … ?
How about + verb + *-ing* … ?
What about + verb + *-ing* … ?
Do you fancy + verb + *-ing* … ?

Responses

OK.
Yes, that's a good idea.
Yes, why not?
I'd rather + infinitive …
I'd rather not.
I'd love to, but I'm afraid I'm busy.
That's very kind of you, but …

When we say *no* to an invitation or suggestion, it is polite to give a reason.

WORD LIST

Weddings

bouquet *n C*	/buːˈkeɪ/
bride *n C*	/braɪd/
bridesmaid *n C*	/ˈbraɪdzˌmeɪd/
ceremony *n C* *	/ˈserəməni/
champagne *n U*	/ˌʃæmˈpeɪn/
church *n C* ***	/tʃɜː(r)tʃ/
groom *n C*	/gruːm/
guest *n C* **	/gest/
honeymoon *n C*	/ˈhʌniˌmuːn/
marriage *n C/U* ***	/ˈmærɪdʒ/
priest *n C* *	/priːst/
reception *n C* *	/rɪˈsepʃ(ə)n/
registry office *n C*	/ˈredʒɪstri ˈɒfɪs/
ring *n C* ***	/rɪŋ/
speech *n C* ***	/spiːtʃ/
wedding cake *n C/U*	/ˈwedɪŋ keɪk/

Relationships

ask (sb) out *phr*	/ɑːsk (sb) aʊt/
be crazy about (sb) *phr*	/bi ˈkreɪzi əˈbaʊt/
be in love with (sb) *phr*	/bi ɪn lʌv wɪð/
divorce *n C* *	/dɪˈvɔː(r)s/
divorced *adj* *	/dɪˈvɔː(r)st/
fall in love with (sb)	/fɔːl ɪn lʌv wɪð/ *phr*
get married to (sb) *phr*	/get ˈmærid tə/
go (out) on a date *phr*	/gəʊ (aʊt) ɒn ə deɪt/
go out with (sb) *phr*	/gəʊ aʊt wɪð/
have an argument about (sth) *phr*	/hæv ən ˈɑː(r)gjʊmənt əˈbaʊt/
have (sth) in common *phr*	/hæv ɪn ˈkɒmən/
partner *n C* ***	/ˈpɑː(r)tnə(r)/
split up *phr*	/splɪt ʌp/

Other words & phrases

anxious *adj* *	/ˈæŋkʃəs/
average *adj* **	/ˈæv(ə)rɪdʒ/
avoid *v* ***	/əˈvɔɪd/
basic *adj* ***	/ˈbeɪsɪk/
calculate *v* **	/ˈkælkjʊleɪt/
cheat (on sb) *v* *	/tʃiːt/
check *v* ***	/tʃek/
close (to) *adj* ***	/kləʊs/
communicate *v* *	/kəˈmjuːnɪkeɪt/
conclusion *n C* ***	/kənˈkluːʒ(ə)n/
confident *adj* ***	/ˈkɒnfɪd(ə)nt/
cover *n C* ***	/ˈkʌvə(r)/
dead *adj* ***	/ded/
disadvantage *n C* **	/ˌdɪsədˈvɑːntɪdʒ/
excuse *n C* **	/ɪkˈskjuːs/
generation *n C* ***	/ˌdʒenəˈreɪʃ(ə)n/
gnome *n C*	/nəʊm/
intelligent *adj* **	/ɪnˈtelɪdʒ(ə)nt/
invent *v* **	/ɪnˈvent/
jacket *n C* **	/ˈdʒækɪt/
magazine *n C* **	/ˌmægəˈziːn/
matter *v* ***	/ˈmætə(r)/
newsagent *n C*	/ˈnjuːzˌeɪdʒ(ə)nt/
prefer *v* ***	/prɪˈfɜː(r)/
prison *n C* ***	/ˈprɪz(ə)n/
professor *n C* *	/prəˈfesə(r)/
promise *v* ***	/ˈprɒmɪs/
realise / realize *v* ***	/ˈrɪəlaɪz/
referee *n C*	/ˌrefəˈriː/
rely on (sb) *v* **	/rɪˈlaɪ ɒn/
romantic *adj*	/rəʊˈmæntɪk/
secure *adj* *	/sɪˈkjʊə(r)/
shame *n U* *	/ʃeɪm/
smile *n C/v* ***	/smaɪl/
solve *v* **	/sɒlv/
statue *n C*	/ˈstætʃuː/
swap *v*	/swɒp/
thief *n C*	/θiːf/
trust *v* ***	/trʌst/
unusual *adj* **	/ʌnˈjuːʒʊəl/
victory *n C* **	/ˈvɪkt(ə)ri/

5A | Tourist trail

Speaking

1 Work in pairs. Discuss these questions.

- What time of year do tourists come to your country?
- Which parts of your country do the tourists go to?
- What do they do there?

Reading

1 You are going to read an article about the place in the photo. Which of these words do you think you will find in the article? Explain why or why not.

city	fast food	jungle
path	ruins	tea bag
train	valley	views

2 Read the article and say if the sentences are true (T) or false (F). Correct the false sentences.

1 Machu Picchu was built in 1911.
2 It is extremely popular with tourists.
3 The only way to Machu Picchu is on foot.
4 Ana Redondo thinks there are too many tourists.
5 Tourists leave their rubbish on the Inca Trail.
6 She thinks the cable car is good for Machu Picchu.
7 Ana's organization is trying to stop the cable car.

3 Underline the arguments for and against the cable car. Who do you agree with?

THE RUINS OF MACHU PICCHU

For centuries, the Inca city of Machu Picchu was lost in the jungle. Then, in 1911, the American explorer, Hiram Bingham, discovered the ruins of the city. It is one of the most extraordinary places in the world. The city ruins, the Inca bridge, the mountain views and the beautiful river valley below are all absolutely breathtaking.

Today it is also one of the most popular tourist destinations in the world. Many people choose to follow the Inca Trail, a centuries-old path of 43 km that takes three or four days on foot. Others take the train and then a bus for the last part of the journey.

Now a hotel company is going to build a cable car to the top of Machu Picchu. 'The cable car is good news for Machu Picchu,' says a company spokesman. 'There are going to be a lot more tourists and that means more jobs for the local people. Looking after the ruins is expensive. With the extra money, we can spend more on looking after them.'

However, the plan is not popular in Peru. Ana Redondo, a tour guide, explains the problem. 'There are already more than 300,000 tourists that go to Machu Picchu every year. The Inca Trail is crowded and dirty with old tea bags and water bottles everywhere. The new cable car is going to bring 400 tourists every hour! The company is also going to build a large hotel and tourist centre with souvenir shops, fast food restaurants and so on. It is the end of Machu Picchu.'

Ana is an activist who belongs to an organization that wants to save Machu Picchu. She says that the organization is going to stop the company's plans. 'Tomorrow we are meeting government ministers. Next week some people from UNESCO[1] are coming here to look at the plans. Next month we are organizing an international conference. We are not going to stop until the cable car idea is dead.'

[1] United Nations Educational, Scientific and Cultural Organization

VOCABULARY: compound nouns

1 We can often put a noun together with another word to make a compound noun. Compound nouns are sometimes written as one word, sometimes as two words and sometimes with a hyphen in the middle. There are no rules, so use a dictionary if you are not sure.

boyfriend *dinner party* *T-shirt*

Read the article again. How many compound nouns can you find?

2 Can you name the objects in the photos below?

3 Match words from column A with words from column B to check your answers.

A	B
back	bag
camping-gas	book
credit	camera
first-aid	card
flash	glasses
guide	kit
insect	knife
mobile	light
pen	pack
sleeping	phone
sun	spray
video	stove

Use a dictionary to find out if the compound nouns are written as one or two words.

4 Work in pairs. You are going to walk the Inca Trail to Machu Picchu. You can take six objects from the photos with you. Decide together which ones you are going to take.

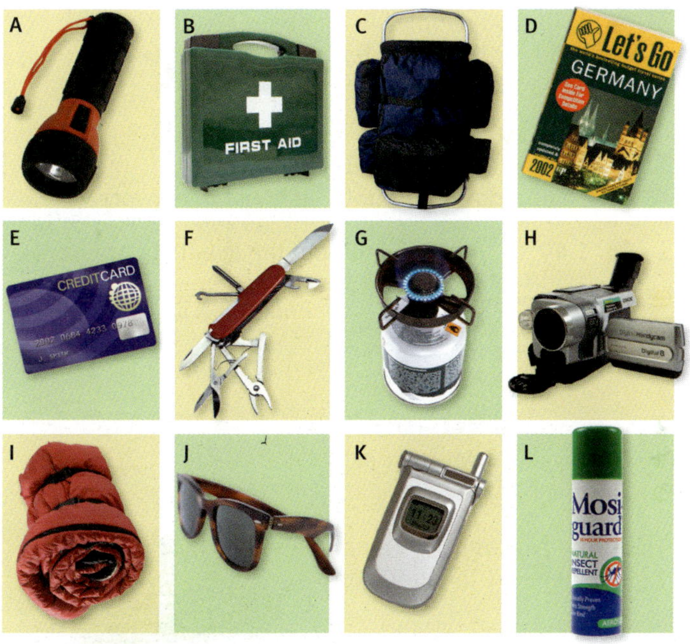

GRAMMAR: future 1 (future plans)

We can use both *am/is/are going to* + infinitive and the present continuous to talk about plans in the future.

The new cable car ***is going to bring*** *400 tourists every hour.*
Some people from UNESCO ***are coming*** *here.*

Often we can use either form, but when we want to show that the plan is more arranged/fixed, we use the present continuous.

The company ***is going to build*** *a large hotel.*
(This is their plan.)
Tomorrow, we ***are meeting*** *government ministers.*
(The plan is fixed in our diaries.)

SEE LANGUAGE REFERENCE PAGE 54

1 Rearrange the words to make questions.

1 after are do going lesson the to what you ?
2 are get going home how to today you ?
3 cooking dinner evening is this who your ?
4 anything are at doing the weekend you ?
5 are birthday doing for next what you your ?
6 are going have holiday next to when you your ?

2 Work in pairs. Ask and answer the questions in exercise 1. Use the expressions in the Useful language box to help you.

Useful language

I'm not sure.
I haven't decided yet.
It depends …

3 Imagine that you are the mayor of your town. How can you make your town a better place for tourists?

Work in pairs. Think of six things that you can do to improve your town for tourists. Tell the rest of your class your ideas.

We're going to build a new airport.

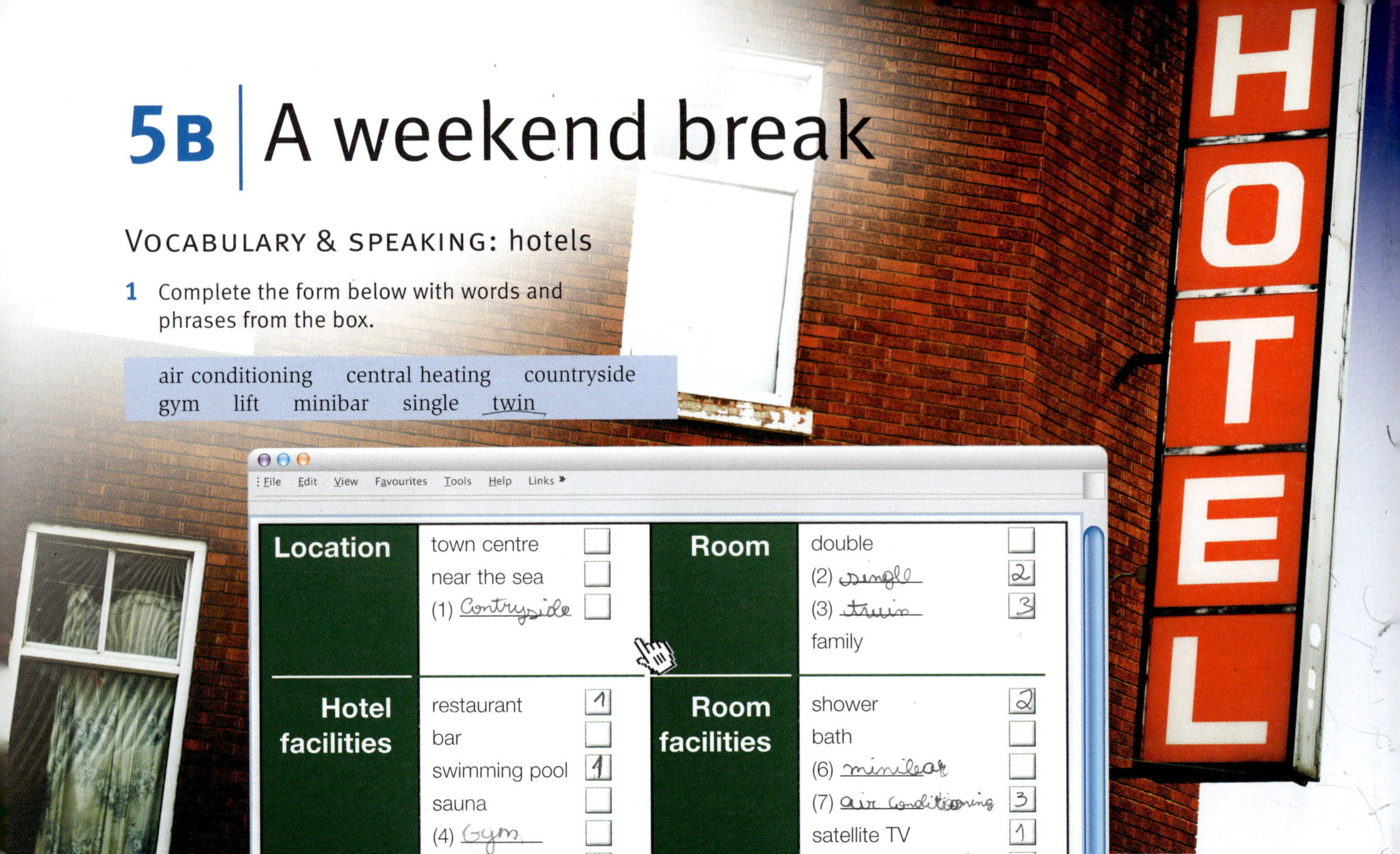

5B | A weekend break

VOCABULARY & SPEAKING: hotels

1 Complete the form below with words and phrases from the box.

> air conditioning   central heating   countryside
> gym   lift   minibar   single   twin

File Edit View Favourites Tools Help Links

Location			Room		
	town centre			double	
	near the sea			(2) single	2
	(1) Contryside			(3) twin	3
				family	
Hotel facilities	restaurant	1	**Room facilities**	shower	2
	bar			bath	
	swimming pool	1		(6) minibar	
	sauna			(7) air conditioning	3
	(4) Gym			satellite TV	1
	free parking	1		(8) Central heating	3
	(5) lift	3		internet connection	2
				room service	2

2 Look at the list of room and hotel facilities again. Choose the four most important facilities from the list for the following people:

1 A family with two children staying at the hotel for two weeks for their summer holiday.
2 A business person staying for three nights at the hotel for a conference.
3 A couple staying one night at the hotel. They are going to arrive late and leave early the next day.

3 What are the most important room or hotel facilities for you? Explain your reasons.

For me, an internet connection is the most important because …

4 What is the best (or worst) hotel you have ever stayed in? Work in pairs. Ask and answer these questions.

- How long ago was it?
- Where was it?
- How long did you stay?
- Why did you go there?
- Who did you go with?
- What was the hotel like?
- Was there anything special about the hotel?

LISTENING

1 Look at the photo of a hotel in Brighton (in the south of England). Would you like to stay there? Why or why not?

2 1.40 Two people went to the hotel for the weekend. Listen to the recording and tick (✔) the problems that they had.

1 broken lift ✓
2 cold shower ✓
3 dirty bathroom
4 no central heating
5 room too small
6 unfriendly hotel manager ✓

3 1.40 Listen again and put the events in order.

[6] They found another hotel.
[1] They arrived at the hotel.
[4] They gave their key to the woman at reception.
[3] They had a cold shower.
[2] They paid for the room.
[7] They went to get their bags.
[5] They went to the cinema.

4 How much can you remember of Nicki and Gavin's experiences? Tell their story.

GRAMMAR: future 2 (*will*)

We use *will ('ll)* + infinitive when we decide something at the moment of speaking.

***I'll fix** the shower this evening, OK?* (He is deciding now.)

We use *am/is/are/going to* + infinitive when we have already made the decision.

***We're going to see** a film at the cinema.* (She decided some time ago.)

SEE LANGUAGE REFERENCE PAGE 54

1 Complete the sentences with *'ll* and a verb from the box.

give see tell think

1 So, outside the cinema at eight o'clock? Yes, OK. I'______ you later.
2 Dad, can I borrow the car for the weekend? I'______ about it.
3 Tell me when you arrive, OK? OK, I'______ you a call.
4 What does this word mean? I'______ you later.

2 You are a friendly hotel manager. Some guests have some problems. What do you say?

1 *I'm sorry, sir. I'll send someone to look at it.*

1 The TV is making a strange noise.
2 We need to get up very early in the morning, but we don't have an alarm clock.
3 There's no water in the minibar.
4 Our room smells of cigarettes. It's horrible.
5 I'm very hungry, but the restaurant is closed.
6 The door to the gym is locked.
7 There's a spider in the bath!

3 Complete the dialogue between a guest and a hotel manager with *'ll* or the correct form of *going to*.

Guest: Excuse me, I (1) ______ visit the old part of town this afternoon. Can you tell me the way?
Manager: Yes, no problem. I (2) ______ give you a map.
Guest: Is it far?
Manager: No, not far. Do you want to walk or take a bus? It's a nice walk.
Guest: Oh, well, I (3) ______ walk, I think.
Manager: Or, if you like, I (4) ______ take you in my car. I (5) ______ do some shopping this afternoon.
Guest: That's kind of you. Thanks. When (6) ______ (you) leave?
Manager: About four o'clock.
Guest: Great. I (7) ______ see you here at four o'clock.
Manager: OK. I (8) ______ see you later.

4 1.41 Listen to the recording to check your answers. Then work in pairs and practise the dialogue.

DID YOU KNOW?

1 What do you think the connection is between Las Vegas, the Eiffel Tower and a waterfall? Read the text to find out.

It is the hotel capital of the world. It has fourteen of the biggest hotels in the world and more than 125,000 hotel rooms. Many of the 37 million tourists who come here every year come to see the hotels. The Rio Hotel, for example, has an Ipanema beach, waterfalls, four swimming pools and sixteen restaurants. At the Venetian Hotel, you can take a gondola, and you can climb the Eiffel Tower or visit the Arc de Triomphe at the Paris Hotel.

Many tourists never go outside their hotels, which have everything you could possibly want: bars, restaurants, sports centres and pools, concerts, cinemas, theatres, casinos – even theme parks. In fact, there is little reason to leave your hotel. The only thing to visit is ... more hotels!

2 Work in pairs. Discuss these questions.

- What else do you know about Las Vegas?
- Do you know anybody who has been there? Would you like to go?
- What famous hotels are there in your country? Why are they famous?

5c Holiday heaven

READING

1 Read the web page and match the photos A–H to the different types of holiday 1–4 in the website below.

File Edit View Favourites Tools Help Links »

HEAVEN HOLIDAYS

Looking for something different? We have the holiday for you.

1 Sea holidays

Scuba Safari
Experience the beauty of the seas of Borneo

Titanic Times
An unforgettable dive to the wreck of the Titanic

Dolphin Days
Swim with the dolphins of the Bahamas

2 Adventure holidays

Route 66
An incredible journey from Chicago to Los Angeles by Harley-Davidson

Mountain Memories
Cycling through the volcanic valleys of Reunion Island

Mach 2
Fly a Russian MiG-29 jet and see the world from above the clouds

3 Haunted holidays

Monster Party
Looking for the Loch Ness monster (includes visits to whisky distilleries)

Feast of Lanterns
Experience the magic of the Hungry Ghost Festival in Malaysia.

Yeti Hunt
Two weeks in the high Himalayas on the trail of the yeti

4 History trails

Great Wall
Explore the villages and temples of Mongolia and northern China

Mayan Treasures
See the lost Mayan pyramids in the rain forest of Mexico.

Alexander the Great
Follow the path of Alexander the Great through the historic cities of Turkey

2 Read about some more holidays. What type of holiday 1–4 are they?

1 **Meet the Shojo**
Explore the Pacific islands of southern Japan in the company of Shojo ghosts

2 **Siberian White Water**
Kayak down the Katun River

3 **Inca Gold**
Follow the trail of the conquistadors and discover the ancient Peruvian cities

4 **Grand Canyon**
Paragliding and sky diving in America's Wild West

5 **Arctic Ice**
A visit by submarine to a wreck under the Arctic ice

6 **1492**
Discover the Jamaica and Puerto Rico of Christoper Colombus

3 Match the paragraphs A–D to the types of holiday 1–4 in the web page advertisement on page 50.

A I'm really looking forward to riding the motorbike. I hope to go with a friend, but if he hasn't got enough money, I intend to go alone. I've got a brother in Los Angeles and I plan to stay with him when I get there.

B We would like to learn some Chinese before we go, because we want to meet lots of people when we're there. My wife is looking forward to seeing the wall, but I'm more interested in finding out about the people who live in that part of the world.

C I know it's going to be difficult so I plan to do a lot of practice on my bike before I go. I intend to take a lot of photos of the volcanoes and the animals and everything. I hope to get some pictures of the monkeys. I want to have an exhibition of the photos when I get back.

D I would really like to see the monster, but it doesn't matter too much. I'm also interested in seeing Scotland and I plan to visit the village where my father was born. My husband is looking forward to tasting all the different whiskies.

4 Which of these holidays do **not** interest you? Why?

Vocabulary: verb patterns

1 Choose the correct form of the verb to complete the sentences.

1 **I hope to** *find / finding* the yeti.
2 **I intend to** *take / taking* some Turkish lessons.
3 **I'm very interested in** *learn / learning* more about the yeti.
4 **I'm looking forward to** *swim / swimming* with the dolphins.
5 **I plan to** *spend / spending* two weeks in the jungle.
6 **I want to** *visit / visiting* the old temples.
7 **I would like to** *read / reading* more about Alexander.

Find the phrases in **bold** in Reading exercise 3 to check your answers.

2 Choose one of the holidays from the advertisement. Prepare answers to these questions.

- Which holiday do you want to go on?
- Would you like to go with another person or alone?
- Why are you interested in that holiday?
- Do you intend to prepare for the holiday in any way?
- What do you plan to take with you?
- What are you looking forward to most in the holiday?
- What do you hope to do when you are there?

3 Now work in pairs. Ask and answer the questions.

Pronunciation: silent letters

1 Circle the silent letters in the words below.

1	castle	6	receipt
2	climb	7	ghost
3	foreign	8	Wednesday
4	hour	9	whole
5	knife	10	wreck

2 1.42 Listen to the recording to check your answers.

3 How many more words can you think of with silent letters?

Speaking

1 Two friends from Australia are coming to visit you for a week. It is their first visit to your country. You are going to be their guide.

First of all, decide what you intend to do with them. Look at the list and use ideas of your own.

- visit different parts of the country
- things to do and see
- means of transport
- places to stay
- places and things to eat
- people to introduce them to
- things to do on the last night

2 Work in pairs and discuss your plans. Then tell the rest of the class.

5D | Planes

A

B

Speaking

1 Work in pairs. Think of a long/interesting/boring/frightening journey you have been on. Describe your journey.

Vocabulary: air travel

1 Find these things in the pictures.

boarding card	check-in	hand luggage
overhead locker	seat belt	security guard

2 Put the phrases in the correct order.

- ☐ **Fasten** your **seat belt** and wait for **take-off**.
- ☐ *1* **Book** your **flight** and get your **ticket**.
- ☐ Get on the plane and find your **seat**.
- ☐ Go to the airport **terminal**.
- ☐ Show your ticket and **passport** at **passport control**.
- ☐ Go to the **departure gate** and show your **boarding card**.
- ☐ Go to the **departure hall** and into the **duty-free shop**.
- ☐ **Pack** your bag(s).
- ☐ Put your **hand luggage** in the **overhead locker**.
- ☐ Go through **security**.
- ☐ Go to the **check-in** and **check in** your **luggage**.

Listening

1 Describe what is happening in the pictures above. Use the vocabulary to help you.

2 1.43–1.45 Listen and match the dialogues 1–3 to the pictures A–C.

3 1.43–1.45 Listen to the dialogues again and choose the correct answer.

1 What is the passenger's seat number?
a) 21A b) 23A c) 23F
2 When does his plane board?
a) 12.00 b) 12.15 c) 12.30
3 What is his departure gate?
a) 21 b) 31 c) 41
4 Where is the passenger going?
a) Dublin b) Glasgow c) London
5 What can't he take on the plane?
a) his comb b) his jacket c) his mobile phone
6 What does the male passenger order to drink?
a) coffee b) hot chocolate c) tea
7 How much does the drink cost?
a) €2.50 b) €3.50 c) €4.50

Functional language: requests
Pronunciation: intonation

1 There are many ways of asking for something and asking another person to do something. Look at audioscripts 1.43–1.45 on page 137. Underline all the requests. Then find different ways of responding to the requests and complete the table opposite.

C

Requests

(Excuse me,)	I'd like	*a glass of water* *a coffee* (noun)	*please*
	I'd like to *Can I* *Could I* *I wonder if I could*	*have a receipt* *see your passport* (infinitive)	
	Can you *Could you*	*stand over here* (infinitive)	

Responses

☺		☹
Yes,	*s _ _ _* *o _ c _ _ _ _ _* *c _ _ _ _ _ _ _ _*	*I'm a _ _ _ _ _ _ that …* *I'm s _ _ _ _ but …*

2 Find five more mistakes in the dialogue and correct them.

Passenger: Excuse me, I like a cup of coffee, please.
Attendant: I'm afraid but we're not serving drinks any more, sir. The plane is going to land in about twenty minutes.
Passenger: Oh, please, could I just have a cup of coffee? Please!
Attendant: I afraid that's not possible, sir. Could you to fasten your seat belt and close the table in front of you, please?
Passenger: Well, OK. Er, I wonder if could I go to the toilet before we land.
Attendant: Yes, of course. But can you being quick, please?

3 **1.46** To make polite requests, we always say *please*. Friendly intonation is also important. Listen to these two sentences said in different ways.

Excuse me, could I have a coffee, please?
Can you stand over here, please?

4 **1.46** Listen and repeat.

5 **1.47** Listen to the requests. Put a tick (✔) if they are polite and a cross (✗) if they are not.

1 Excuse me, can I have a window seat, please?
2 Could I get past?
3 I wonder if I could have another glass of water, please.
4 Can you sit down?
5 I'd like a black coffee.
6 Could you put your bag up there, please?
7 Can I see your passport, please?

6 Work in pairs. Practise the dialogue in exercise 2. Remember to use friendly intonation.

7 Work in pairs, A and B. You are going to do two roleplays.

Roleplay 1

A: You are a passenger on a long-distance flight. You want to request some things from the flight attendant. Decide what you want to ask for. Use the ideas on page 129 to help you.

B: You are a flight attendant. Help the passenger.

Roleplay 2

A: You are a flight attendant. One of your passengers is very difficult. Look at the ideas on page 131 and choose some of the problems.

B: You are a passenger. Listen to what the flight attendant asks you to do.

Self-assessment (tick ✔)

☐ I can understand information in conversations at airports.
☐ I can make requests on a plane and respond to them.
☐ I can describe a journey I have been on.

5 Language reference

GRAMMAR

Going to

We can use *going to* + infinitive to talk about plans in the future. The action has been decided before the person speaks.

*We'**re going to save** money to buy a flat.*
*I'**m going to buy** a present for Amanda. It's her birthday.*

Affirmative & Negative				
I		'm 'm not	going to	phone him tonight.
He/She/It		's isn't		
You/We/They		're aren't		
Question				
When	am is are	I he/she/it you/we/they	going to	phone him tonight?
Short answer				
Are you going to phone?			Yes, I am. / No, I'm not.	
Is she going to phone?			Yes, she is. / No, she isn't.	

When we talk about future plans with the verb *go*, it is normal to 'drop' the infinitive, *to go*.

I'm going to the cinema this evening.
Not ~~*I'm going to go to the cinema this evening*~~.

Present continuous for future

We can also use the present continuous to talk about future plans. We can often use either the present continuous or *going to* without changing the meaning, but when we want to show that the plan is more arranged or more fixed, we use the present continuous.

*The teachers **are going to ask** for more money.* (This is their plan.)
*We'**re meeting** the managers at ten on Monday.* (The plan is fixed in our diaries.)

See page 44 for more information about the present continuous.

Will + infinitive

We use *will* + infinitive when we decide something at the moment of speaking.

*Don't worry. I'**ll ask** my friend to fix the window this afternoon.* (She is deciding now.)

We sometimes use *will* to make offers.

*If you like, I'**ll take** you in my car.*

Affirmative & Negative			
I He/She/It You/We/They		'll won't	phone.
Question			
When	will	I he/she/it you/we/they	phone?
Short answer			
Will you phone?		Yes, I will. / No, I won't.	

FUNCTIONAL LANGUAGE

Requests

I'd like + noun.
I'd like to + infinitive …
Can I + infinitive … ?
Could I + infinitive … (*please*)?
I wonder if I could + infinitive …
Can you + infinitive … ?
Could you + infinitive … ?

Responses

Yes, sure.
Yes, of course.
Yes, certainly.
I'm afraid that …
I'm sorry, but …

When we say *no* to a request, it is polite to give a reason.

Word list

Compound nouns

backpack *n C* /ˈbækˌpæk/
boyfriend *n C* * /ˈbɔɪˌfrend/
cable car *n C* /ˈkeɪb(ə)l kɑː(r)/
camping-gas stove *n C* /ˈkæmpɪŋgæs stəʊv/
credit card *n C* /ˈkredɪt kɑː(r)d/
dinner party *n C* /ˈdɪnə(r) pɑː(r)ti/
first-aid kit *n C* /ˈfɜː(r)steɪd kɪt/
flashlight *n C* /ˈflæʃˌlaɪt/
guide book *n C* * /ˈgaɪdˌbʊk/
insect spray *n U* /ˈɪnsekt spreɪ/
mobile phone *n C* /ˈməʊbaɪl fəʊn/
penknife *n C* /ˈpenˌnaɪf/
sleeping bag *n C* /sliːpɪŋ bæg/
sunglasses *n pl* /ˈsʌnˌglɑːsɪz/
tea bag *n C* /tiː bæg/
tour guide *n C* /ˈtʊə(r) gaɪd/
T-shirt *n C* /tiːʃɜː(r)t/
video camera *n C* /ˈvɪdiəʊ ˈkæm(ə)rə/
water bottle *n C* /ˈwɔːtə(r) bɒt(ə)l/

Air travel

attendant *n C* /əˈtendənt/
board *v* /bɔː(r)d/
boarding card *n C* /ˈbɔː(r)dɪŋ kɑː(r)d/
book *v* * /bʊk/
check in *v* /tʃek ɪn/
check-in *n U* /tʃekɪn/
departure *n C* /dɪˈpɑː(r)tʃə(r)/
duty-free *adj* /ˈdjuːtifriː/
fasten *v* *** /ˈfɑːs(ə)n/
flight *n C* *** /flaɪt/
gate *n C* ** /geɪt/
hall *n C* *** /hɔːl/
hand luggage *n U* /hænd ˈlʌgɪdʒ/
land *v* ** /lænd/
locker *n C* /ˈlɒkə(r)/
luggage *n U* /ˈlʌgɪdʒ/
overhead *adj* /ˌəʊvə(r)ˈhed/
pack *v* * /pæk/
passenger *n C* ** /ˈpæsɪndʒə(r)/
passport *n C* * /ˈpɑːspɔː(r)t/
passport control *n U* /ˈpɑːspɔː(r)t kənˈtrəʊl/
seat *n C* *** /siːt/
seat belt *n C* /ˈsiːt belt/
security *n U* *** /sɪˈkjʊərəti/
security guard *n C* /sɪˈkjʊərəti gɑː(r)d/
take-off *n C/U* /ˈteɪk ɒf/
terminal *n C* /ˈtɜː(r)mɪn(ə)l/
ticket *n C* *** /ˈtɪkɪt/

Hotels

air conditioning *n U* /eə(r) kənˈdɪʃ(ə)nɪŋ/
central heating *n U* /ˈsentrəl ˈhiːtɪŋ/
countryside *n U* ** /ˈkʌntriˌsaɪd/
facility *n C* *** /fəˈsɪləti/
gym *n C* /dʒɪm/
lift *n C* * /lɪft/
location *n C* ** /ləʊˈkeɪʃ(ə)n/
minibar *n C* /ˈmɪniˌbɑː(r)/
room service *n U* /ruːm ˈsɜː(r)vɪs/
satellite *n C* * /ˈsætəlaɪt/
sauna *n C* /ˈsɔːnə/
shower *n C* * /ˈʃaʊə(r)/
single *adj* *** /ˈsɪŋg(ə)l/
twin *adj* /twɪn/
vacancy *n C* /ˈveɪkənsi/

Verb patterns

be interested in + verb + *-ing* *** /bi ˈɪntrəstɪd ɪn/
hope to + *infinitive* *** /həʊp tə/
intend to + *infinitive* *** /ɪnˈtend tə/
look forward to + verb + *-ing* /lʊk ˈfɔː(r)wə(r)d tə/
plan to + *infinitive* *** /plæn tə/
want to + *infinitive* *** /wɒnt tə/
would like to + *infinitive*/ / wʊd laɪk tə

Other words & phrases

activist *n C* /ˈæktɪvɪst/
afterwards *adv* ** /ˈɑːftə(r)wə(r)dz/
ancient *adj* ** /ˈeɪnʃ(ə)nt/
beach *n C* ** /biːtʃ/
beauty *n U* ** /ˈbjuːti/
bell *n C* ** /bel/
breathtaking *adj* /ˈbreθˌteɪkɪŋ/
build *v* *** /bɪld/
calm *adj* ** /kɑːm/
capital *n C* *** /ˈkæpɪt(ə)l/
climb *v* *** /klaɪm/
cloud *n C* *** /klaʊd/
comb *n C/v* /kəʊm/
comfortable *adj* ** /ˈkʌmftəb(ə)l/
crowded *adj* * /ˈkraʊdɪd/
depend *v* *** /dɪˈpend/
destination *n C* * /ˌdestɪˈneɪʃ(ə)n/
discover *v* *** /dɪˈskʌvə(r)/
distillery *n C* /dɪˈstɪləri/
dive *n C/v* /daɪv/
dolphin *n C* /ˈdɒlfɪn/
exhibition *n C* ** /ˌeksɪˈbɪʃ(ə)n/
explore *v* ** /ɪkˈsplɔː(r)/
extraordinary *adj* * /ɪkˈstrɔː(r)d(ə)n(ə)ri/
extremely *adv* *** /ɪkˈstriːmli/
festival *n C* /ˈfestɪv(ə)l/
fix *v* ** /fɪks/
forest *n C* *** /ˈfɒrɪst/
get changed *phr* /get tʃeɪndʒd/
ghost *n C* /gəʊst/
give up *v* /gɪv ʌp/
hand in *v* /hænd ɪn/
historic *adj* /hɪˈstɒrɪk/
horrible *adj* * /ˈhɒrəb(ə)l/
hunt *n C/v* /hʌnt/
ice *n U* ** /aɪs/
in advance *phr* /ɪn ədˈvɑːns/
incredible *adj* /ɪnˈkredəb(ə)l/
jet *n C* * /dʒet/
journey *n C* *** /ˈdʒɜː(r)ni/
jungle *n C/U* /ˈdʒʌŋg(ə)l/
key *n C* *** /kiː/
local *adj* * /ˈləʊk(ə)l/
lock *v* ** /lɒk/
luxury *n U* /ˈlʌkʃəri/
magic *n U* * /ˈmædʒɪk/
map *n C* ** /mæp/
metal *n C/U* *** /ˈmet(ə)l/
mind *v* *** /maɪnd/
minister *n C* ** /ˈmɪnɪstə(r)/
monster *n C* /ˈmɒnstə(r)/
motorbike *n C* /ˈməʊtə(r)ˌbaɪk/
nervous *adj* ** /ˈnɜː(r)vəs/
object *n C* *** /ˈɒbdʒekt/
organization *n C* *** /ˌɔː(r)gənaɪˈzeɪʃ(ə)n/
path *n C* *** /pɑːθ/
receipt *n C* * /rɪˈsiːt/
rubbish *n U* * /ˈrʌbɪʃ/
ruins *n pl* /ˈruːɪnz/
save *v* *** /seɪv/
search *v* ** /sɜː(r)tʃ/
shout *v* *** /ʃaʊt/
sign *n C* *** /saɪn/
smell *n C/v* ** /smel/
souvenir *n C* /ˌsuːvəˈnɪə(r)/
spider *n C* /ˈspaɪdə(r)/
spokesman *n C* /ˈspəʊksmən/
stairs *n pl* ** /steə(r)s/
submarine *n C* /ˈsʌbməriːn/
temple *n C* /ˈtemp(ə)l/
throw *v* *** /θrəʊ/
trail *n C* * /treɪl/
treasure *n C/U* /ˈtreʒə(r)/
valley *n C* * /ˈvæli/
view *n C* *** /vjuː/
volcano *n C* /vɒlˈkeɪnəʊ/
wall *n C* *** /wɔːl/
waterfall *n C* /ˈwɔːtə(r)ˌfɔːl/
wreck *n C* /rek/

6A | Junk food

VOCABULARY: food

1 Look at the items of food from America. Tick (✔) the items on the shopping list that you can see.

2 How often do you eat the food on the list? Which of them do you think are 'junk food'?

READING

1 Look at the photo of Elvis Presley. What sort of food do you think he liked?

2 Now read the book review. While you read, put a **!** next to the facts you find most surprising.

Eating the Elvis Presley Way

David Adler Blake Publishing

There are more than 400 books about Elvis Presley. There are books about his music, his films, his life, his death, his religion – and his food. There is the *Presley Family Cookbook, The Elvis Presley Cookbook, Elvis' Favorite Recipes,* and now *Eating the Elvis Presley Way*. What makes this book different? To begin with, this is not a cookbook. You can find recipes here, but this book is the story of Elvis' life. It is the story of the food that he ate and the people who cooked it for him. And an extremely interesting life it was, too.

The food in the first two or three chapters is quite normal – baby food, boring school dinners, army meals when he was doing his military service, that sort of thing. But later, when Elvis was rich and famous, it is a very different story. With all the money in the world, Elvis chose to eat like a child. Elvis got up late and his first meal of the day was breakfast at five o'clock in the afternoon: bacon and eggs, or sausage and eggs. After that, it was snacks: pizza and hot dogs, hamburgers and fries, chocolate and cakes – all day and every day. Elvis even had a fridge in his bedroom for his favorite snacks.

As the years passed, Elvis' eating problems became really serious. One day, when Elvis was going to the White House to meet the President, he was feeling a bit hungry and ate 250g of chocolate and then 12 donuts in his taxi. Another time, he ordered a large ice cream for breakfast. He ate it quickly, ordered a second, a third, a fourth and a fifth before falling asleep again. Elvis' last meal before he died was four scoops of ice cream with six chocolate cookies.

Elvis was an extremely unhappy man. His food and the drugs that he took made him feel good, but killed him in the end. It's a fairly sad story, but a fascinating one, too.

Recommended ★★★★

3 Read the review again and say if the sentences are true (T) or false (F). Correct the false sentences.

1 This is the first book about Elvis Presley and food.
2 It is different from the other books about Elvis and food.
3 His eating problems started when he was a child.
4 He had breakfast early in the morning.
5 He ate a lot of junk food.
6 He had food in his bedroom.
7 The President gave him a large box of chocolates.
8 Elvis didn't like ice cream very much.

4 Complete the definitions with an adjective from the review.

1 When someone is f______ a lot of people know their name.
2 A f______ story, place or person is very interesting.
3 Your f______ thing or person is the one that you like best.
4 You feel h______ when you want to eat.
5 When you are unhappy, you feel s______.
6 When you have a s______ problem, you are very worried about it.

5 What else do you know about Elvis Presley? Why do you think that Elvis had eating problems?

GRAMMAR: modifiers

We can make an adjective stronger or weaker with a modifier. We put this before the adjective.

Weak
a bit hungry

Medium
quite ______
fairly ______

Strong
very ______
really ______
extremely ______

SEE LANGUAGE REFERENCE PAGE 64

1 Underline examples of modifiers before adjectives in the book review. Use them to complete the examples in the language box.

2 Put the modifiers in the correct place in the sentences.

1 Burger Paradise is always busy. (*very*)
2 I like The New York Donut Shop but the service is slow. (*a bit*)
3 I think that the chicken burgers at The Alabama Chicken are good. (*really*)
4 The fast food shops on Main Square are expensive. (*fairly*)
5 The hot dogs at The Happy Sandwich are nice. (*quite*)
6 The Magic Hamburger in my town is popular. (*extremely*)

3 Make six sentences about places where you can eat out in your town. Use modifiers and adjectives. Here are some more adjectives that you can use.

cheap	dirty	fashionable	friendly	healthy
lively	small	unhealthy		

SPEAKING

1 Do you know any 'theme' restaurants like the Hard Rock Café or Planet Hollywood? What is special about them?

Have you ever been to a 'theme' restaurant? What was it like?

2 Work in pairs. Plan your own 'theme' restaurant. Use these questions to help you.

- What is the theme of your restaurant? (sport, music, cinema, a famous person, a country, a historical period, etc)
- What is the name of your restaurant?
- What kind of food and drink do you serve?
- What does the restaurant look like?
- Do the waiters and waitresses wear uniforms? What kind?
- What kind of music do you play?
- How much does a meal cost in your restaurant?

3 Describe your restaurant to other students in the class. Decide which restaurant is the best.

6B | Slow food

Are You A Foodie?

Answer our questionnaire to find out if you are a foodie.

1 How long is a typical meal in your home?
a) less than 30 minutes
b) 30–90 minutes
c) more than 90 minutes

2 How often do you eat in front of the TV?
a) less than once a week
b) once a week
c) more than once a week

3 How many of the following do you eat at least once a week?
a) crisps
b) chips
c) chocolate biscuits
d) microwave dinner

4 How many recipe books do you have?
a) 0
b) 1–5
c) more than 5

5 How often do you spend more than one hour preparing a meal?
a) less than once a week
b) once a week
c) more than once a week

6 How often do you go to a restaurant (not fast food or pizza!)?
a) less than twice a month
b) 2–4 times a month
c) more than 4 times a month

Answers on page 128.

Speaking

1 Work in pairs and do the quiz. Take it in turns to ask the questions. (A foodie is someone who enjoys eating or cooking different types of food.)

2 Now turn to page 128. Add up your points and read the description for your score. Does it describe you well?

Who is the biggest 'foodie' in the class?

Listening

1 **1.48** Listen to part of a radio interview about food in Italy. Choose the best title for the programme.

1 How to make Bolognese sauce
2 Fast food in Italy
3 Slow food in Bologna
4 Tagliatelle or spaghetti?

Spaghetti Bolognese
(spaghetti with a sauce made with tomatoes, meat, onions and herbs)

2 **1.48** Read the passage below and then listen again. Underline the incorrect information and explain what is wrong.

The radio presenter is in Bologna, not Rome.

The radio presenter is in Rome, an Italian city where people eat Spaghetti Bolognese. Spaghetti is a speciality of Bologna. Bolognese sauce from supermarkets is made from many different ingredients. It is very similar to Ragu sauce. Ragu is quicker to prepare.
'Slow food' is a movement that started in France in 1997. It has members in about twenty countries and they are interested in making food more enjoyable and more traditional.

3 Do you agree with Maura that *good food is slow food*? Why or why not?

What traditional foods are there in your country? What parts of the country do they come from?

VOCABULARY: adjectives (opposites)

1 Complete the words by putting vowels (*a, e, i, o, u*) in the spaces. Then match the adjectives in column A to their opposites in column B.

A	B
1 fresh	a n_t_r_l
2 _nt_r_st_ng	b s_mpl_
3 c_mpl_c_t_d	c stale
4 _rt_f_c__l	d n_rm_l
5 str_ng_	e b_r_ng
6 h__lthy	f tr_d_t__n_l
7 m_d_rn	g _nh__lthy

2 Find an adjective in exercise 1 that you can use with the words below.

1 costume dancing marriage song teacher
traditional

2 face film person picture place

3 air bread food fruit

4 baby diet eating food lifestyle

3 Choose an adjective from exercise 1 and think of five things you can describe with that adjective.

Work in pairs. Tell your partner the five things. Your partner must guess the adjective that you chose.

PRONUNCIATION: word stress 1

1 1.49 Listen to these words and count the syllables.

1 2
heal / thy

1 healthy	6 complicated
2 difficult	7 simple
3 enjoyable	8 artificial
4 modern	9 traditional
5 important	

2 Mark the stress in each word and say the words.

☐
heal / thy

3 1.49 Listen to the recording again to check your answers.

GRAMMAR: comparatives

We use the comparative form to compare two things or people.

We make the comparative of short adjectives with the adjective + *-er* (+ *than*).

slow → *slower* *The service in the restaurant was* ***slower than*** *usual.*

1 When the adjective ends in *-e*, add *-r*.
nice → *nicer* *The sauce is* ***nicer*** *with spaghetti.*

2 When the adjective ends in *-y*, remove the *-y* and add *-ier*.
easy → *easier* *It's* ***easier than*** *you think.*

3 With some adjectives you need to double the last consonant.
big → *bigger* *Can we have a* ***bigger*** *table, please?*

We make the comparative of longer adjectives with *more* + adjective (+ *than*).
It's a ***more traditional*** *recipe.*
Food is ***more interesting than*** *that.*

There are two very common irregular comparatives.
good → *better (than)* *bad* → *worse (than)*

SEE LANGUAGE REFERENCE PAGE 64

1 Correct the mistakes in the sentences.

1 I like ~~traditionaler~~ *more traditional* cooking recipes.
2 Juice is healthyer for you than beer.
3 Chinese food is more interesting English.
4 Bologna is hoter than London.
5 A real sauce is gooder than sauce in a bottle.
6 The Spanish often eat more later than the Dutch.
7 Pizzas are more cheaper than steak and chips.

2 Use comparatives to complete the sentences below about your country.

1 The food in my country is _____ than American food.
2 The food that we eat is _____ than 20 years ago.
3 Fast food is becoming _____.
4 These days, people want to eat _____ food.
5 It's _____ to eat in a restaurant than at home.
6 Restaurants are _____ than they used to be.

Work in pairs. Compare your sentences.

3 Work in pairs. Turn to page 130 and look at the pictures. How many differences can you find?

6c | Coffee break

Coffee Break

1 **Can you imagine getting up in the morning without a coffee for breakfast? What is a good meal without a coffee at the end of it? Coffee is probably the world's favourite drink, but most of us never give it a second thought. How much do you know about coffee?**

2 The Turks gave us the word *coffee* and the Italians gave us *espresso* and *cappuccino*, but Finland is the biggest coffee-drinking country in the world. Coffee originally came from Ethiopia, but Brazil and Colombia are now the most important coffee-producing countries.

3 There are more than 100 different varieties of coffee bean and Jamaican Blue Mountain is said to have the best taste. However, the most expensive coffee in the world (at $660/kilo) is Kopi Luwak. An Indonesian cat called Paradoxurus is especially fond of coffee beans and Kopi Luwak is made from its droppings!

4 We all know coffee addicts – people who can do nothing in the morning until their second or third cup of coffee. The most famous coffee addicts in the world were probably the French writers Balzac (40 cups a day) and Voltaire (more than 50 cups a day). Beethoven was also a coffee lover – he always counted 60 beans for each cup of coffee that he made.

5 The most fashionable coffee bars in the US serve 'coffee art'. Artists in California draw leaves, hearts and other designs in your coffee.

A

B

C

D

E

Speaking

1 Work in pairs. Discuss these questions.

- What is your favourite drink?
- Where and when do you drink it?
- Do you prefer tea or coffee? How do you take it? (white/black, strong/weak, with/without sugar)
- What drinks are traditional in your country?

Reading

1 Read the magazine article about coffee. Match the photos A–E to the paragraphs 1–5.

2 Read the article again. Explain the connection between coffee and the countries below.

1 *Brazil is an important coffee-producing country.*

1 Brazil
2 Finland
3 France
4 Indonesia
5 Jamaica
6 The United States
7 Turkey

3 Find words in the article that match the definitions.

1 at the beginning = o_____
2 kinds, sorts = v_____
3 the fruit of the coffee plant = b_____
4 people who cannot stop taking a drug = a_____

GRAMMAR: superlatives

We use the superlative form to compare more than two things or people.

We make the superlative of short adjectives with *the* + adjective + *-est*.

cheap → *the cheap**est***
large → *the larg**est***
hot → *the hott**est***
happy → *the happi**est***
*Finland is **the biggest** coffee-drinking country in the world.*

We make the superlative of longer adjectives with *the* + *most* + adjective.

the most interesting *the most traditional*
*The **most expensive** coffee in the world is Kopi Luwak.*

There are two very common irregular superlatives.

good → *the best* *bad* → *the worst*
*Jamaican Blue Mountain has **the best** taste.*

SEE LANGUAGE REFERENCE PAGE 64

1 Find six examples of superlatives in the article about coffee.

2 Complete the sentences in the quiz. Put the adjectives in brackets into the superlative form.

Amazing Food Facts

1 _______ (*expensive*) meal in the world was in Bangkok in 2007. For their food and drink, the 15 diners paid
a) £75,000 b) £100,000 c) £150,000.

2 _______ (*good*) caviar in the world comes from
a) the Caspian Sea b) Lake Titicaca in Bolivia
c) the Eastern Mediterranean.

3 _______ (*large*) restaurant in the world is in Syria. It seats
a) 2,500 b) 4,000 c) 6,000 people.

4 _______ (*big*) donut in the world was made in 2007. It was
a) 3m b) 6m c) 10m in diameter.

5 _______ (*long*) hot dog in the world was made in Japan. It measured
a) 8m b) 25m c) 600m.

6 _______ (*popular*) fast food in Britain is
a) hamburgers b) pizzas c) sandwiches.

7 _______ (*heavy*) tomato in the world weighed
a) 3.5 kg b) 5 kg c) 8 kg.

8 Scientists think that _______ (*old*) soup in the world was made from
a) crocodiles b) dinosaurs c) hippopotamuses.

3 Work in pairs. Choose the correct answers in the quiz.

4 1.50 Listen to the recording to check your answers.

5 Work in pairs. Think of places you know where you can drink (cafés, bars, hotels, etc). Make sentences about these places, using superlatives. You can use adjectives from the box or think of your own.

bad big cheap expensive
fashionable friendly good
near to the school traditional

Central Café is the nearest café to the school.

DID YOU KNOW?

1 Read the information about Starbucks™ and discuss the questions.

Starbucks™ started as a small coffee shop in Seattle. In the 1990s, the company grew and it now serves coffee to more than 11 million customers around the world every week. With more than 17,000 stores in about 50 countries around the world, Starbucks™ has become the most famous coffee shop in the world.

- How many of the following can you find near where you live?

Burger King™ Dominos Pizza
Häagen Dazs® Kentucky Fried Chicken™
McDonalds© Starbucks™

- What other big food chains do you know?
- What do you like eating or drinking in these places?

6D | Class meal

SPEAKING

1 Work in pairs. Look at the types of restaurant in the box and discuss these questions.

- Which type of food have you tried?
- Which do you like best?
- Which ones can you find in your city/town?

Italian	French	Chinese	Indian	Mexican

2 What restaurants do you know in your town? Which is:

- the best?
- the most fashionable?
- the most popular?
- the cheapest?

3 Which restaurant in your town would you choose for a class meal. Why?

11/05/12 22.13

La vie en Rose

Your waiter today is 03 Jean-Paul

	£
1 x set menu @	23.00
1 x starter (mixed salad) @	5.50
1 x main course (cassoulet) @	14.50
1 x dessert (lemon sorbet) @	5.00
1 x house red @	17.50
1 x 1 litre mineral water @	6.00
12% Service charge	8.58
Total	**80.08**

Thank you for choosing La Vie en Rose.

Tel: 727 4848
www.manuetgerard.co.uk

VOCABULARY: eating out

1 Look at the restaurant bill and find words that match the definitions.

1 waiter

1 the person who takes your order = waiter
2 the last course = dessert
3 the first course = starter
4 a fixed choice of two or three courses = set menu
5 the money you pay for your waiter/waitress = service charge
6 the most important part of the meal = main course

2 How much do you pay for the items on the bill in restaurants in your town? Is *La Vie en Rose* more or less expensive?

LISTENING & FUNCTIONAL LANGUAGE 1: making a reservation

1 1.51 Listen to a woman booking a restaurant and complete the booking form.

La vie en Rose Booking Form

Customer name ____________

Number of people ______

Day: Mon / Tue / Wed / Thu / Fri / Sat

Time: Lunchtime: 12.00 / 12.30 / 1.00 / 1.30 / 2.00

Evening: 7.00 / 7.30 / 8.00 / 8.30 / 9.00 / 9.30

2 1.51 Listen to the dialogue again. Underline the words that you hear.

1 *Can* / *How may* I help you?
2 I'd like to *book* / *make a booking for* a table.
3 *It's for ten people.* / *There'll be ten of us.*
4 What time *suits you* / *would you like*?
5 Yes, certainly, we can *arrange* / *do* that for you.
6 *Could I take* / *you give me* your name, please?
7 *OK, I've got* / *made a note of* that.
8 We *are looking* / *look* forward to seeing you.

3 Work in pairs. Practise making a restaurant reservation. Take it in turns to be the customer. Choose the day, the time and the number of people. Begin like this:

Good afternoon. This is … . Can I help you?

PRONUNCIATION: emphatic stress

1 1.52 Listen to these phrases and notice the stress.

☐ ☐
*Not **seven**. **Nine**.*

2 Practise saying these phrases in the same way.

1 Friday evening. Not Thursday evening.
2 It's Ms. Not Mrs.
3 Good? It was excellent!
4 No dessert, thanks. Just coffee.

3 1.53 Listen to the recording to check your answers.

LISTENING & FUNCTIONAL LANGUAGE 2: in a restaurant

1 1.54 Listen to three extracts of a dialogue in a restaurant. Answer the questions.

1 Did everybody arrive at the same time?
2 What did the people order to eat?
3 What did they think of the meal?

2 1.54 Listen to the dialogue again. Put the sentences in the correct order.

☐ Are you ready to order?
☐ That was delicious.
☐ Can I take your coats?
☐ Could we have a bottle of mineral water, please?
☐ I have a reservation for ten people.
☐ Let me show you to your table.
☐ Shall we get the bill?
☐ No starters for me, thanks.

3 Work in groups. You are going to act out a short sketch in a restaurant. Decide what kind of restaurant it is and who the waiter is.

Useful language

Would you like …? *I'd like …*	*to have the bill/to see the menu*
Have you got …? *Could we have …?* *I'll have …*	*a drink/something to drink/ the bill/the house white*

Self-assessment (tick ✔)

☐ I can understand general and specific information in a phone conversation.
☐ I can make a reservation in a restaurant.
☐ I can order a meal in a restaurant.
☐ I can use emphatic stress to correct information.

6 Language reference

GRAMMAR

Modifiers

We can make an adjective stronger or weaker with a modifier, for example, *quite*, *very*.

Weak
a bit

Medium
quite
fairly

Strong
very
really
extremely

*I feel **a bit sad**.*
*We usually eat **quite healthy** food.*
*It's an **extremely** expensive restaurant.*

Comparatives & superlatives

We use comparatives to compare two things or people. We use *than* to join the two things we are comparing.

*Fresh sauce is **healthier than** sauce in bottles.*
*This computer is **faster than** the old one.*

We use superlatives to compare more than two things or people. We often use *in* after a superlative.

*He is **the richest** man **in** England.*
*They serve **the best** hamburgers **in** our town.*

With short adjectives, we usually add *-er/-est*.

strong	strong**er**	the strong**est**
weak	weak**er**	the weak**est**

When an adjective ends in *-e*, we add *-r/-st*.

large	large**r**	the large**st**
nice	nice**r**	the nice**st**

When an adjective ends with *-y* after a consonant, we change the *-y* to *-ier/-iest*.

busy	bus**ier**	the bus**iest**
easy	eas**ier**	the eas**iest**

When an adjective with one syllable ends with a consonant after a vowel, we double the consonant.

big	big**ger**	the big**gest**
hot	hot**ter**	the hot**test**

With longer adjectives, we add *more/the most*.

modern	**more** modern	**the most** modern
traditional	**more** traditional	**the most** traditional

Some adjectives have irregular comparative and superlative forms.

good	better	the best
bad	worse	the worst
far	further	the furthest

We can make negative comparisons with *less/the least*.

strong	less strong	the least strong
busy	less busy	the least busy
modern	less modern	the least modern

FUNCTIONAL LANGUAGE

Making a reservation

I'd like to book a table for ...

Certainly, Madam/Sir.
What time would you like?
For how many people?
Could I take your name, please?
We look forward to seeing you.
I'm afraid we're fully booked.

In the restaurant

Can I take your coats?
Let me show you to your table.
Would you like to + infinitive ... ?

I'd like to + infinitive ...
Have you got + noun?
Could we have + noun?
I'll have + noun.

Word list

Food

bacon *n U*	/ˈbeɪkən/
bean *n C*	/biːn/
beer *n C/U* *	/bɪə(r)/
breakfast *n C* **	/ˈbrekfəst/
cake *n C/U* **	/keɪk/
caviar *n U*	/ˈkæviˌɑː(r)/
chicken *n C/U* **	/ˈtʃɪkɪn/
chip *n C* **	/tʃɪp/
chocolate *n C/U* **	/ˈtʃɒklət/
coffee *n C/U* ***	/ˈkɒfi/
cookbook *n C*	/ˈkʊkˌbʊk/
cookie *n C*	/ˈkʊki/
crisp *n C*	/krɪsp/
diet *n C* **	/ˈdaɪət/
dish *n C* **	/dɪʃ/
donut/doughnut *n C*	/ˈdəʊˌnʌt/
egg *n C* ***	/eg/
(French) fries *n pl*	/ˈfrentʃ fraɪz/
fruit *n U* ***	/fruːt/
hamburger *n C*	/ˈhæmˌbɜː(r)gə(r)/
herb *n C*	/hɜː(r)b/
hot dog *n C*	/hɒt dɒg/
ice cream *n C*	/aɪs kriːm/
ingredient *n C*	/ɪnˈgriːdiənt/
junk food *n C*	/dʒʌŋk fuːd/
lemon *n C/U*	/ˈlemən/
meal *n C* ***	/miːl/
meat *n U* ***	/miːt/
microwave *n C/v*	/ˈmaɪkrəˌweɪv/
mineral water *n U*	/ˈmɪn(ə)rəl ˈwɔːtə(r)/
noodles *n pl*	/ˈnuːd(ə)ls/
onion *n C*	/ˈʌnjən/
pasta *n U*	/ˈpæstə/
peanut butter *n U*	/ˈpiːˌnʌt bʌtə(r)/
pizza *n C/U*	/ˈpiːtsə/
potato *n C* **	/pəˈteɪtəʊ/
recipe *n C* **	/ˈresəpi/
salad *n C/U* *	/ˈsæləd/
salt *n U* *	/sɔːlt/
sauce *n C/U* *	/sɔːs/
sausage *n C*	/ˈsɒsɪdʒ/
snack *n C*	/snæk/
sorbet *n U*	/ˈsɔː(r)beɪ/
sparkling *adj*	/ˈspɑː(r)k(ə)lɪŋ/
steak *n C/U*	/steɪk/
strawberry *n C*	/ˈstrɔːb(ə)ri/
sugar *n U* **	/ˈʃʊgə(r)/
tomato *n C*	/təˈmɑːtəʊ/
yoghurt/yogurt *n C/U*	/ˈjɒgə(r)t/

Eating out

bill *n C* ***	/bɪl/
course *n C* ***	/kɔː(r)s/
dessert *n C/U* *	/dɪˈzɜː(r)t/
diner *n C*	/ˈdaɪnə(r)/
main course *n C*	/meɪn kɔː(r)s/
serve *v* ***	/sɜː(r)v/
service *n U* ***	/ˈsɜː(r)vɪs/
service charge *n C*	/ˈsɜː(r)vɪs tʃɑː(r)dʒ/
set menu *n C*	/set ˈmenjuː/
starter *n C*	/ˈstɑː(r)tə(r)/
waiter *n C*	/ˈweɪtə(r)/
waitress *n C*	/ˈweɪtrəs/

Other words & phrases

addict *n C*	/ˈædɪkt/
alcohol *n U* *	/ˈælkəˌhɒl/
army *n C* ***	/ˈɑː(r)mi/
artificial *adj* *	/ˌɑː(r)tɪˈfɪʃ(ə)l/
authentic *adj*	/ɔːˈθentɪk/
bedroom *n C* **	/ˈbedruːm/
boring *adj* **	/ˈbɔːrɪŋ/
box *n C* ***	/bɒks/
busy *adj* ***	/ˈbɪzi/
chapter *n C* ***	/ˈtʃæptə(r)/
chemical *n C* ***	/ˈkemɪk(ə)l/
costume *n C*	/ˈkɒstjuːm/
count *v* ***	/kaʊnt/
customer *n C* ***	/ˈkʌstəmə(r)/
delicious *adj* *	/dɪˈlɪʃəs/
diameter *n C*	/daɪˈæmɪtə(r)/
draw *v* ***	/drɔː/
droppings *n pl*	/ˈdrɒpɪŋz/
drug *n C* ***	/drʌg/
face *n C* ***	/feɪs/
fascinating *adj* *	/ˈfæsɪneɪtɪŋ/
flavour *n C* *	/ˈfleɪvə(r)/
foodie *n C*	/ˈfuːdi/
fresh *adj* ***	/freʃ/
fridge *n C* *	/frɪdʒ/
healthy *adj* **	/ˈhelθi/
heart *n C* ***	/hɑː(r)t/
kill *v* ***	/kɪl/
leaf *n C* ***	/liːf/
lifestyle *n C*	/ˈlaɪfˌstaɪl/
lively *adj*	/ˈlaɪvli/
market *n C* **	/ˈmɑː(r)kɪt/
measure *v* ***	/ˈmeʒə(r)/
military service *n U*	/ˈmɪlɪt(ə)ri sɜː(r)vɪs/
movement *n C* ***	/ˈmuːvmənt/
occasion *n C* ***	/əˈkeɪʒ(ə)n/
order *v* ***	/ˈɔː(r)də(r)/
plant *n C* ***	/plɑːnt/
presenter *n C*	/prɪˈzentə(r)/
progress *n U* ***	/ˈprəʊgres/
scoop *n C*	/skuːp/
shopping list *n C*	/ˈʃɒpɪŋ lɪst/
special *adj* ***	/ˈspeʃ(ə)l/
speciality *n C*	/ˌspeʃiˈæləti/
stale *adj*	/steɪl/
supermarket *n C* *	/ˈsuːpə(r)ˌmɑː(r)kɪt/
taste *n/v* ***	/teɪst/
taxi *n C* ***	/ˈtæksi/
variety *n C* ***	/vəˈraɪəti/
weak *adj* **	/wiːk/
weigh *v* **	/weɪ/

7A | Work experience

Speaking

1 Read this description of a job. What is the job?

I work for the government and I deal with – everything! I work in a beautiful office in Washington. I work with lots of different people. It's very well-paid. It's also temporary. What do I do?

2 Think of another job and make three sentences about it. Work in pairs. Read your sentences to your partner. Your partner must guess the job.

Vocabulary: work

1 Choose the correct words to complete the sentences.

1 Many film stars had very different *jobs / works* before they started their acting *careers / jobs*.
2 Madonna hated her *career / work* at a donut shop, but she needed a *job / work*.
3 Brad Pitt had a *career / job* as a dancing chicken outside a restaurant before he began his *career / job* as an actor.
4 Tom Cruise was thinking of a *career / work* in the church before finding *job / work* in the movies.

2 Complete the sentences in column A with a phrase from column B.

A		**B**	
1	At the donut shop, Madonna was **in charge**	a	**of work**.
2	She was **fired**	b	**as** a model.
3	Brad Pitt used to **work**	c	**for** cleaning the tables.
4	When he was young, he was often **out**	d	**from** the job.
5	For a time, Tom Cruise **earned**	e	**of** the coffee machine.
6	He was **responsible**	f	**a living** in a New York restaurant.

3 Work in pairs. Talk about someone you know who …

- is out of work.
- does not need to earn a living.
- has an interesting career.
- has had lots of different jobs.
- has a very responsible job.
- loves/hates her/his work.

My sister is out of work.
She lost her job when her company closed.
She's finding it very difficult to get another job.

Listening

1 2.1 Listen to three people on a radio talk show. They are speaking about famous people they have met in their jobs. Match the speakers to the stars.

1	Valerio	a	Brad Pitt
2	Michelle	b	Tom Cruise
3	Tony	c	Leonardo DiCaprio
		d	Tom Hanks
		e	Madonna
		f	Angelina Jolie

2 2.1 Listen to the talk show again. Complete the sentences with Valerio (V), Michelle (M) or Tony (T).

1 _____ can't remember a star's name.
2 _____ comes from New Jersey.
3 _____ is Australian.
4 _____ lives in Santa Monica.
5 _____ thought the stars were cute.
6 _____ thought the star was very generous.
7 _____ works as a customer service assistant.

3 Have you ever met anyone famous?

GRAMMAR: present perfect simple

We can use the present perfect simple to talk about our experiences. We often use it with *ever* and *never*.

__Have__ you ever __met__ anyone famous?
Yes, I__'ve met__ Rafael Nadal.
I__'ve__ never __visited__ England.

We use the present perfect simple to focus on the experience, not when or where it happened. If we want to give more details, we use the past simple.

I__'ve met__ Rafael Nadal.
I __met__ him in New York in 2010.

SEE LANGUAGE REFERENCE PAGE 74

1 What are the infinitives of the past participles in the box?

done	driven	drunk	earned	eaten	found
hated	helped	met	served	spoken	worked

Put the verbs into two groups: regular and irregular.

regular *earned*
irregular *done*

2 Complete the dialogue. Put the verbs in brackets into the past simple or the present perfect simple.

A: ____ you ever ____ (*hear*) of Thomas Mapother IV?
B: No, I ____ (*never / hear*) of him. Who is he?
A: He's an actor. He ____ (*make*) loads of famous films.
B: Well, I ____ (*never / see*) a film with him in it.
A: What about *Mission Impossible*? It was on TV last night. ____ you ____ (*see*) it?
B: Yes, but that ____ (*be*) with Tom Cruise.
A: Ah, but Thomas Mapother IV is Tom Cruise's real name. He ____ (*change*) it before he got famous.

3 Work in pairs. Practise the dialogue.

4 Work in groups. Take it in turns to make questions using the prompts below. If the answer is *yes*, ask more questions to find out the details.

Have you ever driven a sports car?
What kind of car was it?

- drive / a sports car
- eat / in an expensive restaurant
- find / anything interesting in the street
- have / a temporary summer job
- live / in a different town
- lose / your job
- stay / in a five star hotel
- work / in an office
- win / a prize or a competition

5 Now tell the class about the people you spoke to.

Helen and John have both had a summer job, but Helen worked in a restaurant and John worked for his father.

PRONUNCIATION: /æ/ & /ʌ/

1 Underline any six words in the table below.

past simple /æ/	past participle /ʌ/
began	begun
drank	drunk
ran	run
sang	sung
swam	swum

2.2 Now listen to the recording and tick (✔) the words you hear. When you hear the six words that you have underlined, say *Bingo*.

2 Work in pairs. Say a word from the table in exercise 1. Your partner must say if they hear a verb in the past simple or a past participle.

7B | Hard work

VOCABULARY & SPEAKING: verb collocations (work)

1 Put the sentences in the correct place in the diagram.

a You apply for a job.
b You finish your studies.
c You get promoted.
d You get the job.
e You go for an interview.
f You go on a training course.

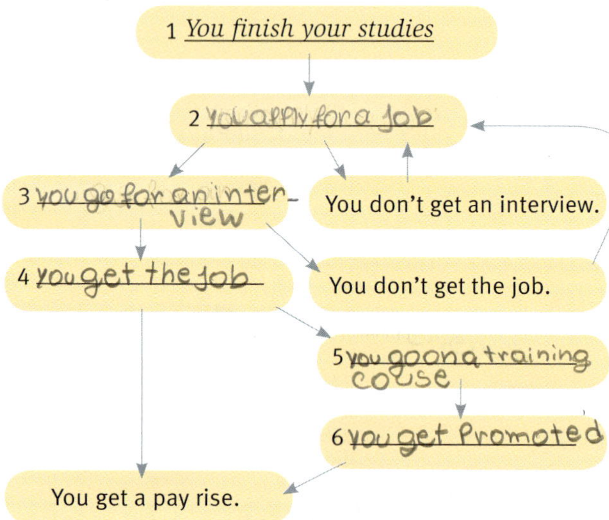

2 Complete the text about Pat Side's experience of work with the verbs in the box.

applied	finished	got (x2)	had	left
lost	was (x2)	went (x2)		

3 2.3 Listen to the recording to check your answers.

4 What kind of work have you done? Describe your own experiences, using the expressions in exercise 1.

READING

1 Read the first paragraph of the magazine article opposite. What do the two women have in common?

2 Read the rest of the article and decide if the sentences are true (T) or false (F). Correct the false sentences.

1 She describes her experience of looking for work.
2 It was difficult to find a job.
3 She had some money problems.
4 She enjoyed her experience.

3 Put the diary extracts a–d into the gaps 1–4 in the article.

a Finally, finally, my unemployment benefit cheque arrived and I went to the post office to cash it. At the same time, I paid the gas and electricity. I've never felt so happy!
b I went for an interview at the Jobcentre today. Mr Mills, my interviewer, gave me application forms for six jobs.
c Tomorrow I return to my old life. My job, my home, my car and no more interviews. This is the hardest four weeks I've ever had and I realize how lucky I am.
I really hope Pat finds a job soon.
d I've done half of the month. I wanted to go out with some friends, but I haven't got enough money.

4 Work in pairs. Discuss these questions.

- What is unemployment benefit (line 15)?
- How much is unemployment benefit in your country?
- Is there an unemployment problem in your country?

CAREER

Back to Work

When Pat Side's children (1) *finished* their studies and (2) ____ home, Pat wanted to find a job. She (3) ____ no qualifications, so she (4) ____ on a training course to become an assistant in a home for retired people. After the course, she (5) ____ for many different jobs. She (6) ____ for a few interviews, but it was six months before she (7) ____ a job. She (8) ____ good at her work and, two years later, she (9) ____ promoted to 'senior assistant'. She also (10) ____ a small pay rise. Unfortunately, the home closed a year after that and Pat (11) ____ her job.

REAL LIFE

Life on the Other Side

Earlier this year, successful journalist Pat Side was preparing an article about the problems of mothers who want to return to work. By chance, she met another woman who had the same name as her and was the same age. The other Pat Side was unemployed and looking for a job. The two women agreed to exchange lives for four weeks and to write about their experiences.

Day 2 (1) ______________

Day 4 Tomorrow, I've got interviews for four different jobs. The salaries are low – more or less the same as my unemployment benefit. But if I don't apply for the jobs, I lose my benefit! It's crazy!

Day 5 I didn't get the jobs. They said I was too old. It's the first time in my new life that I've wanted to cry.

Day 8 Back to the Jobcentre. I waited for three hours to speak to Mr Mills. They said he was in a meeting, but I think he was having a long lunch. He gave me two more application forms ...

Day 12 I've never worried about money too much, but today I got two bills in the post. Gas and electricity. I haven't got the money. What am I going to do?

Day 14 (2) ______________

Day 15 Another interview today. I didn't have the money for the bus so I walked. Five miles in the cold and rain and I didn't get the job. Chips again for dinner.

Day 16 (3) ______________

Day 18 I went for another interview today and took the bus. Surprise, surprise – I didn't get the job. They said I was too qualified.

Day 29 I've filled in seventeen application forms and been to seven interviews, but no success. I begin to think this is all a waste of time.

Day 30 (4) ______________

Two weeks after this article was written, Pat Side found a job in a telephone call centre. She enjoys her new work and says that the money is good.

SPEAKING

1 Imagine that you can exchange your life with the life of someone else for four weeks. Make notes about a typical day in your new life.

2 Work in pairs. Ask and answer questions about your new life.

DID YOU KNOW?

1 Work in pairs. Read the information about different salaries in the United Kingdom and discuss the questions.

- Do you think the differences in salary are fair?
- How would you change the order?
- What is a good salary in your country?
- What are the best and worst paid jobs in your country?

Who has the best-paid job?

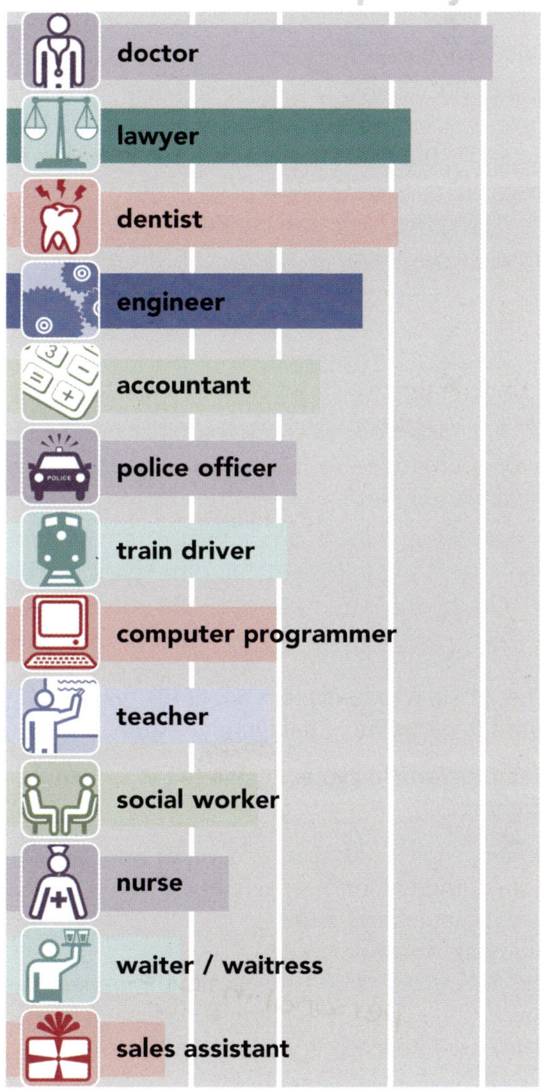

7c Job selection

Reading

1 How often do you read your horoscope? Do you believe what it says?

2 Read the magazine article and choose the best title.

1 Horoscopes are a waste of time
2 Why you should read your horoscope
3 Astrology and the secret police

It's 9 o'clock in the morning and you have already arrived at work. There are a million things to do: check your email, finish something you started yesterday, get ready for that meeting, tidy up your desk … stop, hold it! Have you read your horoscope yet?

or many people, a horoscope is a good way to waste five inutes, but if you haven't looked at your star sign yet, it's ime that you did. Somebody, somewhere has already tudied **your** horoscope and made decisions about **your** uture.

ike it or not, astrology is important. Millions and millions of eople around the world actually believe in it. American residents, the secret police, national football managers and uccessful business people have all used horoscopes in their ork. The great American banker, J P Morgan, once said, illionaires don't use astrology. Billionaires do.'

Every time you write your date of birth on an application form (to apply for a job or promotion, for example), somebody, somewhere will probably look at the astrological information it contains. Does this person have the right personality for the job? Will they work well with the other people? How important is work in their life? Is this person a good traveller? How ambitious are they?

So even if you think that horoscopes are a waste of time, it's often interesting to know what other people are thinking about you. Oh, by the way, have you read your boss's star sign yet?

3 The article was badly torn out of the magazine. What is the first word in each line of paragraphs 2 and 3?

4 Read the article again. Complete the sentences with words from the text.

1 Some people think that horoscopes are a _ _ _ _ _ of time.
2 Many different kinds of people _ _ _ _ _ _ _ in astrology.
3 People sometimes make _ _ _ _ _ _ _ _ _ about your future after studying your horoscope.
4 People can get your astrological information when you fill in an _ _ _ _ _ _ _ _ _ _ _ form for a job.
5 They are interested in finding out about your _ _ _ _ _ _ _ _ _ _ _ .

Grammar: present perfect simple with *already* & *yet*

We usually use *already* in positive sentences. We use it to emphasize that something has happened before now (perhaps earlier than expected).

*It is early in the morning, but she has **already** arrived at work.*

We use *yet* in negative sentences and questions. We use it to talk or ask about something that has not happened, but will probably happen soon.

*Have you checked your email **yet**?*
*No, I haven't done it **yet**.*

See Language Reference page 74

1 Complete the dialogue with *already* or *yet*.

A: Have you finished ______?
B: No, not ______. Another few minutes, OK?
A: But you've ______ taken two hours!
B: I know, but I haven't really understood the problem ______.
A: I've ______ explained it to you twice!
B: Just give me a few more minutes, OK?

2 Work in pairs. Practise the dialogue.

3 Work in pairs, A and B.

A: Turn to page 131. Look at the *Things to do* list. Ask your partner questions.
Have you … yet?

B: Turn to page 132. Look at the *Things to do* list. Answer your partner's questions.
Yes, I have. *No, I haven't.* *No, not yet.*

4 Make sentences that are true for you using the prompts. For each sentence, give some extra information.

1 I haven't finished my studies yet. I'm going to take my final exams next year.

1 finish my studies
2 find the perfect job
3 meet the love of my life
4 buy my own home
5 travel to lots of different countries

VOCABULARY: adjectives & nouns (personality)

1 What star sign are you? Think of three people you know. What are their star signs?

Now read the star signs for you and for them. Do you agree with the information?

2 Complete the table with words from the horoscope.

definition	adjective	noun
wants to be successful	(1) ____	ambition
shows strong feelings	(2) ____	emotion(s)
can create new ideas	imaginative	(3) ____
does not need other people	(4) ____	independence
can understand things quickly	intelligent	(5) ____
does not mind waiting	patient	(6) ____
has special abilities	skilled	(7) ____
can understand what other people are feeling	(8) ____	sensitivity

SPEAKING

1 Work in groups. Discuss the jobs in the box. Decide which are the most important qualities people need to do these jobs and explain why. Use the words and phrases in the horoscope to help you.

lawyer   police officer   sales person   teacher

Good police officers are calm people because they often have to deal with dangerous situations.

Now choose the best star sign for each job.

2 Imagine the perfect boss. Describe her/him in eight sentences.

The perfect boss …
has a lot of patience.
gives you a bonus every year.

ARIES
21/03 – 20/04
When they stop thinking about themselves, they are excellent managers. Well-organized and with very good people skills, they need to learn a bit more patience.

TAURUS
21/04 – 21/05
Not the most imaginative people in the world, but they are the best people to have near you if you are looking for action. When they do things, they do them well.

GEMINI
22/05 – 21/06
Their independence is important to them and they work better on their own than in a team. Lots of imagination and ideas, but they get bored quickly.

CANCER
22/06 – 23/07
They seem calm and organized, but Cancers have a secret sensitivity. Look after them well, and they will look after you.

LEO
24/07 – 23/08
Strong, patient and skilled, Leos want to be boss – and they often are. They have great ambition, but be careful of them if they do not get what they want.

VIRGO
24/08 – 23/09
They often live for their work and they are not very emotional people. They learn quickly and do not need a lot of help. Calm, but sometimes too calm.

LIBRA
24/09 – 23/10
Librans are a happy balance of many opposites: imagination and hard work, patience and speed. They are liked by other people.

SCORPIO
24/10 – 22/11
Their main strength is their ability to change. With their natural intelligence, they understand situations quickly and know what to do next.

SAGITTARIUS
23/11 – 21/12
Honest and straightforward in the way they work, but when things don't go well, they can get worried. Patient and kind with other people.

CAPRICORN
22/12 – 20/01
Naturally skilled managers, they are independent and strong. They are more sensitive than they seem and they are good listeners.

AQUARIUS
21/01 – 19/02
They like their work and they enjoy working with other people. They do not usually show their emotions. Quite ambitious, but they make good friends.

PISCES
20/02 – 20/03
Intelligent and imaginative, they have good people skills, but they find it difficult to make important decisions.

7D | The recruitment agency

SPEAKING

1 Work in pairs. Discuss these questions.

- What's the best way to find a job? Make a list. (For example, go to a recruitment agency.)
- Is it easy or difficult to find work in your town?

VOCABULARY: curriculum vitae

1 Look at extracts 1–6 from a CV (curriculum vitae). Match them to the highlighted words or phrases in the recruitment agency advertisement.

(1)
1. Mr R. Dailly (college tutor), Doncaster University, Box 478B, Doncaster
2. Mrs Mary Whitehead (General Manager), Socks Are Us, High Street, Halifax

(2)
2008–2010 Socks Are Us, Halifax (Manager)
2007–2008 Street Wear, (Assistant Manager)

(3)
Alison Peabody
Date of birth: 4 March 1984
Address: 39d, Victoria Road, Halbridge
Tel: 0719 376488
Email: ali.peabody@quickmail.com

(4)
2006 DMS (Diploma of Marketing and Sales)
2005 BA Business Studies
2002 Three A levels: English, Business Studies, History

(5)
2002–2005 University of Doncaster
1996–2002 Brunel School for Girls, Halifax

(6)
Cinema, travel, tennis, eating out

2 Work in pairs. Ask and answer questions using the words and phrases in the advertisement.

Could you tell me about your education?
What qualifications have you got?

Can't find a job?
Want to find a new job?
Looking for a better job?
Not sure what to do?

SRT

Sayers Recruitment & Training can help!

Send us a short letter/CV with your personal details and information about your education, qualifications, professional experience and personal interests. Include the names of two referees.

We can find the right job for you! Speak to one of our experienced career advisers.

For more information, visit our website
www.sayers-rt.com
or send your CV to davinasayers@srt.net

LISTENING

1 2.4 Listen to a dialogue in a recruitment agency. Underline the correct information in the notes below.

SRT

Name:	Miss / Ms Ruby Tuesday
Qualifications:	none / MA Philosophy
Interests:	computers / cooking
Present job:	fast food restaurant / shop assistant
Ideal job:	restaurant manager / she doesn't know

2 2.4 Listen to the dialogue again. Tick (✔) the advice that the consultant gives to Ruby.

1 Write a fuller CV.
2 Get a qualification.
3 Mention personal interests on the CV.
4 Invent some information on the CV.
5 Do a course in computer skills.
6 Arrive for interviews on time.
7 Improve her appearance.
8 Move to another town.

3 Do you agree with the consultant's advice? What would you say to Ruby?

FUNCTIONAL LANGUAGE: advice

Asking for advice
What should I do?
Should I + infinitive ?

Giving advice
You should/shouldn't + infinitive
I (don't) think you should + infinitive
(If I were you,) I'd + infinitive
Why don't you + infinitive … ?
What about + verb + *-ing* … ?

1 Rearrange the words to make questions and sentences that give/ask for advice.

1 go I I or should should stay ?
2 decide quickly shouldn't too you
3 about don't it think why you ?
4 ask friends I should think you your
5 a get if I I'd job new were you
6 a about agency going recruitment to what ?

2 Work in pairs. A friend of yours has some problems at work. Give your friend some advice.

1 Why don't you write him a letter?
I think you should speak to his boss!

1 My boss never listens to my ideas.
2 I've got a new job and no one talks to me in the office.
3 I want to take a day off next Friday and I don't want to tell my boss.
4 My boss was angry with me because I was late for the third time this week.
5 I've got too much work to do and I'm feeling really stressed.

3 You are going to ask for some careers advice. Think about your answers to these questions. Make notes if necessary.

- What do you do now?
- What other jobs have you had?
- What qualifications do you have?
- What are you good at? (organizing, working with people, etc)
- What are you interested in? (music, sport, etc)
- What is important for you in a job? (money, travel, working regular hours, etc)
- What kind of job would you most like to do?

4 Work in pairs. Take it in turns to interview each other, using the questions in exercise 3. Give your partner some careers advice.

PRONUNCIATION: email & website addresses

1 2.5 Listen to the email and website addresses.

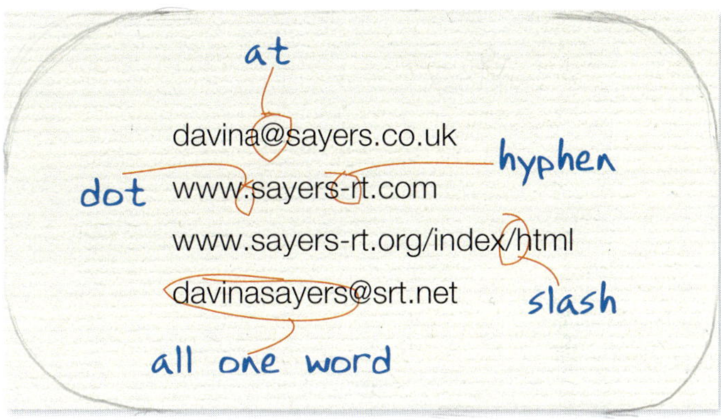

2 Work in pairs, A and B.

A: Turn to page 129.
B: Turn to page 131.

Dictate the addresses to your partner.

3 Write four more email or website addresses and dictate them to your partner.

Self-assessment (tick ✔)

☐ I can understand a conversation in a recruitment agency.
☐ I can understand the main details of a curriculum vitae.
☐ I can ask for and give advice about careers.
☐ I can say and understand email and website addresses.

7 Language reference

GRAMMAR

Present perfect simple 1

We use the present perfect simple to talk about general or personal experiences.

*I **have had** many different jobs.*

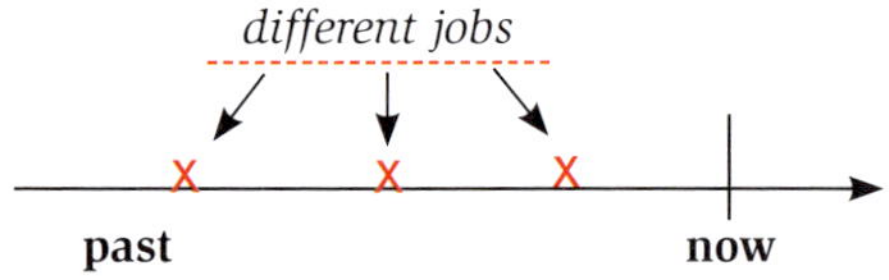

We do not usually refer to a specific time when we use the present perfect simple. We only know that the action (or actions) happened before now.

*I **have visited** many countries.* (= in my life)

We use the past simple when we refer to a specific time.

*I **worked** as a waitress **last summer**.*

We make the present perfect simple with *have/has* + past participle.

Affirmative & Negative			
I		've haven't	worked abroad.
He/She/It		's hasn't	worked abroad.
You/We/They		've haven't	worked abroad.
Question			
Where	have	I	worked abroad?
Where	has	he/she/it	worked abroad?
Where	have	you/we/they	worked abroad?
Short answer			
Have you worked abroad?			Yes, I have. / No, I haven't.
Has he worked abroad?			Yes, he has. / No, he hasn't.

We use *ever* in questions when we want to ask about a person's life up to the present time.

***Have** you **ever worked** in a restaurant?*
(= at any time in your life?)

Already* & *yet

We can use the present perfect simple with *already* and *yet*.

We use *already* in positive sentences and we usually put it before the past participle. We use *already* with completed actions that happen before now or sooner than expected.

*I've **already** found a job.*
*She's **already** finished her studies.*

We use *yet* in questions and negative sentences and we put it at the end of the sentence. We use *yet* to ask if an action is complete or to say that it is not complete. We use it when we think the action will happen soon.

*Have you read your horoscope **yet**?*
*I haven't checked the mailbox **yet**.*

See page 104 for more information about the present perfect simple.

FUNCTIONAL LANGUAGE

Asking for advice

What should I do?
Should I + infinitive?

Giving advice

You should + infinitive …
You shouldn't + infinitive …
I (don't) think you should + infinitive …
(If I were you,) I'd (wouldn't) + infinitive …
Why don't you + infinitive?
What about + verb + *-ing*?

Word list

Work

boss *n C* ***	/bɒs/
application form *n C*	/ˌæplɪˈkeɪʃ(ə)n fɔː(r)m/
apply for *v* ***	/əˈplaɪ fə(r)/
be fired (from a job)	/biː ˈfaɪə(r)d/
career *n C* **	/kəˈrɪə(r)/
CV (curriculum vitae) *n C*	/ˌsiː ˈviː/ (/kəˌrɪkjʊləm ˈviːtaɪ/)
deal (with) *v* ***	/diːl/
diploma *n C*	/dɪˈpləʊmə/
do (sth) for a living *phr*	/duː fə(r) ə ˈlɪvɪŋ/
earn *v* **	/ɜː(r)n/
education *n U* ***	/ˌedjʊˈkeɪʃ(ə)n/
in charge (of sth/sb)	/ɪn tʃɑː(r)dʒ/
interview *n C* **	/ˈɪntə(r)ˌvjuː/
job *n C* ***	/dʒɒb/
office *n C* ***	/ˈɒfɪs/
out of work *phr*	/aʊt əv ˈwɜː(r)k/
pay rise *n C*	/ˈpeɪ raɪz/
professional *adj* ***	/prəˈfeʃ(ə)nəl/
(be/get) promoted *v* **	/prəˈməʊtɪd/
promotion *n C/U* *	/prəˈməʊʃ(ə)n/
qualification *n C* *	/ˌkwɒlɪfɪˈkeɪʃ(ə)n/
recruitment *n U*	/rɪˈkruːtmənt/
referee *n C*	/ˌrefəˈriː/
responsible (for sth) *adj* ***	/rɪˈspɒnsəb(ə)l/
retired *adj*	/rɪˈtaɪə(r)d/
salary *n C* *	/ˈsæləri/
temporary *adj* ***	/ˈtemp(ə)rəri/
training *n U* ***	/ˈtreɪnɪŋ/
well-paid *adj*	/welpeɪd/

Jobs

accountant *n C*	/əˈkaʊntənt/
chauffeur *n C*	/ˈʃəʊfə(r)/
computer *n C* ***	/kəmˈpjuːtə(r)/
programmer *n C*	/ˈprəʊˌgræmə(r)/
dentist *n C*	/ˈdentɪst/
doctor *n C* ***	/ˈdɒktə(r)/
engineer *n C* *	/ˌendʒɪˈnɪə(r)/
journalist *n C* **	/ˈdʒɜː(r)nəlɪst/
lawyer *n C* **	/ˈlɔːjə(r)/
manager *n C* **	/ˈmænɪdʒə(r)/
nurse *n C* **	/nɜː(r)s/
police officer *n C*	/pəˈliːs ˈɒfɪsə(r)/
sales assistant *n C*	/seɪls əˈsɪst(ə)nt/
social worker *n C*	/ˈsəʊʃ(ə)l wɜː(r)kə(r)/
teacher *n C* ***	/ˈtiːtʃə(r)/
train driver *n C*	/ˈtreɪn draɪvə(r)/
waiter *n C*	/ˈweɪtə(r)/
waitress *n C*	/ˈweɪtrəs/

Personality

ambition *n C/U* *	/æmˈbɪʃ(ə)n/
ambitious *adj*	/æmˈbɪʃəs/
emotion *n C/U* **	/ɪˈməʊʃ(ə)n/
emotional *adj* **	/ɪˈməʊʃ(ə)nəl/
honest *adj* *	/ˈɒnɪst/
imagination *n U* *	/ɪˌmædʒɪˈneɪʃ(ə)n/
imaginative *adj*	/ɪˈmædʒɪnətɪv/
independence *n U* **	/ˌɪndɪˈpendəns/
independent *adj* ***	/ˌɪndɪˈpendənt/
(well) organized *adj*	/ˈɔː(r)gənaɪzd/
patience *n U*	/ˈpeɪʃ(ə)ns/
patient *adj* **	/ˈpeɪʃ(ə)nt/
sensitive *adj*	/ˈsensətɪv/
sensitivity *n U*	/ˌsensəˈtɪvəti/
skill *n C/U* ***	/skɪl/
skilled *adj*	/skɪld/

Other words & phrases

ability *n C/U* ***	/əˈbɪləti/
adviser *n C* *	/ədˈvaɪzə(r)/
angry *adj* ***	/ˈæŋgri/
appearance *n U* ***	/əˈpɪərəns/
assistant *adj/n C* **	/əˈsɪst(ə)nt/
astrology *n U*	/əˈstrɒlədʒi/
balance *n U* **	/ˈbæləns/
basic *adj* ***	/ˈbeɪsɪk/
billionaire *n C*	/ˌbɪljəˈneə(r)/
by chance *phr*	/baɪ ˈtʃɑːns/
cash *v*	/kæʃ/
celebrity *n C* *	/səˈlebrəti/
cheque *n C* *	/tʃek/
contain *v* ***	/kənˈteɪn/
crazy *adj* **	/ˈkreɪzi/
cute *adj*	/kjuːt/
dot *n C*	/dɒt/
downtown *adj/adv*	/ˌdaʊnˈtaʊn/
gas *n C/U* ***	/gæs/
horoscope *n C*	/ˈhɒrəˌskəʊp/
hyphen *n C*	/ˈhaɪf(ə)n/
loads of *phr*	/ləʊdz əv/
marketing *n U*	/ˈmɑː(r)kɪtɪŋ/
mile *n C* ***	/maɪl/
millionaire *n C*	/ˌmɪljəˈneə(r)/
movies *n pl*	/ˈmuːviz/
natural *adj* ***	/ˈnætʃ(ə)rəl/
naturally *adv* *	/ˈnætʃ(ə)rəli/
philosophy *n U* *	/fɪˈlɒsəfi/
post office *n C*	/ˈpəʊst ɒfɪs/
recently *adv* ***	/ˈriːs(ə)ntli/
sales *n pl*	/seɪls/
situation *n C* ***	/ˌsɪtʃuˈeɪʃ(ə)n/
slash *n C*	/slæʃ/
smart *adj* *	/smɑː(r)t/
star *n C* ***	/stɑː(r)/
star sign *n C*	/ˈstɑː(r) saɪn/
strength *n U* ***	/streŋθ/
stressed *adj*	/strest/
successful *adj* ***	/səkˈsesf(ə)l/
suit *n C* **	/suːt/
team *n C* ***	/tiːm/
tidy (up) *v* *	/ˈtaɪdi/
traveller *n C* *	/ˈtræv(ə)lə(r)/
tutor *n C*	/ˈtjuːtə(r)/
unemployed *adj* *	/ˌʌnɪmˈplɔɪd/
unemployment *n C* **	/ˌʌnɪmˈplɔɪmənt/
benefit *n U* **	/ˈbenɪfɪt/
waste *v* **	/weɪst/
worried *adj* *	/ˈwʌrid/

8A | The futurological conference

Speaking

1 Work in pairs. Discuss these questions.

- What are the films in the box called in your language?

Alien *Iron Man 2* *Star Wars*
Men in Black *Resident Evil* *The Matrix*

- What science fiction films have you seen?
- What happens in them?

In Alien, *a crew on a spaceship discover they have an alien on board and have to fight the alien to survive.*

Reading

1 You are going to read about a futurological conference. (*Futurology* is the study of the ***future***.)

Look at the titles for the talks. Three of the titles do **not** come from this conference. Put a cross (✗) by these three titles.

a An exciting new theory of time travel
b Armstrong – the first man on the moon
c The world is growing older
d Life in front of the computer screen
e Salyut and Mir – early space stations
f Prisons in space
g Star wars: fact or fiction?
h The advantages of new energy sources
i The end of English lessons?
j The invention of the laser

4TH INTERNATIONAL FUTUROLOGICAL CONFERENCE

22ND–25TH MAY DES MOINES, IOWA

PROGRAMME

1 ______________

Dr Judith Amos (author of *Clean New World*)

It might not be long before the sun, the wind and the sea become our main sources of energy. We will live in a cleaner, healthier world. Will it be a safer one, too?

2 ______________

Professor J B Gartenberg (University of London)

Research scientists will find cures for most of the world's diseases in the next 50 years. We will all live longer and, by the year 2020, there will be more than one billion people over 60 years old. How will this change our society and how will we pay for the elderly?

3 ______________

Randy Oakes (journalist)

The 21st century is the age of the internet. More and more, people are using the internet for business, education, shopping and even to make friends. This talk will explore how internet use will increase in the next 20 years.

4 ______________

Duncan Hague (Institute of Sociology)

In the US and the UK, prisons are almost full and crime is increasing every day. Soon, there won't be enough room for all our prisoners. Where will we put them? Space stations may be the answer.

5 ______________

Dr Mikhaïl Radvanyi (Lingua Foundation)

Learning a foreign language may soon be a thing of the past. This talk will look at new developments in automatic translation machines.

6 ______________

Xavier M Berman (author of *Light Years Away*)

A hundred years ago many scientists said that space travel was impossible. Now they say that we will never be able to travel in time. But new theories of time suggest that they might be wrong.

7 ______________

Stella May Roche (War on War)

American military scientists are developing new laser technology that may change the world for ever. Laser guns on military satellites will be unstoppable and the future for the smaller countries of the world is extremely frightening.

Glossary
elderly *n* old people

2 Now read about the conference talks. Match the titles a–j in exercise 1 to the descriptions 1–7.

3 Complete the sentences with words from the box.

cures	energy	satellites	source	technology	theory

1 The sun is the most important ___ of light for our planet.
2 At the moment, most of our ___ comes from oil.
3 We will need to find ___ for new diseases.
4 Gödel's ___ of time travel says that we will need to travel faster than the speed of light.
5 American military ___ is becoming more and more advanced.
6 ___ in space carry many different kinds of equipment.

4 Which of the talks at the conference would you like to go to? Why?

I'd like to go to the talk by Judith Amos because I'm interested in green politics.

Grammar: predictions 1 (*may, might* & *will*)

We can use *will/won't* + infinitive to talk about things we are sure will happen in the future.

*There **will be** more than 1 billion people over 60 years old.*
*We **won't be** able to travel in time.*

We can use *may/might* + infinitive when we are less sure things will happen in the future.

*The world **may become** more dangerous.*
*Scientists **might find** life on other planets.*

sure	not sure	sure
will	*may/might*	*won't*

See Language Reference page 84

1 Correct the mistakes in the sentences.

1 I think that our teacher will gives us a test next week.
2 I may be go to America soon.
3 I may not to get married.
4 I think my country might wins the next World Cup.
5 I'll always remembering the people in this class.
6 I think that it will rains tomorrow.
7 I'll never living in another country.
8 I won't to become rich or famous.

2 Change the sentences in exercise 1 so that they are true for you.

3 How will life be different for you/your family:

- in one year's time?
- in ten years' time?

Work in pairs. Talk about the topics in the box.

appearance	home	money	work

Pronunciation: contractions 2

1 2.6 Listen to these contractions and repeat.

I'll it'll there'll we'll what'll you'll

2 Match a phrase in column A with a response in column B.

A		B	
1	Aren't you ready yet? Hurry up!	a	I'll be OK.
2	Be careful – it's very dangerous.	b	I won't be long.
3	I wonder where they are.	c	You'll like it.
4	Let's have a drink before the film starts.	d	We'll be late.
5	What's this? I've never eaten that before.	e	They'll be here soon.

3 2.7 Listen to the recording to check your answers.

4 Work in pairs. Practise the exchanges in exercise 2.

Speaking

1 2.8–2.10 Listen to three people speaking. Match the speakers 1–3 to three of the topics a–j below.

The future of:

a	computers	f	medicine
b	crime	g	my country
c	education	h	restaurants
d	holidays	i	shops
e	languages	j	space travel

2 Choose a topic from the list. You must talk about the topic for thirty seconds without stopping. Before you speak, spend some time preparing what you are going to say.

8B Space tourists

Listening

1 You are going to listen to a radio programme. All the words in the box appear in the programme. What do you think it is about?

blast off	contestant	game show
museum	rocket	tourist

2 2.11 Listen to check your answers.

3 2.11 Listen again and answer the questions.

1 How many space tourists have there been?
2 How much did they pay to go into space?
3 Who is organizing the new game show?
4 What countries will the contestants come from?
5 Where will the game show be filmed?
6 What is the prize?
7 Will the winner visit the International Space Station?
8 Who thinks that space tourism is too dangerous?

4 Would you like to go into space? Why or why not?

Vocabulary: compound nouns with numbers

1 Look at audioscript 2.11 on page 140 and find these phrases. Which phrase is correct?

1 20-million dollar cheque / 20-million dollars cheque
2 thirteen-part show / thirteen-parts show
3 eight-day trip / eight-days trip

2 Match the words from column A with the words from column B to complete the sentences.

A	B
eight-hour	break
five-star	course
million-dollar	day
ten-minute	hotel
20-euro	house
two-week	note

1 He went to England for a ______ in business English.
2 Have you got change for a ______?
3 I've never stayed in a ______.
4 Let's stop for a ______ and a cup of coffee.
5 I usually work an ______ but sometimes I do more.
6 She lives in a ______ in the Hollywood Hills.

GRAMMAR: predictions 2 (*maybe, probably, certainly,* etc)

We can use words like *possibly* and *perhaps* to make our predictions sound more or less probable.

100%

maybe	*probably*	*certainly*
perhaps	*definitely*	
possibly		

We usually put *maybe* and *perhaps* at the beginning of the sentence.

***Perhaps** it will be you.*

Possibly, probably, certainly and *definitely* come after *will* in positive sentences and before *won't* in negative sentences.

*The contestants will **certainly** need to be very fit.*
*The winner **possibly** won't visit the space station.*

SEE LANGUAGE REFERENCE PAGE 84

1 Put the words in brackets into the correct place in the sentences.

1 We won't discover life on other planets. (*probably*)
2 China will be the first country to land a person on Mars. (*possibly*)
3 Ordinary people won't be able to travel in space for a very long time. (*definitely*)
4 There will be hotels in space in the next twenty years. (*perhaps*)
5 Engineers will build factories in space. (*certainly*)
6 We will stop spending money on space exploration. (*maybe*)

Do you agree with the sentences above?

2 Choose one of the questions below for a class survey. Ask the other students in the class what they think. Use the words in the box in your answers.

definitely	probably	possibly	definitely not

1 Will you ever speak very good English?
2 Will you ever be in trouble with the police?
3 Will you lose your teeth or your hair?
4 Will you have more than five children?
5 Will you live to be 100?

3 Tell the rest of the class the results of your survey in exercise 2.

SPEAKING

1 Think of someone you know who would be a good contestant for *Star Quest*. Why would they be good? Make notes about the following:

- their personality
- their practical skills
- their appearance and health
- other reasons

2 Work in groups. Take it in turns to describe your person. Then decide as a group who is the best person to go on the game show.

PRONUNCIATION: word stress 2

1 Underline the word in each group that has a different stress pattern.

1	certainly	energy	probably	<u>unhappy</u>
2	businessman	engineer	president	scientist
3	dangerous	internet	invention	satellite
4	advantage	computer	conference	contestant
5	equipment	exciting	possible	remember

2 2.12 Listen to the recording to check your answers.

8c | Great ideas

Listening & speaking

1 2.13 Listen to the recording and match the descriptions 1–5 to the gadgets A–E.

2 Work in pairs. Discuss these questions.

- Which of these gadgets would you like to buy? For who?
- Which of these will sell the most? Put the gadgets in order (1 = best seller ➔ 5 = worst seller).

Reading

A Great Idea?

Ash Sharma, a second-year business studies student at Thames Valley University, thinks he has found a good way to make money. He needs £5,000 to get his idea off the ground, but his father has refused to help. What do you think? Read both sides of the story and decide for yourself.

My idea is very simple, really. I already have a small website called businessessays.com (1) ______. Business students at university log on to the site and download essays. They have an essay to write for homework, for example, but they need some help with it. On the site, they find the essay they need, download it (2) ______. At the moment, the site is free but if I can improve it, that will change.

I want to make the site much bigger and my idea is to make it really international. I have found some software that can translate the essays into sixteen different languages. It will be easy to use for people from all round the world.

I need about two months to do all the programming (3) ______. When everything is ready, people will pay $2.99 a month to use my service. If it's successful, I will be able to sell advertising, too.

Of course, I can't continue with my university studies and set up the site at the same time. And if I wait, someone else will take my idea (4) ______

I would like to help my son, but my wife and I agree that it is not a good idea to lend him £5,000 now. There are two main reasons for our decision.

My son has an interesting idea (5) ______. Will his idea work? At the moment, it's impossible to say. Are there any other websites that offer a similar service? How successful are these other sites? How many customers will he need before he starts to make money? If the site is successful, will he need to employ other people? How many? How much will he pay his staff (6) ______? And finally – is it legal to help students with their homework? When he has a business plan and when he has the answers to these questions, I will think again.

We also think that it is important for our son to finish his university studies before he starts this website. If he leaves now, it will be too risky. What will happen to him if his idea doesn't work? He will find himself with no job and no qualification, (7) ______, he will find it is difficult to get a good job. There are some things in life that we must wait for (8) ______. After he finishes his studies, we will talk about his idea again.

1 Read the magazine article on page 80 and answer the questions.

1 How does Ash think that he can make money?
2 Why does Ash want to leave university?
3 Why doesn't Ash's father want to help him?

2 Read the article again and put the phrases a–h into the gaps 1–8.

a and Ash is still very young
b and I need money to buy the software
c and if he does not have a qualification
d and it is very successful
e and it will be too late
f and use it for their work
g and who will look after the finances
h but he does not have a business plan

3 Work in pairs. Discuss these questions.

- Is the website a good idea?
- Is Ash's father right to refuse to lend him the money?
- Is it wrong to download essays from the internet?

Vocabulary: adjectives with infinitives

1 Complete these sentences with an infinitive from the box.

to finish   to get   to help   to say   to use

1 It will be easy _____ the new website.
2 It is impossible _____ if Ash's idea will work.
3 Is it legal _____ students with their homework?
4 It's important for my son _____ his studies.
5 It's difficult _____ a good job without a qualification.

Look at the article again to check your answers.

2 How many different sentences can you make from the table?

It	is will be used to be	easy possible usual legal dangerous healthy difficult impossible unusual illegal safe unhealthy	to be to drink to find to have to meet to see to begin to eat to get to make to say to stop	…

Grammar: present tense in future time clauses (first conditional)

When we are talking about future time in clauses with *if, when, after* and *before*, we use the present tense. We can use *will* in the main clause of the sentence.

subsidiary clause	main clause
If it's successful,	*I will be able to sell advertising.*
When everything is ready,	*people will pay $2.99.*
After he finishes his studies,	*we will talk about his idea again.*

The subsidiary clause can also come after the main clause.
*I will be able to sell advertising **if it's successful**.*

See Language Reference page 84

1 Complete the text. Put the verbs in brackets into the correct tense. Use *will* or present simple.

A modelling agency has offered a job in Japan to a sixteen-year-old English school student, Emily. She has decided to take the job. 'If I (1) _____ (*not take*) the job, I (2) _____ (*not get*) the chance again,' she said. Before she (3) _____ (*go*), she (4) _____ (*have*) a big party for all her friends. 'I'm so excited,' she said. 'When I (5) _____ (*say*) goodbye to my boyfriend at the airport, I (6) _____ (*be*) very sad. But after I (7) _____ (*arrive*) in Japan, everything (8) _____ (*be*) OK.' If she (9) _____ (*be*) successful, the agency (10) _____ (*give*) her more work. 'I've never done this before,' she said, 'but I'm sure I (11) _____ (*be*) good at it when I (12) _____ (*have*) a little experience.'

2 Emily's boyfriend does not want her to go. He thinks she will have problems. Make sentences from the prompts.

1 When she arrives, she won't speak the language.

1 When / arrive / not speak the language
2 If / not speak the language / not make friends
3 If / not make friends / feel very lonely
4 If / feel very lonely / want to come home
5 When / come home / not have any qualifications

3 Can you think of any other possible problems that Emily will have? Make sentences with *if, when, before* or *after*.

4 Complete the sentences so that they are true for you.

1 If I don't go out this weekend, I ….
2 I … when I have enough money.
3 After I leave the school today, I …
4 I … before I am 65.

8D | Help!

Speaking

1 Work in pairs. Ask and answer these questions.

- Do you have a computer at home?
- What do you use it for?
- Are you connected to the internet?
- How often do you use the internet?
- What do you do online?
- Do you know any older people (eg grandparents) who use the internet? What do they do?

Vocabulary: computer actions

1 Label the computer icons A–L with words from the box.

attach	close	copy	cursor	delete	find
open	paste	print	save	send	undo

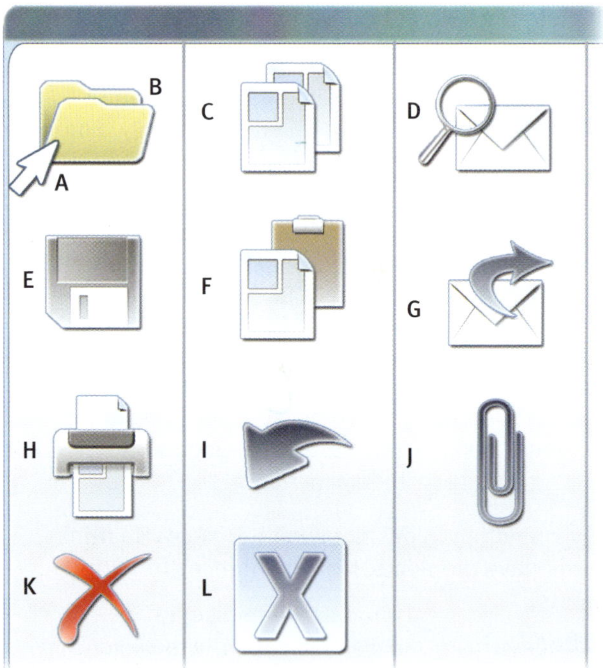

2 Use the words in exercise 1 to complete the sentences.

1 Before you ______ an email, you need to connect to the internet.
2 Do you want to ______ this in colour or black and white?
3 If you make a mistake, you can always ______ it.
4 It's very easy to ______ a picture into a document.
5 Move the ______ to the 'Open document' icon and click on it.
6 Please ______ your CV to your application form.
7 Use a memory stick or a CD to ______ the work you have done.

Listening

1 2.14 Listen to a dialogue between a young woman, Karen, and her grandfather. Answer the questions.

1 How much does the grandfather know about computers?
2 What does the grandfather want to do?
3 Does he succeed?

2 2.14 Listen to the dialogue again and put the instructions for sending an email in the correct order.

- ☐ Attach your document to the message.
- ☐ Click on the email icon.
- ☐ Connect to the internet.
- ☐ Click on 'Write Mail'.
- ☐ Log off.
- ☐ Send the message.
- ☐ Type the address.
- ☐ Write your message.

3 Is the order of the instructions the same for your computer? If not, how is it different?

FUNCTIONAL LANGUAGE: giving instructions

We give instructions with:
1 *you* + present simple
__You type__ your address there.

2 the imperative form
__Click__ on that button. *__Don't forget__ to log off.*

We can make the order of the instructions easier to understand with sequencing adverbs.

First of all, … Then, …/After that, … Next, …/Afterwards, … Finally, …

1 Look at audioscript 2.14 on page 141. Underline all the instructions and sequencing adverbs.

2 Put the instructions in the correct order.

Checking your English spelling
☐ add it to the languages on the right. You will now
☐ and find 'Tools'. Then, select
☐ be able to use the spell check program in
☐ English on your computer.
☐ First of all, you click on 'Start' at the bottom of your
☐ 'Language Settings'. Finally, find 'English' and
☐ screen. After that, you click on the 'Program' arrow

3 Work in pairs. A friend is writing an essay and wants to find a different word for *world*. Look at the pictures and give her/him instructions.

1 *First of all, highlight the word that you want to change.*

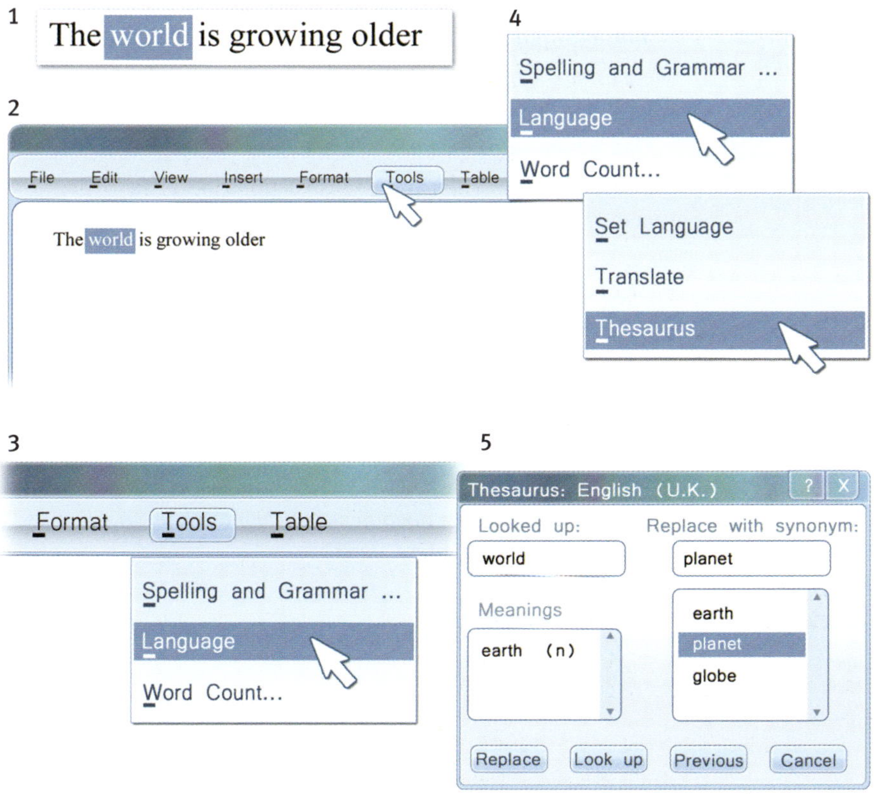

DID YOU KNOW?

1 Read the information about computer games in the US. Do you think the facts are the same or different for your country?

- More than 60% of all Americans over the age of six play computer games.
- About 75% of game players are over eighteen. The average age is 35.
- 60% are men. 40% are women.
- Every year, Americans buy more than 200 million computer games.
- Some people play games on their own but more than 60% play with their friends.

2 Work in pairs. Discuss these questions.

- What are the most popular computer games in your country?
- Have you ever played any computer games? Which ones? How do the games work?

Self-assessment (tick ✔)

☐ I can follow instructions for sending an email.
☐ I can ask and answer questions about computers, computer games and the internet.
☐ I can give instructions for how to use a computer program.

8 Language reference

GRAMMAR
Predictions

Modal verbs (*may, might & will*)
We can use *will* + infinitive to talk about things we are sure *will* happen in the future.

*Most people **will live** in cities, not in the country.*
*I **will** never **be** famous.*
*We **won't win** the match next weekend.*

We can also begin the sentence with *I think/don't think/ hope/expect*.

***I think** (that) they **will get** married.*

We can use *may/might* + infinitive when we are less sure that things will happen in the future.

*Scientists **may find** a cure for cancer.*
*I **might go** to New Zealand for my holidays.*

sure — not sure — sure

will — *may/might* — *won't*

Adverbs (*maybe, probably, certainly,* etc)
We can use adverbs like *perhaps* and *probably* to make our predictions sound more or less certain.

100%

maybe	*probably*	*certainly*
perhaps		*definitely*
possibly		

We usually put *maybe* and *perhaps* at the beginning of the sentence.

***Perhaps** you'll pass all your exams and become a doctor.*

We put *possibly, probably, certainly* and *definitely* after *will* in positive sentences and before *won't* in negative sentences.

*I **will probably** pass my exams.*
*The winner **certainly won't** need to work again.*

Present tense in future time clauses (first conditional)

All sentences have a main clause. We can use *will* + infinitive to talk about future time in a main clause.

Sometimes, we also need a subsidiary clause to give information about the time of an action. These clauses can begin with *if, when, after* and *before*. When we want to talk about future time in the subsidiary clause, we use a present tense. We do not use *will* in these subsidiary clauses.

subsidiary clause	main clause
When he has a business plan,	his parents will think again.
After he improves the site,	people will pay for the service.
If his idea doesn't work,	what will happen to him?

We usually separate the two clauses with a comma.

We can also put the subsidiary clause after the main clause. In this case, we do not usually separate the two clauses with a comma.

What will happen to him if his idea doesn't work?

FUNCTIONAL LANGUAGE
Giving instructions

We can give instructions with *you* + present simple.

***You highlight** the word, then **you click** the spell check icon.*

We can also use the imperative form.

***Save** your work before you log off.*
***Don't press** that button!*

We can make the order of the instructions easier to understand with sequencing adverbs.

First, ...
First of all, ...

Then, ...
Next, ...
After that, ...
Afterwards, ...

Finally, ...

***First of all**, find the document you want. **Then** attach it to the email. **Finally**, press 'send'.*

Word list

Compound nouns with numbers

When we make compound nouns that include numbers, the middle noun is singular.

20-million **dollar** cheque	/twenti mɪljən ˈdɒlə(r) tʃek/
thirteen-**part** show	/ˌθɜː(r)ˈtiːn ˈpɑː(r)t ʃəʊ/
eight-**day** trip	/eɪt ˈdeɪ trɪp/

Computer actions

arrow *n C*	/ˈærəʊ/
attach *v* *	/əˈtætʃ/
button *n C* **	/ˈbʌt(ə)n/
click *n C/v*	/klɪk/
connect *v* ***	/kəˈnekt/
copy *v* ***	/ˈkɒpi/
cursor *n C*	/ˈkɜː(r)sə(r)/
delete *v*	/dɪˈliːt/
document *n C* ***	/ˈdɒkjʊmənt/
download *n C/v*	/ˌdaʊnˈləʊd/
edit *v*	/ˈedɪt/
format *n U/v* *	/ˈfɔː(r)mæt/
highlight *v* *	/ˈhaɪˌlaɪt/
icon *n C*	/ˈaɪkɒn/
insert *v*	/ɪnˈsɜː(r)t/
log off *v*	/lɒg ɒf/
log on *v*	/lɒg ɒn/
look up *v*	/lʊk ʌp/
memory stick *n C*	/ˈmem(ə)ri stɪk/
message *n C* ***	/ˈmesɪdʒ/
paste *v*	/peɪst/
print *n C/v* *	/prɪnt/
program *n C/v* ***	/ˈprəʊgræm/
replace *v* ***	/rɪˈpleɪs/
save *v* ***	/seɪv/
screen *n C* **	/skriːn/
select *v* *	/sɪˈlekt/
site *n C* ***	/saɪt/
software *n U* ***	/ˈsɒf(t)ˌweə(r)/
synonym *n C*	/ˈsɪnənɪm/
table *n C* ***	/ˈteɪb(ə)l/
thesaurus *n C*	/θɪˈsɔːrəs/
tool *n C* **	/tuːl/
type *v*	/taɪp/
undo *v*	/ʌnˈduː/

Adjectives with infinitives

dangerous ***	/ˈdeɪndʒərəs/
difficult ***	/ˈdɪfɪk(ə)lt/
easy ***	/ˈiːzi/
healthy **	/ˈhelθi/
illegal **	/ɪˈliːg(ə)l/
impossible ***	/ɪmˈpɒsəb(ə)l/
legal ***	/ˈliːg(ə)l/
possible ***	/ˈpɒsəb(ə)l/
safe ***	/seɪf/
unhealthy	/ʌnˈhelθi/
unusual **	/ʌnˈjuːʒʊəl/
usual ***	/ˈjuːʒʊəl/

Other words & phrases

advanced *adj* *	/ədˈvɑːnst/
airport *n C* ***	/ˈeə(r)ˌpɔː(r)t/
alien *n C/adj*	/ˈeɪliən/
automatic *adj* *	/ˌɔːtəˈmætɪk/
blast off *v*	/blɑːst ɒf/
brilliant *adj* *	/ˈbrɪljənt/
businessman *n C*	/ˈbɪznəsmæn/
consortium *n C*	/kənˈsɔː(r)tiəm/
contestant *n C*	/kənˈtestənt/
crew *n C* **	/kruː/
cure *n C* *	/kjʊə(r)/
development *n C* ***	/dɪˈveləpmənt/
disease *n C* ***	/dɪˈziːz/
earth *n sing* ***	/ɜː(r)θ/
elderly *adj* **	/ˈeldə(r)li/
energy *n U* ***	/ˈenə(r)dʒi/
equipment *n U* ***	/ɪˈkwɪpmənt/
essay *n C* *	/ˈeseɪ/
exploration *n U*	/ˌekspləˈreɪʃ(ə)n/
fact *n C* ***	/fækt/
fiction *n U* **	/ˈfɪkʃ(ə)n/
film *v*	/fɪlm/
finances *n pl*	/ˈfaɪnænsəs/
foreign *adj* ***	/ˈfɒrɪn/
freaky *adj*	/ˈfriːki/
frightening *adj* *	/ˈfraɪt(ə)nɪŋ/
game show *n C*	/ˈgeɪm ʃəʊ/
grow *v* ***	/grəʊ/
hill *n C* ***	/hɪl/
increase *v* ***	/ɪnˈkriːs/
invention *n C* *	/ɪnˈvenʃ(ə)n/
invisible *adj*	/ɪnˈvɪzəb(ə)l/
knowledge *n U* ***	/ˈnɒlɪdʒ/
laser *n C*	/ˈleɪzə(r)/
lend *v* ***	/lend/
litre *n C*	/ˈliːtə(r)/
luck *n U* **	/lʌk/
machine *n C* ***	/məˈʃiːn/
matrix *n C*	/ˈmeɪtrɪks/
medicine *n U* **	/ˈmed(ə)s(ə)n/
military *adj* **	/ˈmɪlɪt(ə)ri/
modelling *n U*	/ˈmɒd(ə)lɪŋ/
moon *n C* **	/muːn/
museum *n C* ***	/mjuːˈziːəm/
offer *v* ***	/ˈɒfə(r)/
oil *n U* ***	/ɔɪl/
permission *n U* **	/pə(r)ˈmɪʃ(ə)n/
pick (sth) up	/pɪk ʌp/
planet *n C* *	/ˈplænɪt/
prisoner *n C* **	/ˈprɪz(ə)nə(r)/
privilege *n C*	/ˈprɪvəlɪdʒ/
product *n C* ***	/ˈprɒdʌkt/
quest *n C*	/kwest/
refuse *v* ***	/rɪˈfjuːz/
risky *adj*	/ˈrɪski/
rocket *n C*	/ˈrɒkɪt/
satellite *n* *	/ˈsætəlaɪt/
science fiction *n U*	/ˈsaɪəns fɪkʃ(ə)n/
scientist *n C* ***	/ˈsaɪəntɪst/
similar *adj* ***	/ˈsɪmɪlə(r)/
society *n U* ***	/səˈsaɪəti/
source *n C* **	/sɔː(r)s/
space *n U* ***	/speɪs/
space ship *n C*	/ˈspeɪsˌʃɪp/
space station *n C*	/speɪs ˈsteɪʃ(ə)n/
suggest *v* ***	/səˈdʒest/
survey *n C* **	/ˈsɜː(r)veɪ/
talk *n C* ***	/tɔːk/
text *n C* ***	/tekst/
theory *n C* **	/ˈθɪəri/
thirsty *adj* *	/ˈθɜː(r)sti/
title *n C* ***	/ˈtaɪt(ə)l/
translation *n C/U* *	/trænsˈleɪʃ(ə)n/
trip *n C* **	/trɪp/
ultraviolet *adj*	/ˌʌltrəˈvaɪələt/
unstoppable *adj*	/ʌnˈstɒpəb(ə)l/
war *n C* ***	/wɔː(r)/
wind *n U* ***	/wɪnd/

9A What's on

SPEAKING & LISTENING

1 Look at the events below. Think of one person you know who would like to go to each event.

Work in pairs. Tell your partner about the people you have thought of. What other things do these people like doing?

WHAT'S ON ...

A The Moscow State Circus
Victoria Park
Tues to Sun 7.30pm

B Camille Pissarro in London
Paintings of London by the French Impressionist
National Gallery, Trafalgar Square
Daily 10am–6pm

C Dance Crazy
An exciting afternoon of international dance from Spain, France and Switzerland
Canary Wharf
Saturday 1–5pm

D Verdi's Requiem
Verdi's masterpiece conducted by Patrick Davin
Royal Albert Hall
Friday 7.30pm

E Brazilian Club Night
Top DJs play house, techno, R & B and hip hop
Downstairs at The Sound Barrier, Oxford Street
Saturday 10pm–2am

F Mamma Mia – the Musical
Aldwych Theatre
Mon–Sat 7.30pm, also Sat 3pm

G Lady Gaga
Wembley Arena
Thursday, Friday, Saturday
7.30pm

2 2.15 Listen to part of a radio programme. Put the events in exercise 1 in the order that they are mentioned.

- ☐ The Moscow State Circus
- ☐ Camille Pissarro in London
- ☐ Dance Crazy
- ☐ Verdi's *Requiem*
- ☐ Brazilian Club Night
- ☐ *Mamma Mia* – the Musical
- ☐ Lady Gaga

3 2.15 Listen to the programme again. The reporter makes eight mistakes. Underline the information in the events that is different from the information on the programme.

G Lady Gaga
Wembley Arena
Thursday, Friday, Saturday
7.30pm

4 Match the events in column A with the adjectives that the reporter uses in column B.

A		B	
1	The Moscow State Circus	a	cool
2	Camille Pissarro in London	b	depressing
3	Dance Crazy	c	enjoyable
4	Verdi's *Requiem*	d	exciting
5	Brazilian Club Night	e	fantastic
6	*Mamma Mia* – the Musical	f	fascinating
7	Lady Gaga	g	fun

5 Look at audioscript 2.15 on page 141 to check your answers. Do you agree with the reporter's adjectives?

6 Work in pairs. Imagine you are in London. Ask and answer these questions.

- Which of these events would you like to go to?
- What other things would you like to do in London?
- What kinds of entertainment are available in your town?
- What is on at the moment?

VOCABULARY: *-ing* & *-ed* adjectives

1 In the sentences below, which adjective describes how the speaker feels? Which adjective describes the thing that makes her/him feel this way?

1 I think that kind of music is really *relaxing*.
2 That kind of music makes me really *relaxed*.

2 Complete the dialogues with the correct word.

1 **A:** I'm so *exciting / excited*. I've got tickets for the Lady Gaga concert.
B: Lady Gaga? I think her music is *boring / bored*.
2 **A:** I'm really *tiring / tired*. I didn't get home until three o'clock this morning.
B: I know. And it was extremely *annoying / annoyed* that you came home singing!
3 **A:** I think this music is really *relaxing / relaxed*.
B: Really? It makes me feel *depressing / depressed*.
4 **A:** The concert was a bit *disappointing / disappointed*, wasn't it?
B: Yes, I was *surprising / surprised*. Celine Dion is usually so good.

3 **2.16** Listen to the recording to check your answers. Work in pairs and practise the dialogues.

4 Complete the sentences so that they are true for you.

1 I find … quite frightening.
2 I sometimes feel depressed when …
3 I think that … is/are really fascinating.
4 … is the most boring place in the world.
5 I usually feel relaxed when …
6 I was disappointed when …

PRONUNCIATION: diphthongs

1 Put the words in the box in the correct place in the table.

~~don't~~ down fame find go home house kind
most out place quite show sound Spain state
stay time town twice

night /aɪ/	**know** /əʊ/	**now** /aʊ/	**name** /eɪ/
	don't		

2 **2.17** Listen to the recording to check your answers.

3 Think of two other words for each column.

DID YOU KNOW?

1 Read the information about leisure activities in the UK (listed in order of popularity) and discuss the questions.

- What are the favourite leisure activities of people in your country?
- What about you? What do you like doing?
- Are you typical of the people in your country?

9B | Reality TV

VOCABULARY: TV programmes

1 Match the types of TV programmes in the box to a programme description.

> chat show   current affairs programme
> documentary   game show   sitcom
> soap opera   sports programme

EVENING

18.30 — 19.00

Wheel of Fortune (1) ________
The winner takes the jackpot prize of $500,000.

Bill Zucker Presents (2) ________
Bill's guests this week are Hollywood legend, Al Pacino and British designer Stella McCartney.

Friends (3) ________
More laughs in tonight's episode as Chandler and Joey look after baby Ben, but leave him on the bus. When they get him back, have they got the right baby? (repeat from second series)

Match of the Day (4) ________
All the goals from today's World Cup games plus news of today's play at Wimbledon.

EastEnders (5) ________
Problems in Walford. Alfie is not welcome at Kat's wedding, but she still loves him. Can he stop the wedding in time?

Horizon (6) ________
Prize-winning film about the life of an urban kangaroo.

Newsbrief (7) ________
An in-depth look at what is happening in the world this week.

2 Describe examples of the different kinds of TV programmes in your country.

3 Work in pairs. Ask and answer these questions.

- Which of these kinds of programmes do you like to watch? Why?
- What are your favourite programmes on TV?
- Are there too many programmes of one kind on TV?

READING

1 Read the article below. Match the paragraphs 1–3 to the descriptions a–e. There are two descriptions that you do **not** need.

a Why people like reality TV
b The beginnings of reality TV
c The end of reality TV
d Making money from reality TV
e Problems with reality TV

Reality TV love it or leave it

1 **The first reality TV show in the world was called *Expedition Robinson* and it was shown in Sweden in 1997. Half the population of the country watched the final episode and a new kind of TV programme was born.** Two years later in Holland, the first series of *Big Brother* was filmed. Again, it was a fantastic success and the final programme was watched by 15 million people. There are now over 70 countries around the world which have had *Big Brother, Survivor* or something very similar on their TV screens. The ordinary people who take part in the programmes are known by millions of people in their own countries and reality TV has become big, big business.

2 For the TV producers, reality TV is a dream come true because many of the programmes cost nothing to make. At some point, the television viewers are asked to telephone the programme – to vote or to apply to take part in the show. It is the cost of these telephone calls that pays for the shows. One of the most popular shows is *The X Factor* (the programme is called different things in different countries). In the show, a group of attractive young people are made into pop stars. TV viewers vote for their favourite person on the show. The winner makes a record, his or her pictures are published on the covers of magazines, millions of copies of the record are sold and then … they are quickly forgotten.

3 But not everyone is happy about reality TV. In Portugal, two TV channels got into trouble because they showed too much of the private lives of the people in the shows. In France, reality TV is called 'rubbish TV' and the studios of *Loft Story* (*Big Brother*) were attacked three times in one week. In Greece, *Big Brother* was described as 'an insult to human rights and civilization'. But despite the problems, reality TV continues to do well in most countries and it will be here for some time to come.

***Big Brother*, India**

2 Read the article again and tick (✔) the things that are mentioned in the text.

1 Reality TV started in Sweden.
2 The prize money for *Survivor* is $1 million.
3 Many countries have reality TV shows.
4 Some people get married after being on a reality TV show.
5 In the UK, *Big Brother* is more popular than *Survivor*.
6 Reality TV makes money when the viewers make phone calls.
7 *Loft Story* and *The X Factor* are the names of reality TV shows.
8 *Loft Story* has been very successful in France.

3 Which reality TV shows are popular in your country? Do you like reality TV shows? Why or why not?

Grammar: passive

In a normal (active) sentence, we put the agent (the person or thing that does the action) before the verb.

agent verb

The viewers vote for their favourite programme.

But sometimes:
1 we do not know the agent of the action.
2 the agent is not important.
3 the agent is obvious.
In these cases we can use the passive.

We form the passive with *to be* + past participle.

*The viewers **are asked** to call the programme.* (present simple)
The studios of Loft Story ***were attacked***. (past simple)

See Language Reference page 94

1 Find three examples of the passive form in paragraph 3 of the article.

2 Complete the text with the passive form of the verbs in the box.

allow	choose	film	give
invite	send	show	teach

Star Academy
Thousands of young people apply to take part in this programme. They send video tapes to the producers and a group of them (1) <u>are chosen</u> to take part. During the series, they live in a castle, where they (2) ______ to sing and dance. They (3) ______ not ______ to speak to their friends or family and every moment of their life in the castle (4) ______. Their lives (5) ______ on TV every evening and, on Saturday, there is a special show. A famous TV star (6) ______ on the show and one of the contestants sings a song with him or her. At the end of the programme, there is a vote and one person (7) ______ home. At the end of the series, the winner (8) ______ a contract to make an album.

3 2.18 Listen to the recording to check your answers.

4 Choose the correct verb form to complete the sentences.

For Love or Money
1 This programme *showed / was shown* on American TV for the first time in 2003.
2 In this programme, fifteen women *tried / were tried* to win the heart of a rich young man.
3 In the first episode, the women *learnt / were learnt* that there was also a prize of $1 million.
4 The women *told / were told* to keep the prize a secret from the young man.
5 The man and the women *took / were taken* to different Californian cities to go out on dates.
6 At the end of each week, one woman *left / was left* the show.
7 In the final show, the last woman *told / was told* she must choose between the man and the money.

5 Think of a reality TV programme that you know. Complete the sentences below to describe the programme.

The contestants are The winner is The programme is	taken given asked shown filmed invited not allowed sent	…

Speaking

1 Work in groups. You are going to plan your own reality TV show. Use these questions to help you.

- What do the people on the show do?
- Where is the show filmed?
- What is the show called?
- How many people take part?
- What sort of people are they?
- Are there any famous people in the show?
- How is the winner decided?
- What is the prize?

2 You all work for a TV company. Take it in turns to sell your show to the other groups. Then, as a class, vote for the best idea.

9c | Oscars® and raspberries

Speaking

1 Work in pairs. Ask and answer these questions.

- How often do you go to the cinema?
- When was the last time you went?
- Who did you go with?
- What did you see?
- What did you think of the film?

Vocabulary: films

1 Read the information about *Avatar* below and find words or phrases that match these definitions.

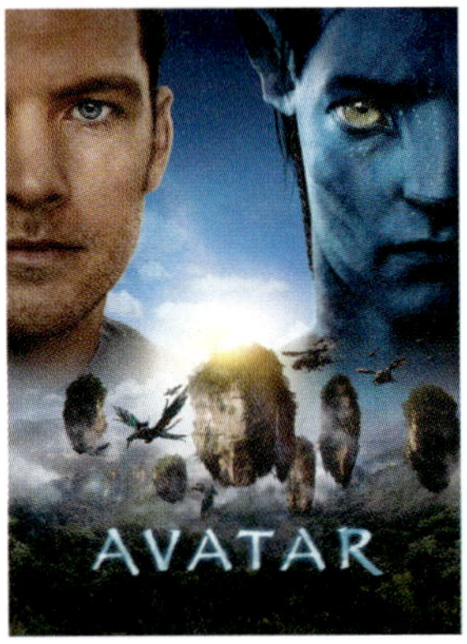

1 music that is played during a film
2 takes place
3 the main actors are
4 the person in charge of making a film
5 unusual images that are made for a film

Avatar

Written and directed by James Cameron, *Avatar* is set on a distant planet in the 22nd century. It stars Sam Worthington, Zoe Saldana and Sigourney Weaver. One of the most successful films of all time.

Avatar was nominated for 9 Oscars® including

• BEST FILM • BEST DIRECTOR • • BEST SOUNDTRACK • • BEST SPECIAL EFFECTS •

2 Work in pairs. Discuss these questions.

- Which films can you see at the cinema at the moment in your town?
- What do you know about the stars, the director, the soundtrack, the setting and the story of these films?

Reading

1 Read the magazine article and explain the connection between Oscars® and raspberries.

Oscars® night

Channel 1	
22.00	This year's Razzies®
22.30	This year's Oscar® nominees
23.30	The stars arrive
24.00	The Oscars® ceremony – live

Tonight is the night that all Hollywood is waiting for. The stars are wearing their best designer clothes and some of them are thinking about the speech they are hoping to make later. The limousines arrive at the red-carpeted entrance to the luxury Kodak Theatre and the stars are photographed by hundreds of hungry paparazzi. There are thousands in the audience, and the ceremony is watched by millions of TV viewers around the world. The winners are instant celebrities and they will earn mega-bucks with more ticket sales and new contracts. Yes, folks, it's Oscars® time.

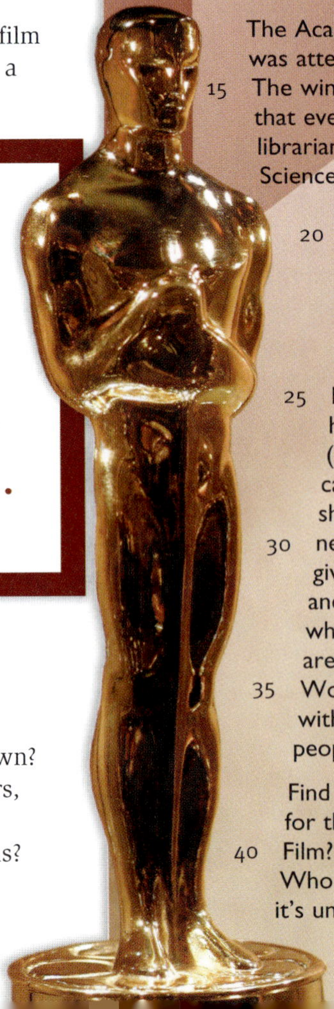

The Academy Awards started back in 1929 and the first ceremony was attended by 250 people, who paid $10 for a dinner ticket. The winners' names were published by the newspapers earlier that evening, so there were no surprises. Two years later, a librarian at the American Academy of Motion Picture Arts and Sciences said that the statue awards looked like her Uncle Oscar. The Academy Awards became Oscars® and now, over 75 years later, TV companies pay more than $20 million for the rights to the show. For the advertisers and designers, the record companies and the film studios, for the investors and businessmen, and for the stars themselves, the Oscars® is big business.

Meanwhile, on the other side of town in a Santa Monica hotel, the winners of the Golden Raspberry Awards® (the Razzies) are announced. The ceremony is shown on cable TV channels and CNN reports the winners. The show costs only $5,000 to produce and the awards are never collected. The Razzies® – in their 25th year – are given to actors and film directors for being bad, really bad, and worse than bad. They were started by John Wilson, who says that most Hollywood films are rubbish. There are prizes for Worst Actor and Actress, and Worst Film. Worst Actress of the 20th century was won by Madonna, with Sylvester Stallone taking the men's prize. 'Some of these people are so bad,' said Wilson, 'they should take up knitting.'

Find out who gets this year's Razzies® (22.00), and stay tuned for this year's Oscars® ceremony (24.00). Who will get Best Film? Who will make this year's most embarrassing speech? Who will wear the most ridiculous dress? It's all good fun and it's unmissable television.

2 Read the article again and say if the sentences below refer to the Oscars® (O) or the Golden Raspberries (R).

1 A ticket for the ceremony cost $10.
2 This ceremony takes place first.
3 Madonna won a top award for acting.
4 They started 25 years ago.
5 The winners make speeches when they get their award.
6 Millions of people watch the ceremony on TV.
7 The ceremony takes place in a Santa Monica hotel.
8 They are named after someone's uncle.

3 What are the best and worst films you have ever seen? Why?

GRAMMAR: passive with agent

In passive sentences, we often don't include the agent of an action (see page 89).

On the other side of town, the winners of the Golden Raspberries ***are announced.***

Sometimes we want or need to include the agent. We use *by* to include the agent.

The ceremony is watched ***by millions of TV viewers*** *around the world.*
The stars are photographed ***by hundreds of hungry paparazzi.***
The first ceremony was attended ***by 250 people.***

SEE LANGUAGE REFERENCE PAGE 94

1 Complete the sentences. Put the verbs in brackets into the past simple passive.

1 An early form of cinema _____ (*invent*) by the Lumière brothers in the 1890s.
2 Their first film _____ (*see*) by 35 people in a Parisian café.
3 The first talking movie, *The Jazz Singer*, _____ (*make*) by Warner Brothers™ in 1927.
4 In the same year, the world's biggest cinema _____ (*open*) by Samuel Rothapfel with seats for 6,000 people.
5 The first James Bond in the cinema _____ (*play*) by Sean Connery.
6 The James Bond books _____ (*write*) by Ian Fleming, a British spy.
7 The 1981 American presidential election _____ (*win*) by Ronald Reagan, a movie actor.
8 For a short time, Fidel Castro _____ (*employ*) by Hollywood studios as an extra.

2 Rewrite the sentences beginning with the words that are given.

1 An iceberg hits a ship.
A ship _____.
2 Andy's mother throws away most of his toys.
Most of Andy's toys _____.
3 Nicole Kidman plays the role of the cabaret singer.
The role of the cabaret singer _____.
4 A boy and his friends help an alien to return home.
An alien _____.
5 The director used the most advanced technology.
The most advanced technology _____.
6 The producers divided this film into two parts.
This film _____.
7 Ridley Scott directed this story of ancient Rome.
This story of ancient Rome _____.

3 Now match the sentences 1–7 to the films in the box. See page 127 for the answers.

Avatar *Gladiator* *Harry Potter and the Deathly Hallows*
ET *Toy Story 3* *Moulin Rouge* *Titanic*

4 Work in pairs. Use the prompts and your own ideas to make five sentences about films, books or TV programmes you know.

(Film) (Book) (TV programme)	was	made in (a year, a country). written by (name of an author). shown on (name of a TV channel). directed by (name of a director).

5 Work in pairs. Make quiz questions from your sentences in exercise 4.

Spider Man *was made in 2002.* *When was* Spider Man *made?*

6 Work with another pair of students. Ask and answer the quiz questions.

SPEAKING

1 Work in pairs. Practise this short dialogue from *Avatar*. At this moment in the film, Neytiri has just saved Jake's life, and he has thanked her.

Neytiri: Don't thank! You don't thank for this! This is sad. Very sad, only.
Jake: OK, I'm sorry. Whatever I did – I'm sorry.
Neytiri: All this is your fault! They did not need to die!
Jake: They attacked me. How am I the bad guy here?
Neytiri: Your fault! You are like a baby, making a noise, you don't know what to do. You should not come here, all of you! You only come and make problems.
Jake: OK, fine, you love your little forest friends. So why not just let them kill me?

2 Perform your dialogue in front of the class and listen to the dialogues of other students. Which students will win an Oscar®?

9D | Box office

Speaking

1 Work in pairs. Look at the programme for a concert hall.

- Who have you heard of?
- Who would you like to see?

Pronunciation: dates

1 Can you say these numbers?

1st	11th	21st
2nd	12th	22nd
3rd	13th	23rd
4th	15th	24th
5th	16th	31st
6th	20th	

2.19 Listen to the recording to check your pronunciation.

2 There are many different ways of writing dates.

20th September	20 September
September 20	September 20th
20/9	20/09

2.20 Listen to two different ways of saying these dates. Complete the missing words in the spaces below.

1 September _____ twentieth
2 _____ twentieth _____ September

3 **2.21** Listen to the recording and complete the concert programme with the missing dates.

4 Work in pairs. Write four dates that are important for you.

Ask your partner what their dates are and why they are important.

20/9 – That's my daughter's birthday.

Metropolitan Hall

AUGUST – DECEMBER

7 Aug	**Los Van Van (Cuban salsa)**	8.00
(1) _____	**Justin Timberlake**	8.00
(2) _____	**Coldplay**	8.00
3–4 Sep	**Red Hot Chili Peppers**	8.00
(3) _____	**An Evening with Cecilia Bartoli**	7.30
27–31 Oct	**Swan Lake (Tchaikovsky)**	1.45 (27–28 Oct) & 7.45 (all dates)
(4) _____	**Shakira**	8.00
(5) _____	**Handel's Messiah**	8.15
(6) _____	**A Night with Mr Bean**	8.30
22 Nov	**Wynton Marsalis Septet**	7.45
(7) _____	**Justin Bieber**	8.00
4 Dec	**A Tribute to The Beatles**	8.30
17–24 Dec	**Beauty and the Beast**	2.00 & 7.00
(8) _____	**Johann Strauss New Year Concert**	9.30

LISTENING

1 Complete the questions with a word or phrase from the box.

booking fee   box office   circle   credit card   matinee   sold out

1 When you buy tickets for a show, do you usually go to the ______ or to a ticket agency?
2 When you buy tickets at an agency or on the internet, is there a ______? How much is it?
3 When you buy tickets, do you prefer to pay in cash or by ______?
4 Have you ever wanted to buy tickets for a show that was ______?
5 At the theatre, do you prefer an evening performance or a ______?
6 Do you prefer to sit downstairs in the stalls or upstairs in the ______?

2 Work in pairs. Ask and answer the questions in exercise 1.

3 2.22–2.25 Listen to four people telephoning the box office of a concert hall. For each person, complete the information in the table.

	speaker 1	speaker 2	speaker 3	speaker 4
concert	Beauty and the Beast	(3) ______	(6) ______	Cecilia Bartoli
date	23 December	(4) ______	3 September	21 September
kind of ticket	stalls	circle	stalls	(9) ______
number of tickets	(1) ______	(5) ______	(7) ______	2 tickets
price	(2) ______	£76.00	(8) ______	(10) ______

4 2.22–2.25 Listen to the dialogues again to check your answers.

FUNCTIONAL LANGUAGE: at the box office

1 Complete column A with a phrase from column B.

A		B	
1	What date would	a	details please?
2	Would you like the matinee	b	do you want?
3	How many tickets	c	fee of five pounds.
4	What sort of seats	d	for you.
5	I'll see what seats	e	or the evening performance?
6	I'll just check	f	pounds altogether.
7	I'm sorry, sir,	g	would you like?
8	There's a booking	h	we're sold out.
9	That's seventy-six	i	we've got available.
10	Could I take your	j	you like?

Look at audioscripts 2.22–2.25 on page 142 to check your answers.

2 Work in pairs, A and B.

A: Choose a show at the Metropolitan Hall that you would like to see. Telephone the box office and book your tickets.
B: You work at the box office of the Metropolitan Hall. Answer the telephone and decide what tickets you have available for the different shows.

SPEAKING

1 Think of a concert you have been to. You are going to talk to a partner about it. Use these questions to prepare what you are going to say.

- What concert was it? When and where?
- Who did you go with?
- How much did you pay for the tickets?
- Why did you go to this concert?
- What kind of music was it?
- How well could you see and hear?
- Did you dance or sing?
- How long was the concert?
- Did you have a good time?

2 Work in pairs. Tell your partner about the concert.

Useful language

The worst/best concert I've been to was …
I've always been a fan of/interested in …
What I liked most about the concert was …

Self-assessment (tick ✔)

☐ I can pronounce dates.
☐ I can understand dates in a telephone conversation.
☐ I can understand conversations and book tickets for a show using the phone.
☐ I can describe an event I have been to.

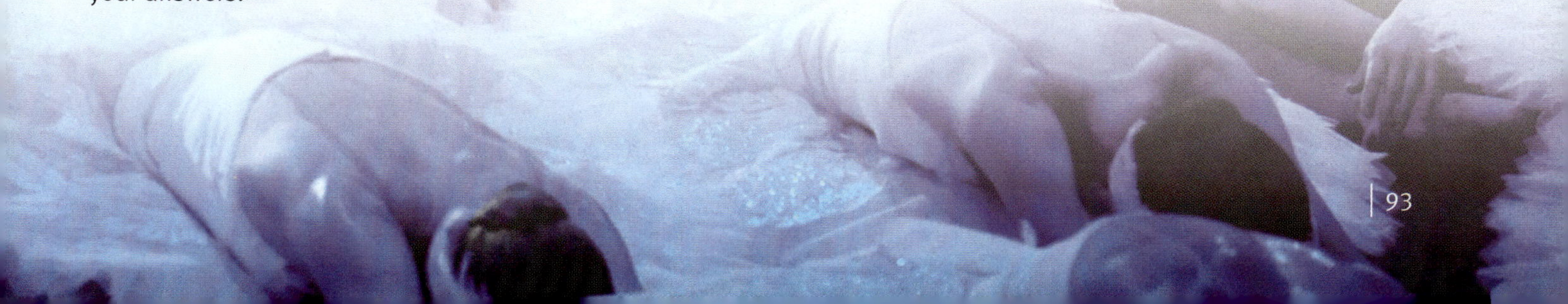

9 Language reference

Grammar

Passive

In a normal (active) sentence, we put the agent (the person or thing that does the action) before the verb.

agent verb

The viewers vote for their favourite programme.

But sometimes:

1 we do not know the agent of the action.
2 the agent is not important.
3 the agent is obvious.

In these cases we often use the passive.

The TV studios ***were attacked*** *last night.*
A famous TV star ***is invited*** *on the show.*
He ***was arrested*** *for driving too fast.*

We make the passive with *to be* + past participle.

Present simple passive

Affirmative & Negative			
I		'm 'm not	photographed all the time.
He/She/It		's isn't	
You/We/They		're aren't	
Question			
Why	am	I	photographed all the time?
	is	he/she/it	
	are	you/we/they	

Past simple passive

Affirmative & Negative			
I He/She/It		was wasn't	invited to the party.
You/We/They		were weren't	
Question			
Why	was	I he/she/it	invited to the party?
	were	you/we/they	

We often don't include the agent of an action in passive sentences.

The winners ***are announced*** *at the end of the show.*

Sometimes, we want or need to include the agent. We use *by* to include the agent.

The final episode of Big Brother *was watched* ***by 15 million people****.*
The Olympics were started ***by the Greeks****.*

Functional language

At the box office

What	*date(s)* *kind of seats*	*would you like?* *do you want?*
Which performance		
How many tickets		

Where would you like to sit?
I'll see what seats we've got available.
I'll just check for you.
I'm sorry, sir, we're sold out.
There's a booking fee of …
That's 58 pounds altogether.
Could I take your details, please?

Word list

-*ing* & -*ed* adjectives

amazing *	/əˈmeɪzɪŋ/
annoyed **	/əˈnɔɪd/
annoying *	/əˈnɔɪɪŋ/
bored **	/bɔː(r)d/
boring **	/ˈbɔːrɪŋ/
depressed *	/dɪˈprest/
depressing *	/dɪˈpresɪŋ/
disappointed *	/ˌdɪsəˈpɔɪntɪd/
disappointing	/ˌdɪsəˈpɔɪntɪŋ/
excited **	/ɪkˈsaɪtɪd/
exciting **	/ɪkˈsaɪtɪŋ/
fascinated	/ˈfæsɪneɪtɪd/
fascinating *	/ˈfæsɪneɪtɪŋ/
frightened *	/ˈfraɪt(ə)nd/
frightening *	/ˈfraɪt(ə)nɪŋ/
relaxed *	/rɪˈlækst/
relaxing	/rɪˈlæksɪŋ/
surprised **	/sə(r)ˈpraɪzd/
surprising **	/sə(r)ˈpraɪzɪŋ/
tired ***	/ˈtaɪə(r)d/
tiring	/ˈtaɪərɪŋ/

TV programmes

chat show *n C*	/ˈtʃæt ʃəʊ/
current affairs programme *n C*	/ˈkʌrənt ˈfeə(r)z prəʊgræm/
documentary *n C*	/ˌdɒkjʊˈment(ə)ri/
game show *n C*	/ˈgeɪm ʃəʊ/
sitcom *n C*	/ˈsɪtkɒm/
soap opera *n C*	/səʊp ˈɒp(ə)rə/
sports programme *n C*	/spɔː(r)tz prəʊgræm/

Films

acting *n U*	/ˈæktɪŋ/
actor *n C* ***	/ˈæktə(r)/
actress *n C*	/ˈæktrəs/
costume *n C*	/ˈkɒstjuːm/
direct *v* **	/dɪˈrekt/
director *n C* ***	/dəˈrektə(r)/; /daɪˈrektə(r)/
extra *n C*	/ˈekstrə/
producer *n C* *	/prəˈdjuːsə(r)/
role *n C* ***	/rəʊl/
setting *n C* *	/ˈsetɪŋ/
soundtrack *n C*	/ˈsaʊn(d)ˌtræk/
special effects *n pl*	/ˈspeʃ(ə)l ɪfekts/
star v ***	/stɑː(r)/
studio *n C* **	/ˈstjuːdiəʊ/

Other words & phrases

agent *n C* *	/ˈeɪdʒ(ə)nt/
album *n C*	/ˈælbəm/
announce *v* *	/əˈnaʊns/
arena *n C*	/əˈriːnə/
attack *v* ***	/əˈtæk/
attend *v* **	/əˈtend/
available *adj* **	/əˈveɪləb(ə)l/
award *n C* **	/əˈwɔː(r)d/
bedtime *n U*	/ˈbedˌtaɪm/
boat *n C* ***	/bəʊt/
booking fee *n C*	/ˈbʊkɪŋ fiː/
building *n C* ***	/ˈbɪldɪŋ/
cabaret *n C/U*	/ˈkæbəreɪ/
cable TV *n U*	/ˈkeɪb(ə)l tiː viː/
channel *n C* **	/ˈtʃæn(ə)l/
circle *n C* ***	/ˈsɜː(r)k(ə)l/
civilization *n C/U*	/ˌsɪvəlaɪˈzeɪʃ(ə)n/
classical music *n U*	/ˈklæsɪk(ə)l mjuːzɪk/
conduct *v* **	/kənˈdʌkt/
contestant *n C*	/kənˈtestənt/
contract *n C* ***	/ˈkɒntrækt/
cost *v* ***	/kɒst/
cruise *n C*	/kruːz/
dance *v* ***	/dɑːns/
designer *n C* *	/dɪˈzaɪnə(r)/
detail *n C* ***	/ˈdiːteɪl/
dream *n C/v* ***	/driːm/
election *n C* ***	/ɪˈlekʃ(ə)n/
entertainment *n U* **	/ˌentə(r)ˈteɪnmənt/
entrance *n C* ***	/ˈentrəns/
episode *n C*	/ˈepɪsəʊd/
event *n C* ***	/ɪˈvent/
exhibition *n C* **	/ˌeksɪˈbɪʃ(ə)n/
expedition *n C*	/ˌekspəˈdɪʃ(ə)n/
fantastic *adj*	/fænˈtæstɪk/
festival *n C*	/ˈfestɪv(ə)l/
gallery *n C*	/ˈgæləri/
get into trouble *phr*	/get ɪntə ˈtrʌb(ə)l/
human rights *n pl*	/ˈhjuːmən raɪtz/
iceberg *n C*	/ˈaɪsˌbɜː(r)g/
idol *n C*	/ˈaɪd(ə)l/
impressionist *n C*	/ɪmˈpreʃ(ə)nɪst/
in-depth *adj*	/ɪndepθ/
insult *v* *	/ˈɪnsʌlt/
invent *v* **	/ɪnˈvent/
investor *n C*	/ɪnˈvestə(r)/
jackpot *n C*	/ˈdʒækˌpɒt/
kangaroo *n C*	/ˌkæŋgəˈruː/
knitting *n U*	/ˈnɪtɪŋ/
legend *n C*	/ˈledʒ(ə)nd/
limousine *n C*	/ˌlɪməˈziːn/
line-up *n C*	/laɪnʌp/
loft *n C*	/lɒft/
masterpiece *n C*	/ˈmɑːstə(r)ˌpiːs/
matinee *n C*	/ˈmætɪneɪ/
musical *n C*	/ˈmjuːzɪk(ə)l/
nominee *n C*	/ˌnɒmɪˈniː/
old-fashioned *adj* *	/ˌəʊld ˈfæʃ(ə)nd/
painting *n C/U* **	/ˈpeɪntɪŋ/
panic *n U/v*	/ˈpænɪk/
paparazzi *n pl*	/ˌpæpəˈrætsi/
performance *n C* ***	/pə(r)ˈfɔː(r)məns/
plus *prep* *	/plʌs/
pronounce *v* *	/prəˈnaʊns/
publish *v* ***	/ˈpʌblɪʃ/
raspberry *n C*	/ˈrɑːzbəri/
reality *n U* ***	/riˈæləti/
record *n C* ***	/ˈrekɔː(r)d/
report *v* ***	/rɪˈpɔː(r)t/
requiem *n C*	/ˈrekwiəm/
ridiculous *adj*	/rɪˈdɪkjʊləs/
series *n C* ***	/ˈsɪəriːz/
session *n C* **	/ˈseʃ(ə)n/
sink *v* **	/sɪŋk/
sold out *adj*	/səʊld aʊt/
spy *n C*	/spaɪ/
stalls *n pl*	/stɔːlz/
statue *n C*	/ˈstætʃuː/
stay tuned	/ˈsteɪ tjuːnd/
survivor *n C*	/sə(r)ˈvaɪvə(r)/
take part (in sth) *phr*	/ˈteɪk pɑː(r)t/
talented *adj*	/ˈtæləntɪd/
unmissable *adj*	/ʌnˈmɪsəb(ə)l/
urban *adj* *	/ˈɜː(r)bən/
video tape *n C*	/ˈvɪdiəʊˌteɪp/
viewer *n C*	/ˈvjuːə(r)/
weekly *adj*	/ˈwiːkli/
wharf *n C*	/wɔː(r)f/

10A | Animal lovers

Speaking

1 Work in pairs. Discuss these questions.

- What kinds of animals do people have as pets in your country?
- Choose a pet from the box for the people in the photos. Explain your reasons.

cat	dog	goldfish	hamster	lizard
monkey	parrot	rabbit	rat	

- Which is your favourite animal? Why?

Reading

1 Do you know any famous Americans who have pets? Make a list.

Now read the article and underline the famous people it mentions. Were they on your list?

2 The writer gives four reasons for why he thinks that Americans are crazy about animals. Tick (✔) the reasons that he mentions.

1 Some hotels have special services for dogs.
2 For some people, pets are more important than children.
3 Some Americans have strange pets (for example, lizards).
4 There are fashion shows for pets.
5 Some people ask the vet to do strange things.
6 Some people take their pets to psychiatrists.
7 Americans spend a lot of money on their pets.

3 Are people in your country crazy about animals?

THE UNITED STATES OF ANIMALS

For years, I have thought that we Americans are probably crazy. Crazy about animals, that is. But now I am sure. I saw an ad in the paper the other day for the Ritz Hotel in Miami which has been open since September 2002. It has a special dog program, with dog menus, dog movies and dog music in the library. It sounds perfect for Oprah Winfrey, who never travels without her dogs. I wonder what the hotel does for other animals of the stars. Leonardo DiCaprio, for example, has had a lizard (called Blizzard) for many years.

In the same newspaper was an article which proves my point. The article, *Hollywood's Super-Vet Tells All*, was about Dr Amy Attas. Dr Attas sounds perfectly normal, unlike some of her customers. Dr Attas has run a veterinary practice, called CityPets, for the last ten years. Her customers are the rich and famous and, since she began the practice, she has looked after the pets of people like Naomi Campbell, Joan Rivers and Uma Thurman.

One of her best stories is about a late-night phone-call that she received from the wife of hockey star, Wayne Gretzky. Their dog was crying and Wayne could not sleep. If Wayne doesn't sleep, he doesn't play good hockey, said the wife. The vet visited the house and examined the dog which had a – cold! Another time, she had a call from Cher, who was in Italy. Cher wanted to bring an Italian dog home with her. It had a skin problem and she wanted Dr Attas to come to the airport to look after it. At midnight.

Crazy stuff, huh? No, the really crazy stuff came from another article, this one in the *Wall Street Journal*. Since this time last year, the US has spent $30 billion on pets. That's about the same as the gross national product of a medium-sized South American country. And that's what I call really crazy.

GRAMMAR: present perfect simple with *for* & *since*

We use the present perfect simple for states that began in the past and continue into the present. The states are unfinished.

*How long **have you had** your pet? **I've had** it **for** many years.*
*I've **had** it **since** my sixteenth birthday.*

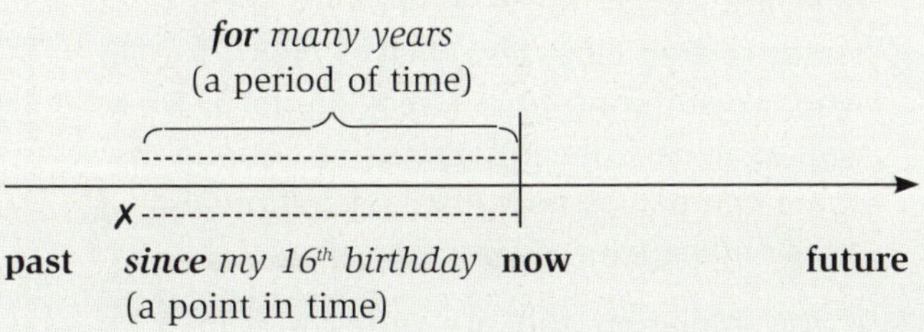

We use the past simple for actions and states that are finished. Compare these examples.

Present perfect simple
*She's **had** it for many years* (and she still has it).

Past simple
*She **had** it for many years* (but she doesn't have it now).

SEE LANGUAGE REFERENCE PAGE 104

1 Complete the text. Put the verbs in brackets into the present perfect simple or the past simple.

Oscar Werbeniuk, who is 61, (1) ______ (*live*) all his life in the same New Jersey house. He (2) ______ (*love*) animals, especially cats, since he was a child. He (3) ______ (*find*) his first cat, Tabatha, in the street in 1981, and he (4) ______ (*find*) another 43 cats since then. But Tabatha – who died in 1990 – (5) ______ (*have*) babies and Oscar soon (6) ______ (*have*) more than a hundred cats. For the last fifteen years, there (7) ______ (*be*) more than two hundred cats in his house. Oscar is lucky because his parents (8) ______ (*be*) very rich, so he (9) ______ (*never / worry*) about money. In fact, since 1999, Oscar (10) ______ (*be*) so busy that he (11) ______ (*not / leave*) his house.

2 **2.26** Listen to the recording to check your answers.

3 Complete the phrases with *for* or *since*.

1 ______ 2002
2 ______ a day or two
3 ______ Monday
4 ______ yesterday
5 ______ I left school
6 ______ three years
7 ______ a few weeks
8 ______ an hour
9 ______ the lesson started
10 ______ five minutes
11 ______ half past six
12 ______ last week

4 How many different ways can you complete the questions?

1 How long have you been … ?
2 How long have you had … ?
3 How long have you known … ?

5 Work in pairs. Ask and answer the questions in exercise 4.

SPEAKING

1 Work in pairs. Turn to page 132.

Take it in turns to choose one of the animals in the picture. Ask and answer *yes/no* questions to find out which animal it is. Use these questions and your own ideas.

- Has it got four legs?
- Is it a farm animal?
- Is it a kind of bird?
- Do people keep it as a pet?
- Does it eat other animals?
- Can it run very fast?
- Is it dangerous?

10B Stress

How often have you had a headache in the last twelve months? How many stomach aches have you had? Have you sometimes found it difficult to breathe? Have you had any skin problems? How often have you felt sad or nervous for no good reason? How often have you wanted to cry? How often have you got angry?

If your answer to three or more of these questions is 'too often', you are probably suffering from stress. And if you are suffering from stress, you are not alone. Over half of the adult population has had stress-related symptoms in the last year and many of them have needed help of some kind. Stress is now the major health problem of our times.

Stress, itself, is not an illness, but it can certainly contribute to illnesses, some of them serious. When you feel under stress, your body produces more of the hormones adrenaline and cortisol. As a result, the body needs more oxygen and your heart rate and blood pressure go up. At its most serious, this can lead to heart problems, but stress is also related to weight problems, coughs and colds. Scientists have also discovered that stress can lead to the loss of brain cells.

The most common cause of stress is over-work, but a difficult boss or problems with your colleagues are also common causes. Some jobs are more stressful than others, with teachers and police officers at the top of the scale and beauty therapists at the bottom. From time to time, we hear of celebrities suffering from stress, football managers like Kenny Dalglish or the American actress, Winona Ryder. But stress can affect us all and the figures prove it. 40 million working days are lost in the UK every year because of stress-related illnesses. What is more, people who are suffering from stress do not work as well as usual. The situation is so serious that some companies now offer relaxation and stress management classes.

If you think you, too, are suffering from stress, it's important to know if it is causing you health problems. If it is, see your doctor and talk about it.

Speaking & reading

1 Work in pairs. Which of the jobs in the box do you think are especially stressful? Explain why or why not.

accountant beauty therapist nurse doctor computer programmer gardener police officer teacher unemployed person

Being a doctor is stressful because …

2 Read the article and choose the best title.

1 Adrenaline and cortisol
2 Are you suffering from stress?
3 The most stressful jobs

3 Read the article again and answer the questions.

1 What are three symptoms of stress?
2 How many adults suffer from stress?
3 Which hormones does the body produce when it is under stress?
4 What illnesses are related to stress?
5 Name two stars who have suffered from stress.
6 How many working days are lost in Britain every year because of stress?
7 What are some companies doing about stress?

4 How stressful is your work and day-to-day life?

GRAMMAR: present perfect simple for unfinished time

We use the present perfect simple to talk about finished states that happened in a period of time which is not finished. The time phrases we use (for example *this week, in the last twelve months*) are connected to present time.

I've had two days off work ***this week***. (*This week* is not finished.)
How often have you had a headache ***in the last twelve months***? (*In the last twelve months* includes this month.)

We use the past simple to talk about finished actions and states that happened in a period of time that is also finished. The time phrases we use (for example, *last Friday, two years ago*) are not connected to present time.

I was ill ***last Friday***.
He went to relaxation classes ***two years ago***.

SEE LANGUAGE REFERENCE PAGE 104

1 Mark the phrases unfinished time (U) or finished time (F).

yesterday	last month	this month
in 1998	last week	this week
in my life	one year ago	today
in the last month	since last year	this morning

2 Complete the sentences with the correct verb form.

1 I *have been / went* for a walk a few days ago.
2 I*'ve done / did* a lot of sport this month.
3 I*'ve made / made* some good friends this year.
4 I *have been / was* very busy last month.
5 I*'ve been / was* quite tired in the last two weeks.
6 I *haven't had / didn't have* much free time this week.
7 I *have had / had* a big party for my last birthday.

3 Now change the sentences so that they are true for you.

4 Complete the sentences. Put the verbs in brackets into the present perfect simple or the past simple.

1 How many cups of coffee _____ (*you / drink*) yesterday?
2 How many films _____ (*you / see*) this month?
3 How many times _____ (*you / take*) a train/bus this week?
4 How much money _____ (*you / spend*) today?
5 How much junk food _____ (*you / eat*) last week?
6 How often _____ (*you / be*) late for school/work this year?
7 How often _____ (*you / be*) ill last year?
8 Which countries _____ (*you / visit*) in the last five years?

5 Work in pairs. Ask and answer the questions in exercise 4.

VOCABULARY & SPEAKING: collocations with *get*

1 Complete column A with a phrase from column B.

A
1 They **got into** financial **difficulties**
2 She **got promoted**
3 They **got into trouble**
4 They **got divorced**
5 He **got fired**
6 She **got** very **ill**
7 They **got married**

B
a and the children stayed with their mother.
b and they closed their company.
c and took two months off work.
d because he was always late.
e with the police.
f in a beautiful church.
g because her work was so good.

2 Many events in our lives can cause stress. Put the events in exercise 1 in order of stressfulness.

3 Work in groups. Compare and discuss your lists. As a group, decide on the four most stressful events.

I think that getting divorced is the most stressful because …

I don't think that getting promoted is very stressful.

4 These suggestions come from books about stress. Which ones work for you?

What else do you do when you are feeling stressed?

DEALING WITH STRESS

Do some breathing exercises.
Go shopping and buy something you like.
Eat some fruit or vegetables.
Listen to some music.
Think of something positive.
Ask a friend to brush your hair.
Have a ten minute break from what you are doing.
Go for a walk.
Talk to a friend.

10c | Marathon men

Speaking & vocabulary: sport

1 Look at these sentences. Mark each one like this:

✔✔ very true for me
✔ true for me
✗ not true for me

1 I am fit.
2 I enjoyed sport at school.
3 My health is very important to me.
4 I like lots of different sports.
5 I would like to run a marathon.

2 Work in pairs. Compare your answers to exercise 1. For each sentence, give some extra information.

3 Match the sports in the box to the pictures A–I.

aerobics   cycling   golf   running   squash
swimming   tennis   weight training   yoga

4 Put the sports in exercise 3 into three groups according to the verbs they go with.

do	go	play
aerobics		

5 Which are the best sports to keep fit? Which are the best sports to watch?

Listening

1 You are going to listen to part of a sports radio programme. All the things shown in photos A–F appear in the programme. What do you think it is about?

A Ranulph Fiennes and Mike Stroud

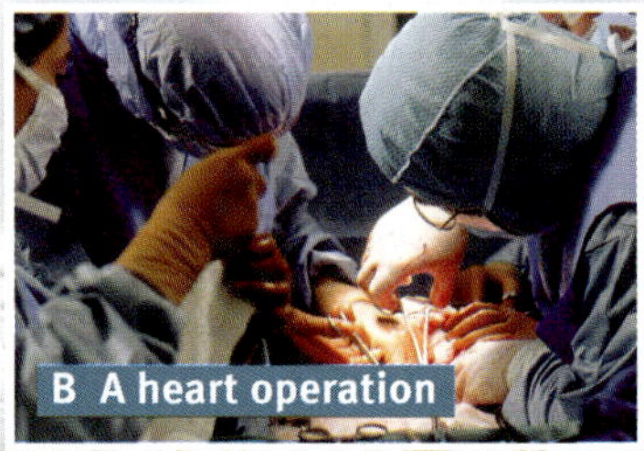
B A heart operation

C Cairo

D The New York Marathon

E Millions of pounds

F The Antarctic

2 2.27 Now listen to the programme to find out if you were right.

3 2.27 Listen again and choose the correct answers.

1 The winner of the men's marathon was *Martin Lel. / Rodgers Rop.*
2 The fastest woman ran the race in *2 hours 10 minutes and 30 seconds. / 2 hours 22 minutes and 31 seconds.*
3 They ran their first marathon in *the North Pole. / Patagonia.*
4 In the last seven days, Fiennes and Stroud have been to *Sydney, Singapore and Cairo. / the Andes, the Amazon and the desert of Oman.*
5 They have raised more than *two / four* million pounds for a multiple sclerosis research centre.
6 Ranulph Fiennes is going *into hospital / to work* soon.

4 Who are the greatest sports heroes in your country? What have they done?

GRAMMAR: present perfect simple with *been* & *gone*

1 Match sentences 1 and 2 to the diagrams below.

1 Ranulph has gone to Singapore.
2 Ranulph has been to Singapore.

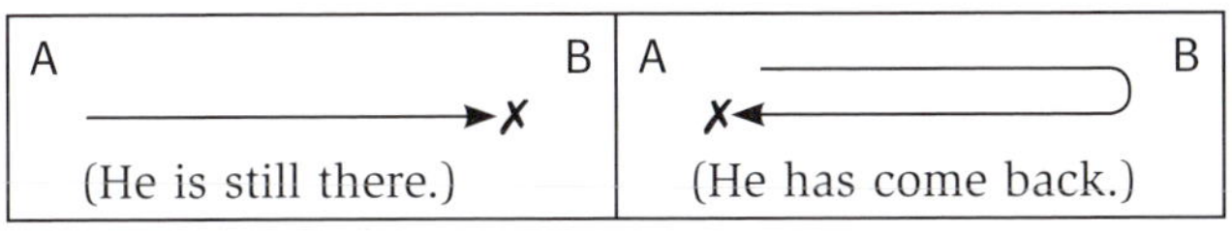

2 Complete the dialogue with *been* or *gone*.

Jane:	Hello.
Mark:	Hi, it's Mark here. Is Rick there please?
Jane:	Hi, Mark. No, I'm sorry. He's (1) _____ away for the week.
Mark:	Oh? Work? Holiday?
Jane:	Both. He's (2) _____ to Patagonia – for a walk.
Mark:	Oh, I've (3) _____ there. Twice. It's really nice. Why didn't you go with him?
Jane:	Because my boss has (4) _____ to Nepal on business so I'm in charge of the office.
Mark:	Nepal? Nice!
Jane:	Have you (5) _____ there, too?
Mark:	Yes, I've (6) _____ a few times, actually.
Jane:	Really? I've only (7) _____ there once. I liked it.
Mark:	Yes, it's an excellent place for walking.
Jane:	Yes. Well, I'll tell him you called.
Mark:	OK. Thanks. Bye, Jane.
Jane:	Bye, Mark.

3 2.28 Listen to the recording to check your answers. Then work in pairs and practise the dialogue.

PRONUNCIATION: /ɔː/

1 What are the missing letters in the words below? All the words have the same vowel sound.

1 bef_re	6 c_lled
2 f_ _r	7 sp_rt
3 New Y_rk	8 s_rt
4 n_rth	9 th_ _ght
5 rep_rt	10 w_lking

2 Which of these words contain the same sound (/ɔː/)?

1 awful	6 morning
2 caught	7 squash
3 cause	8 thought
4 daughter	9 walk
5 important	10 would

3 2.29 Listen to the recording to check your answers.

DID YOU KNOW?

1 Read the information about sport in Australia and discuss the questions.

Australia is one of the most sporting countries in the world. Although the population is quite small (about 22 million), it has a large number of world champions in many different sports.

About three quarters of all Australians do some kind of sport. The most popular are walking, swimming, aerobics, cycling, tennis and golf. They also enjoy watching sport. The most important events in the sporting calendar are the Grand Final of Australian Rules Football, international cricket matches, the Melbourne Cup (horse racing), international basketball and soccer matches, and the Australian Grand Prix (motor racing).

- What are the most popular sports in your country?
- What are the most important sporting events in your country?
- Describe a sporting event that you have attended.

10D | Doctor, doctor

VOCABULARY & SPEAKING: body & health

1 Label the parts of the body A–J in the picture with the words in the box.

back	chest	ear	eye	head	mouth	neck
nose	stomach	throat				

How many other parts of the body can you name?

2 What do you think is wrong with the people in the doctor's waiting room? Use the language in the boxes to describe them.

He She	's got	a headache. a stomach ache. a cold. a cough. flu. a hangover. a temperature. a pain in his/her back/neck, etc.
His Her	back head stomach throat	hurts.

3 Which person in the picture above needs these things?

1 some **aspirin** or **paracetamol**
2 a **prescription** for **antibiotics**
3 an **appointment** with a **specialist**

4 Work in pairs. Ask and answer these questions.

- When was the last time you were ill? What was the matter?
- Did you see a doctor? Did the doctor give you a prescription?
- Did you take any time off work/school?

LISTENING

1 2.30–2.31 Listen to two people at the doctor's. Why are they quite happy when they leave?

2 2.30–2.31 Listen to the dialogues again. Complete the doctor's notes for both patients.

back	cold	cough	depressed	eyes	flu
paracetamol	specialist	stomach ache	stress		

Name: Sarah Hanning

Symptoms: She's got a headache, a cold and a (1) ______. She's also got pains in her (2) ______, chest and neck. Her temperature is 39°.

Diagnosis: (3) ______

Other notes: Problems at work. She's feeling (4) ______.

Treatment / Medicine: strong (5) ______

Name: Roger Hunter

Symptoms: He is extremely nervous. He's got a (6) ______, but he also says he feels hot and (7) ______. His (8) ______ hurt.

Other notes: He doesn't eat well – he lives on coffee.

Diagnosis: (9) ______

Treatment / Medicine: Appointment with a (10) ______.

3 How often do you go to the doctor's? How do you feel about going to the doctor's?

FUNCTIONAL LANGUAGE: at the doctor's

1 Look at the phrases. Who is speaking: the doctor (D) or the patient (P)?

a I feel awful.
b I think you should take a few days off work.
c I'll give you a prescription.
d I'll have a look at you.
e Is there anything I can take for it?
f It's nothing to worry about.
g It's very painful.
h What's the matter?
i What's wrong with me?
j Where does it hurt?

2 Complete the dialogue with phrases a–j from exercise 1.

Doctor: Come in. Take a seat.
Patient: Thank you.
Doctor: Now, (1) ______
Patient: (2) ______ It's my back.
Doctor: (3) ______
Patient: Here and here.
Doctor: OK. (4) ______ Take off your shirt. Does this hurt?
Patient: Yes, it does. (5) ______ Is it serious?
Doctor: No, (6) ______
Patient: (7) ______ Do you know?
Doctor: I think you've pulled a muscle.
Patient: (8) ______
Doctor: Yes, (9) ______
Patient: Thank you. And what about work? Is it OK to work?
Doctor: No, not at the moment. (10) ______ And come back and see me in ten days.
Patient: OK. I'll make an appointment with the receptionist. Thank you. Bye.

3 2.32 Listen to the recording to check your answers. Then work in pairs and practise the dialogue.

4 Work in pairs, A and B.

A: You are the patient. Describe how you feel.
B: You are the doctor. Ask the patient questions about how they are feeling and suggest what she/he should do.

Use the phrases in exercise 1 to help you.

PRONUNCIATION: sentence stress

1 2.33 Listen to a joke. Notice how the important words are stressed.

Patient: Doctor, doctor, what did the X-ray of my head show?
Doctor: Absolutely nothing!

2 Work in pairs. Practise reading these jokes. Stress the words that are underlined.

1 **Patient:** Doctor, doctor, I'm seeing double.
Doctor: Take a seat, please.
Patient: Which one?

2 **Patient:** Doctor, doctor, I've got a memory problem.
Doctor: How long have you had this problem?
Patient: What problem?

3 **Patient:** Doctor, doctor, I feel very nervous. This is the first operation I've ever had.
Doctor: Don't worry. It's my first time, too.

3 2.34–2.36 Listen to the recording to check your pronunciation.

10 Language reference

GRAMMAR

Present perfect simple 2

We use the present perfect simple to show the connection between present time and past time.

We use the present perfect simple for states that began in the past and continue into the present. The states are unfinished.

*How long **have** you **had** your dog?*
*I'**ve had** it for many years.*

We use the past simple for finished actions and states. Compare these examples.

Present perfect simple

*She'**s had** a dog for many years* (and she still has it).

Past simple

*She **had** a dog for many years* (but she doesn't have it now).

We can also use the present perfect simple to talk about finished states that happened in a period of time which is not finished. The time phrases we use (for example, *this week, in the last twelve months*) are connected to present time.

*I've been ill twice **this year**.*
*How often have you been ill **this year**?*
(this year is not finished*)*

We use the past simple to talk about finished actions and states that happened in a period of time that is also finished. The time phrases we use (for example, *last Friday, two years ago*) are **not** connected to present time.

*I was ill three times **last year**.* (*last year* is finished)

Time phrases

The following time phrases include present time. They are often used with the present perfect simple.

today
***this** week/month/year*
***in** the last week/the last year/my life*

The following time phrases are not connected to present time. They are not usually used with the present perfect simple.

in 1992
***last** week/year*
yesterday
*one week/two days **ago***

With some time phrases, the connection to the present depends on the time of speaking. *This morning* is connected to present time if it is now before midday. It is not connected to present time if it is now after midday.

*I'**ve read** three reports this morning.*
(spoken at 11.00 am)
*I **read** three reports this morning. (spoken at 3.00 pm)*

We use *for* to talk about periods of time.

*I've lived here **for** three years.*
*He studied **for** ten minutes.*

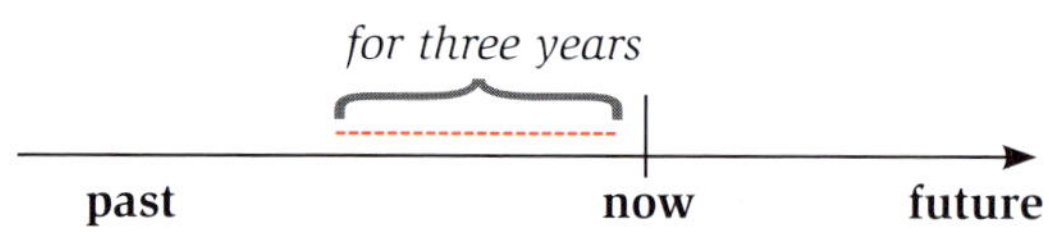

We use *since* to talk about the starting point of an action or state.

*She's been ill **since** Monday.*
*I haven't spoken to them **since** we had an argument.*

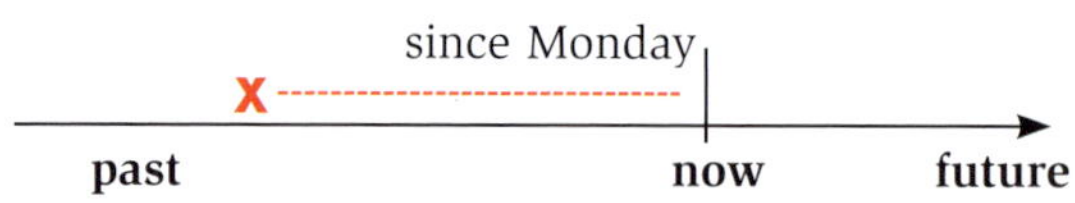

Been & gone

The verb *go* has two past participles: *been* and *gone*.

We use *gone* to show that a person has left a place.

*He has **gone** to Singapore.*

We use *been* to show that a person has left a place and returned.

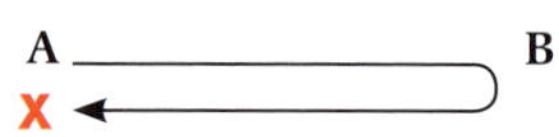

*He has **been** to Singapore.*

See page 74 for more information about the present perfect simple.

Functional language

At the doctor's

What's the matter?
What's wrong with you?
Where does it hurt?

I feel awful.
It's very painful.
It hurts.

I'll have a look at you.
I'll give you a prescription.
I think you should take a few days off work.
It's nothing to worry about.

Word list

Animals

cat *n C* *** /kæt/
dog *n C* *** /dɒg/
goldfish *n C* /ˈgəʊldˌfɪʃ/
hamster *n C* /ˈhæmstə(r)/
lizard *n C* /ˈlɪzə(r)d/
monkey *n C* /ˈmʌŋki/
parrot *n C* /ˈpærət/
rabbit *n C* /ˈræbɪt/
rat *n C* /ræt/

Collocations with *get*

get divorced *phr* /get dɪˈvɔː(r)st/
get fired *phr* /get ˈfaɪə(r)d/
get ill *phr* /get ɪl/
get into (financial) difficulties *phr* /get ɪntə (faɪnænʃ(ə)l) ˈdɪfɪk(ə)ltiz/
get into trouble *phr* /get ɪntə ˈtrʌb(ə)l/
get married *phr* /get ˈmærid/
get promoted *phr* /get prəˈməʊtɪd/

Sport

aerobics *n U* /eəˈrəʊbɪks/
champion *n C* * /ˈtʃæmpiən/
cricket *n U* /ˈkrɪkɪt/
cycling *n U* /ˈsaɪklɪŋ/
final *n C* /ˈfaɪn(ə)l/
golf *n U* * /gɒlf/
horse racing *n U* /ˈ hɔː(r)s reɪsɪŋ/
marathon *n C* /ˈmærəθ(ə)n/
motor racing *n U* /ˈməʊtə(r) reɪsɪŋ/
race *n C* *** /reɪs/
running *n U* /ˈrʌnɪŋ/
soccer *n U* /ˈsɒkə(r)/
squash *n U* /skwɒʃ/
swimming *n U* /ˈswɪmɪŋ/
tennis *n U* /ˈtenɪs/
weight training *n U* /ˈweɪt treɪnɪŋ/
yoga *n U* /ˈjəʊgə/

Body & health

adrenaline *n U* /əˈdrenəlɪn/
antibiotic *n C* /ˌæntibaɪˈɒtɪk/
appointment *n C* *** /əˈpɔɪntmənt/
aspirin *n C/U* /ˈæsprɪn/
back *n C* *** /bæk/
blood pressure *n U* /ˈblʌd preʃə(r)/
brain *n C* ** /breɪn/
breast cancer *n U* /ˈbrest kænsə(r)/
breathe *v* ** /briːð/
cell *n C* ** /sel/
check-up *n C* /tʃek ʌp/
chest *n* *** /tʃest/
cold *n C* *** /kəʊld/
cough *n C/v* * /kɒf/
diagnosis *n C* /ˌdaɪəgˈnəʊsɪs/
ear *n C* *** /ɪə(r)/
examine *v* *** /ɪgˈzæmɪn/
exhausted *adj* /ɪgˈzɔːstɪd/
eye *n C* *** /aɪ/
flu *n U* /fluː/
hangover *n C* /ˈhæŋˌəʊvə(r)/
headache *n C* * /ˈhedeɪk/
heart attack *n C* /ˈhɑː(r)t ətæk/
heart rate *n U* /ˈhɑː(r)t reɪt/
hormone *n C* /ˈhɔː(r)məʊn/
hurt *v* *** /hɜː(r)t/
illness *n C* *** /ˈɪlnəs/
mouth *n C* *** /maʊθ/
multiple sclerosis *n U* /ˈmʌltɪp(ə)l sklərəʊsɪs/
muscle *n C* ** /ˈmʌs(ə)l/
neck *n C* *** /nek/
nose *n C* *** /nəʊz/
operation *n C* *** /ˌɒpəˈreɪʃ(ə)n/
oxygen *n U* /ˈɒksɪdʒ(ə)n/
pain *n C* *** /peɪn/
painful *adj* * /ˈpeɪnf(ə)l/
paracetamol *n C/U* /ˌpærəˈsiːtəmɒl/; /ˌpærəˈsetəmɒl/
prescription *n C* /prɪˈskrɪpʃ(ə)n/
skin *n U* *** /skɪn/
specialist *n C* * /ˈspeʃəlɪst/
stomach ache *n C/U* /ˈstʌmək eɪk/
stress *n U* * /stres/
suffer (from sth) *v* *** /ˈsʌfə(r)/
symptom *n C* ** /ˈsɪmptəm/
temperature *n C/U* *** /ˈtemprɪtʃə(r)/
throat *n C* ** /θrəʊt/
treatment *n U* *** /ˈtriːtmənt/
vitamin *n C* /ˈvɪtəmɪn/
weight *n U* *** /weɪt/
X-ray *n C* /ˈeks reɪ/

Other words & phrases

achievement *n C* ** /əˈtʃiːvmənt/
affect *v* *** /əˈfekt/
arrival *n C/U* ** /əˈraɪv(ə)l/
beauty therapist *n C* /ˈbjuːti ˈθerəpɪst/
brush *v* * /brʌʃ/
calendar *n C* /ˈkælɪndə(r)/
cause *v* *** /kɔːz/
celebrate *v* ** /ˈseləˌbreɪt/
continent *n C* ** /ˈkɒntɪnənt/
contribute *v* *** /kənˈtrɪbjuːt/
crazy about (sth) *adj* /ˈkreɪzi əbaʊt/
cry *v* *** /kraɪ/
deep *adj* *** /diːp/
desert *n C/U* ** /ˈdezə(r)t/
event *n C* *** /ɪˈvent/
farm *n C* /fɑː(r)m/
foundation *n C* ** /faʊnˈdeɪʃ(ə)n/
gardener *n C* /ˈgɑː(r)d(ə)nə(r)/
gross national product (GNP) *n U* /ˈgrəʊs næʃ(ə)nəl prɒdʌkt/
hockey *n U* /ˈhɒki/
memory *n C* *** /ˈmem(ə)ri/
official *adj* *** /əˈfɪʃ(ə)l/
over-work *n U* /ˌəʊvə(r)ˈwɜː(r)k/
point *n C* *** /pɔɪnt/
previous *adj* *** /ˈpriːviəs/
prove *v* *** /pruːv/
raise *v* *** /reɪz/
scale *n C* *** /skeɪl/
spectator *n C* /spekˈteɪtə(r)/
stopover *n C* /ˈstɒpˌəʊvə(r)/
stressful *adj* /ˈstresf(ə)l/
stuff *n U* *** /stʌf/
up to date *adj* /ʌp tʊ deɪt/
vet *n C* /vet/
veterinary practice *n U* /ˈvet(ə)nri ˈpræktɪs/

11A | Things

VOCABULARY & SPEAKING: personal possessions

1 Label the pictures A–K with the words.

2 Which of these things are important to you? Why? Which things could you live without?

3 Work in pairs. Describe one of your favourite things.

- What is it?
- How long have you had it?
- Where did you get it?
- Why is it important to you?

A ______

B ______

Can you live without …
a computer • a phone
a credit card • a car
a motorbike • a TV
a watch • lipstick
an MP3 player
sunglasses • a pen

K ______

C ______

D ______

E ______

J ______

I ______

G ______

H ______

F ______

LISTENING

1 Look at the photos. When were these things fashionable?

2 2.37–2.38 Listen to Susan and Katy talking about things they really wanted when they were younger. Which of the things do they mention?

3 2.37–2.38 Listen again and complete the sentences with Susan (S) or Katy (K).

1 ______ asked her sister for permission.
2 ______ saw someone else with it.
3 ______ still has it.
4 ______ thought it was very sexy.
5 ______ used it in a restaurant.
6 ______ waited two years before buying it.
7 ______ wanted to be independent.
8 ______ wanted to impress her clients.

GRAMMAR: infinitive of purpose

We can use the infinitive (with *to*) to talk about why we do things. It explains the reason or purpose of our actions.

She wanted a credit card ***to pay*** *for meals in restaurants.*
She filled out a form ***to get*** *a card.*

SEE LANGUAGE REFERENCE PAGE 114

1 Underline the infinitives in the following sentences. Which ones are infinitives of purpose?

1 I got a credit card to pay for my clients' meals.
2 I started to spend more money with my new card.
3 I used it to pay for my shopping.
4 I was saving up to buy a Mini.
5 I needed a car to get to work.
6 I used to live a long way from the city centre.

2 Make sentences by joining the phrases in columns A and B with *to*.

I worked overtime to earn more money.

A	B
1 I worked overtime	a buy a car.
2 I saved £5,000	b earn more money.
3 I wanted a car	c see if I liked it.
4 I went to a garage	d help me choose.
5 I asked a friend to come with me	e pay for it.
6 We went for a drive in one car	f look at the new cars.
7 Then we went back to the garage	g go away at the weekends.

3 Work in pairs. Talk about all the different things you do with the things in the box.

car   mobile phone   computer   credit card

I use my car to go to work.

FUNCTIONAL LANGUAGE: paraphrasing

1 Sometimes you need to paraphrase when you don't know the right word for something.

2.39–2.40 Listen to two people talking and complete the sentences.

1 It's a kind of ______.
It's a thing you ______.

2 They're a sort of ______.
You use them to ______.

2 Work in pairs. Turn to page 126. Take it in turns to choose one of the objects and use the phrases in exercise 1 to describe it. Your partner must decide which object you are describing.

PRONUNCIATION: /θ/ & /ð/

1 2.41 Listen to the sound at the beginning of these words.

/θ/	/ð/
thanks thing thousand	than this those

2 Put the words in the box into the correct column in the table in exercise 1.

theatre   their   theory   there   they   think
thirteenth   thought   three   Thursday

3 2.42 Listen to the recording and repeat these phrases.

What do you think of their theory?
Do they think the same thing as the others?
Let's meet on Thursday the thirteenth at three o'clock.
They thought the theatre was over there.

11B | Fashion victim

Speaking

1 Work in groups. Discuss these statements.

- You can judge a person's personality by their clothes.
- Clothes are more important for women than for men.
- It's important to look smart at work and when you go out.
- Young people are more fashionable than their parents.

Vocabulary: clothes

1 Match the pictures A–S with the words in the box.

boots	cardigan	dress	jacket	jeans	jersey
scarf	shirt	shorts	skirt	socks	suit
sweatshirt	tie	top	trainers	trousers	
T-shirt	underwear				

2 In exercise 1, which word(s):

- is always singular/uncountable? _______
- are always plural? _______ _______ _______

3 Work in pairs. How much can you remember about the other students in your class? What were they wearing in the last lesson?

Reading

1 Look at the newspaper headline and photo. Why do you think the man on the right is wearing those clothes?

Read the article to find out if you were right.

OFFICE WORKER FLIP FLOPS OUT OF A JOB

'You can't wear those here!' It was a hot summer day, and instead of the usual 'Good morning' from his boss, Philip Dale was told to go home and change out of his casual shorts and flip flops. He refused and, by the end of the morning, he was out of a job.

'I work in an office and we don't have to meet clients. Why can't I wear what I want?' said Mr Dale. 'It's sexual discrimination. Women can wear skirts and shorts. Why do men have to wear hot trousers and ties?'

But the company disagreed. 'This is work, not a holiday on the beach,' said a company spokeswoman. 'It is true that Mr Dale does not have to work with customers, but he has to go in and out of the building and we must think about our image. What is more, Mr Dale's contract says very clearly "Employees must wear suitable clothes in the workplace." It's a question of professionalism. Shorts and flip flops are not formal enough.'

However, Mr Dale's lawyer said: 'This is a question of human rights. Companies cannot tell their employees what to wear. Of course, employees should wear clothes that are suitable for their work, but there is nothing wrong with shorts in the summer. We're talking here about a very old-fashioned company. In a modern company, like Adidas®, for example, employees can wear what they want. But the really important question here is the question of sexual discrimination. If they must have rules about clothes, they cannot have some rules for men and others for women. It's very simple, really.'

The case continues.

2 Read the article again and say if the sentences are true (T) or false (F). Correct the false sentences.

1 Mr Dale's boss told him to change his clothes.
2 Mr Dale didn't want to change his clothes.
3 He went home to change into different clothes.
4 He often takes his clients out to dinner.
5 There are different rules in the company for men and women.
6 The company thinks that Mr Dale's clothes are too casual.
7 The employees of some companies can choose what they wear.
8 Mr Dale's lawyer thinks that the question of sexual discrimination is very complicated.

3 Work in pairs. Discuss these questions.

- Do you agree with Mr Dale or his company?
- What do you think are the most suitable clothes for work in an office?
- Are there any rules in your country about what you can wear to work?

GRAMMAR: modals of obligation (present time)

We use *must* or *have to* to talk about rules and things that are necessary.

*Employees **must** wear suitable clothes.*
*Mr Dale **has to** go in and out of the building.*

We use *don't have to* to say that something is not necessary (but it is possible or allowed).

We ***don't have to*** meet the clients.

When we ask about rules, we usually use *have to*, not *must*.

*Why **do** men **have to** wear trousers?*

We use *can* to say that something is possible or allowed.

*Women **can** wear skirts and shorts.*

We use *can't* to say that something is not possible or not allowed.

*You **can't** wear those here.*

SEE LANGUAGE REFERENCE PAGE 114

1 Complete the texts with the correct verb form.

Most men in London's financial offices (1) *can't / have to* wear dark suits to work, but on Fridays everything is different. 23% of companies have a 'dress down' day, when they (2) *do not have to / must* put on their usual suit. Most of them are happy that they (3) *can / can't* wear anything they like at the end of the week.

(4) *Do children in your country have / Have children in your country* to wear a uniform to school? At most private schools in England, children (5) *can't / have to* wear a uniform. In most state schools, children (6) *have to / can't* wear a school sweatshirt, but they (7) *can / don't have to* choose their own trousers or skirt.

Students at the very traditional Oxford University (8) *don't have to / must* wear black gowns when they take their exams. At some colleges, they also (9) *can't / have to* wear the gowns at dinner. At Cambridge, on the other hand, students (10) *can / must* wear normal clothes.

2 Work in pairs. Discuss the rules in the place where you work or study. Talk about the topics in the box.

clothes	times of work/study	days off
responsibilities	other rules	

3 Think about what you discussed with your partner in exercise 2 and try to complete all of the sentences below. If necessary, speak to your partner from exercise 2 again.

1 I can leave work at 5 o'clock on Fridays and she can, too.

1 I can _____ and she/he can, too.
2 I can't _____, but she/he can.
3 She/He can _____, but I can't.
4 I have to _____ and she/he has to, too.
5 I have to _____, but she/he doesn't.
6 She/He doesn't have to _____, but I do.

11c | Camden Market

Reading

1 Look at the two photos above. Are there places like this where you live? Have you ever bought anything in places like this?

2 Read the article and explain the connection between the photos.

3 Read the article again and put the events in the correct order.

- ☐ Her friends helped her.
- ☐ Her mother couldn't go to the market.
- ☐ Kyra and her mother stopped selling food.
- ☐ She left school.
- ☐ Her mother started working at the market.
- ☐ She received a book about candles.
- ☐ She sold her first candles.
- ☐ She started making candles.

4 Have you ever worked in a shop or a market? Would you like to? Do you know anyone who has their own business?

Home comforts

With the opening this week of a new branch of *Home Comforts*, Kyra Komac now has 25 stores in her successful international chain of home and furniture shops. But the new store, in London's Camden High Street, takes her back to where it all started. She talks about how the business began.

When I was little, my mother began selling vegetarian food from a stall at Camden Market. She couldn't leave me at home on my own, so I had to go to the market with her.

To begin with, I didn't have to do anything. I just sat there, and my mum told me jokes and stories so I didn't get bored. When I got older, I gave my mum a hand and I really enjoyed it.

Then, one year, my uncle gave me a book for Christmas. It was all about making candles and I loved it. I was fourteen, and I didn't have to go to the market anymore because Mum could leave me at home on my own. I spent my free time making candles of all different shapes and sizes. I made hundreds of them.

One day, my mother was ill so I had to go to the market on my own. I decided to take some candles with me and see if I could sell them. They were sold out in twenty minutes! The next week, my mum gave me some money to buy some wax to make more candles. Again, they sold out really quickly.

Six months later, we decided to stop doing the vegetarian food. My mum and I couldn't make enough candles during the week, so some of my school friends started to help us. I paid them one pound for every candle, and we used to sell them for four or five times that. It was fun and my friends worked with me at the stall.

You could leave school at sixteen and I was in a hurry to leave. My uncle lent us some money and I opened my first shop in Portobello Road. Since then, I've never looked back. In the first store, we only sold incense and candles, but now we sell everything from designer furniture to silver jewellery. Oh, and candles, of course.

GRAMMAR: modals of obligation (past time)

1 Complete the grammar box. Put the phrases a–d in the gaps 1–4.

a This was necessary.
b This wasn't necessary.
c This was possible.
d This wasn't possible.

We use modal verbs to ask and talk about obligation and possibility in the past. We do not usually use *must* or *mustn't* when we are talking about the past.

could **+ infinitive**
*You **could leave** school at sixteen.*
(1) ________

couldn't **+ infinitive**
*She **couldn't leave** me at home.*
(2) ________

had to **+ infinitive**
*I **had to go** to the market with her.*
(3) ________

didn't have to **+ infinitive**
*I **didn't have to go** to the market.*
(4) ________

SEE LANGUAGE REFERENCE PAGE 114

2 Complete the text with *had to, didn't have to, could* or *couldn't.*

My twin brother and I are the oldest in a family of seven. When I was a teenager, I (1) ____ look after my brothers and sisters until my parents came home from work. My brother was really lucky – because he was a boy, he (2) ____ do anything. I (3) ____ see my friends or go out because I (4) ____ do my homework when my parents got home. I wanted to go to college, but I (5) ____ get a place because I did badly in my exams. I got a job where I (6) ____ work in the evenings, so I (7) ____ go to evening school. For ten years I (8) ____ work and study really hard, but I finally got the qualification that I wanted and I became a teacher.

3 2.43 Listen to the recording to check your answers.

4 Think about when you were a child. Complete each sentence in three different ways.

1 I had to …
2 I didn't have to …
3 I could …
4 I couldn't …

Work in pairs. Compare your sentences.

DID YOU KNOW?

1 Read the information about shopping in London. How many different kinds of shops are mentioned?

PORTOBELLO ROAD is famous for its street market (weekends), but it also has a lot of interesting antique shops. Notting Hill Gate

OXFORD STREET is London's main shopping street with all the international chains (Gap®, H & M, Zara, etc), large department stores and two mega-stores for CDs, DVDs and games. Bond Street, Oxford Circus

For books, the best place to go is Charing Cross Road. There are three enormous bookshops and many small specialist bookshops. Tottenham Court Road

Go to **TOTTENHAM COURT ROAD** for computers, hi-fi, TVs and other electronic equipment. Tottenham Court Road

COVENT GARDEN is a lively and popular area with street theatre and music, bars and restaurants. You can find all the usual clothes shops, but also lots of small specialist shops. Covent Garden

BOND STREET is one of the most expensive streets in London. Chanel®, Calvin Klein, DKNY, Versace, Prada – all the big names are here. Bond Street, Green Park

2 Work in pairs. Discuss these questions.

- Have you ever been to London?
- Which parts of the city did you visit?
- What did you like most and least?
- Would you like to visit any of these areas of London?

SPEAKING

1 Work in pairs. Choose a shopping area of your town. Look at these questions and prepare a short presentation.

- Where is the area that you are going to talk about?
- How can you get there? (bus, underground, etc)
- What kind of shops are there?
- What are your favourite shops?
- Are there any shops that you don't recommend?
- What are the cafés/restaurants in the area like?
- Is there anything else that is good or bad about this area?

11D Looking good

Speaking

1 Work in pairs. Discuss these questions.

- Do you like shopping for clothes? What about your friends/family?
- Which are your favourite shops for clothes?
- Where did you buy the clothes that you are wearing?
- Do you prefer to buy clothes with friends or alone? Why?

Vocabulary: *fit, go with & suit*

1 Match the phrases in column A with phrases that mean the same in column B.

A	B
1 Your tie doesn't **go with** your shirt.	a It's the right size for you.
2 That suit **fits** you.	b You look good in that.
3 That dress really **suits** you.	c It isn't a good idea to wear those things together.

2 Work in small groups. Look at the people in the pictures below.

- Do all their clothes fit?
- Do the clothes of each person go well together?
- Do their clothes suit them?

3 Look at the clothes of the other people in your group. Is anyone in your group wearing something that would:

- fit you?
- go with something you are wearing?
- suit you?

Listening

1 Look at the four photos on page 113. Describe what you can see.

2 2.44–2.47 Listen and match the dialogues 1–4 to the photos A–D.

3 Rearrange the words to make sentences from the dialogues.

1 kind of really suits that thing you .
That ______________________________.
2 have if let's my see size they .
Let's ______________________________.
3 don't go I they think together .
I ______________________________.
4 I mean see you'll what .
You'll ______________________________.
5 better bigger fit one size would you .
One ______________________________.
6 about length looks right the .
The ______________________________.
7 always back can come I tomorrow .
I ______________________________.

4 2.44–2.47 Listen to the dialogues again to check your answers.

Pronunciation: word linking

1 2.48 Listen to these phrases from the dialogue. Notice how some of the words are joined together.

What‿do‿you think?
Let's go‿and have‿a‿look.
Why don't‿you try‿it‿on?
That's‿a‿thought.
I'm going to‿think‿about‿it.

2 Practise saying the phrases in exercise 1 quickly.

FUNCTIONAL LANGUAGE: in a clothes shop

1 Complete the dialogues 1–5 with the phrases in the box.

can I help you	excuse me
have you got it	how would you like
I'll take this	I'm afraid not
I'm just looking	I'm looking for
try this on	what size

1 **A:** Good morning, sir. ________________?
B: No, thanks. ________________.

2 **A:** ________________.
B: Yes, madam. How can I help you?
A: ________________ a black jacket.
B: Certainly. ________________ are you?
A: Medium.

3 **A:** Can I ________________, please?
B: Of course, the changing room is over there.

4 **A:** How does it fit?
B: Fine, fine. ________________ in green?
A: ________________, sir.

5 **A:** ________________, please.
B: Certainly, madam. ________________ to pay?
A: Credit card.

2 2.49 Listen to the dialogues to check your answers.

3 Work in pairs, A and B.

A: You work in an expensive clothes shop. A customer walks in. Help the customer. Remember to be polite and friendly. You want the customer to spend lots of money.
B: You are a customer in a clothes shop. You enjoy shopping and you like trying on lots of different things. You are not planning to buy anything today.

Self-assessment (tick ✔)

- ☐ I can ask and answer questions about shopping for clothes.
- ☐ I can ask and answer questions in a clothes shop.
- ☐ I can talk about people's clothes and how they look.

11 Language reference

GRAMMAR

Infinitive of purpose

We can use the infinitive with *to* to talk about why we do things. It explains the reason or purpose of our actions. We can also use *in order to* + infinitive.

He went to the bank ***to get*** *some cash.*
He went to the bank ***in order to get*** *some cash.*

Modals of obligation

Modal verbs are followed by an infinitive, without *to*. The form is the same for all persons.

Present time
We use *must, mustn't* and *have to* to talk about rules and things that are necessary.

Students ***must*** *return books to the library.*
You ***mustn't*** *use your mobile phone in a plane.*
You ***have to*** *park here. That street is closed.*

We use *don't have to* to say that something is not necessary (but it is possible or allowed).

Children at this school ***don't have to*** *wear a uniform.*

We use *have to* to ask about rules.

Do I ***have to*** *wear a suit at the wedding?*

We use *can* to say that something is possible or allowed.

Children over the age of ten ***can*** *use the swimming pool.*

We use *can't* to say that something is not possible or not allowed.

You ***can't*** *park your car outside the school..*

Past time
We don't use *must* to talk about past time. Instead we use *had to*. We use *had to* to talk about rules and things that were necessary.

She ***had to*** *start work at 6.00 am every morning.*

We use *didn't have to* to say that something was not necessary (but it was possible or allowed).

I ***didn't have to*** *wear a uniform at school.*

We use *did* + subject + *have to* to ask about rules.

Did you have to *do any homework when you were a child?*

We use *could* to say that something was possible or allowed.

I ***could*** *stay out until ten o'clock when I was sixteen.*

We use *couldn't* to say that something was not possible or not allowed.

She ***couldn't*** *go to college because she failed her exams.*

FUNCTIONAL LANGUAGE

Paraphrasing

It's a kind of …
It's a thing you …
They're a sort of …
You use them to + infinitive …

In a clothes shop

(How) can I help you?
What size do you take/are you?
How would you like to pay?

I'm just looking.
I'm looking for …
Can I try this on, please?
I'll take this.

WORD LIST

Personal possessions

car *n C* ***	/kɑː(r)/
CD player *n C*	/ˈsiː diː pleɪə(r)/
computer *n C* ***	/kəmˈpjuːtə(r)/
credit card *n C*	/ˈkredɪt kɑː(r)d/
lipstick *n C/U*	/ˈlɪpˌstɪk/
motorbike *n C*	/ˈməʊtə(r)ˌbaɪk/
MP3 player *n C*	/ˌem piː θriː pleɪə(r)/
pen *n C* **	/pen/
phone *n C* ***	/fəʊn/
sunglasses *n pl*	/ˈsʌnˌglɑːsɪz/
TV *n C* ***	/ˌtiː viː/
watch *n C* **	/wɒtʃ/

Clothes

boot *n C* **	/buːt/
cardigan *n C*	/ˈkɑː(r)dɪgən/
changing room *n C*	/ˈtʃeɪndʒɪŋ ˌruːm/
dress *n C* ***	/dres/
fit *v* ***	/fɪt/
flip flops *n pl*	/ˈflɪp flɒpz/
go with *v*	/gəʊ wɪð/
gown *n C*	/gaʊn/
jacket *n C* **	/ˈdʒækɪt/
jeans *n pl* **	/dʒiːnz/
jersey *n C*	/ˈdʒɜː(r)zi/
scarf *n C*	/skɑː(r)f/
shirt *n C* ***	/ʃɜː(r)t/
shorts *n pl*	/ʃɔː(r)ts/
skirt *n C* **	/skɜː(r)t/
sock *n C*	/sɒk/
suit *n C* **	/suːt/
suit *v* ***	/suːt/
sweatshirt *n C*	/ˈswetˌʃɜː(r)t/
tie *n C* *	/taɪ/
top *n C* ***	/tɒp/
trainers *n pl*	/ˈtreɪnə(r)z/
trousers *n pl* **	/ˈtraʊzə(r)z/
try on *v*	/traɪ ɒn/
T-shirt *n C*	/tiːʃɜː(r)t/
underwear *n U*	/ˈʌndə(r)ˌweə(r)/

Other words & phrases

antique *n C*	/ænˈtiːk/
awful *adj* **	/ˈɔːf(ə)l/
bargain *n C*	/ˈbɑː(r)gɪn/
bloke *n C*	/bləʊk/
branch *n C* **	/brɑːntʃ/
candle *n C*	/ˈkænd(ə)l/
case *n C* ***	/keɪs/
casual *adj*	/ˈkæʒuəl/
chain *n C* **	/tʃeɪn/
clearly *adv* ***	/ˈklɪə(r)li/
client *n C*	/ˈklaɪənt/
contract *n C* ***	/ˈkɒntrækt/
department store *n C*	/dɪˈpɑː(r)tmənt stɔː(r)/
discrimination *n U* *	/dɪˌskrɪmɪˈneɪʃ(ə)n/
electronic *adj* **	/ˌelekˈtrɒnɪk/
employee *n C* **	/ɪmˈplɔɪiː/; /ˌemplɔɪˈiː/
enormous *adj* **	/ɪˈnɔː(r)məs/
formal *adj* ***	/ˈfɔː(r)m(ə)l/
furniture *n U* **	/ˈfɜː(r)nɪtʃə(r)/
garage *n C* *	/ˈgærɑːʒ/; /ˈgærɪdʒ/
give (sb) a hand *phr*	/gɪv ə hænd/
human rights *n pl*	/ˈhjuːmən raɪtz/
hurry *v* *	/ˈhʌri/
image *n C* ***	/ˈɪmɪdʒ/
impress *v* **	/ɪmˈpres/
incense *n U*	/ˈɪnsens/
instead (of) *adv* ***	/ɪnˈsted/
investment *n C* ***	/ɪnˈves(t)mənt/
jewellery *n U* **	/ˈdʒuːəlri/
joke *n C* *	/dʒəʊk/
judge *v* **	/dʒʌdʒ/
medium *adj* **	/ˈmiːdiəm/
mega-store *n C*	/ˈmegəˌstɔː(r)/
metallic *adj*	/mɪˈtælɪk/
mum *n C* **	/mʌm/
overtime *n U*	/ˈəʊvə(r)ˌtaɪm/
professionalism *n U*	/prəˈfeʃ(ə)nəˌlɪz(ə)m/
recommend *v* **	/ˌrekəˈmend/
roof *n C* ***	/ruːf/
sell out *v*	/sel aʊt/
seriously *adv* **	/ˈsɪəriəsli/
sexy *adj*	/ˈseksi/
shape *n C* ***	/ʃeɪp/
sign *v* ***	/saɪn/
silver *n C* *	/ˈsɪlvə(r)/
size *n C* ***	/saɪz/
smart *adj* *	/smɑː(r)t/
spokeswoman *n C*	/ˈspəʊksˌwʊmən/
stall *n C*	/stɔːl/
store *n C* **	/stɔː(r)/
suitable *adj* ***	/ˈsuːtəb(ə)l/
uniform *n C* **	/ˈjuːnɪfɔː(r)m/
vegetarian *adj*	/ˌvedʒəˈteəriən/
wax *n U*	/wæks/
wheel *n C* ***	/wiːl/

12A | Around the world

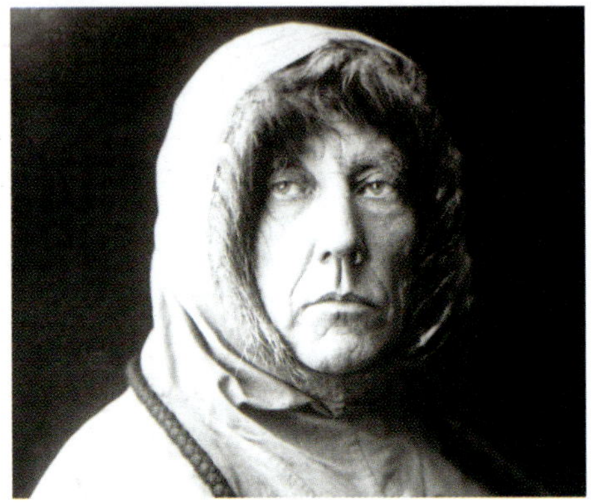

Speaking

1 Work in groups. Answer these questions.

- What do you know about the people below?
- Where did they come from?
- Why are they famous?
- What else do you know about them?

Christopher Columbus
Neil Armstrong
Jacques Cousteau
Roald Amundsen
Marco Polo

Compare your answers with another group.

2 Do you know of any explorers or adventurers from your country?

Grammar: prepositions of movement

1 Match the prepositions in the box to the pictures A–H.

across	along	around	into	out of
over	past	through		

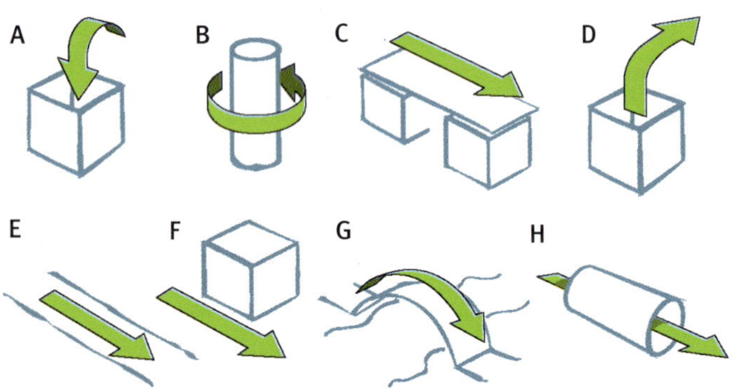

2 Choose the correct preposition to complete these sentences.

1 **1434** The Portuguese explorer, Gil Eannes, was the first European to sail *over / past* Cape Bojador on the coast of Africa.
2 **1492** Columbus first sailed *across / along* the Atlantic Ocean.
3 **1522** Juan Sebastian del Cano became the first man to sail *around / through* the world.
4 **Around 1800** The Scottish explorer, Mungo Park, travelled on horse and on foot *along / into* the Niger River in West Africa.
5 **Around 1800** The German explorer, Alexander von Humboldt, travelled *out of / through* the Amazon jungle and collected plants.
6 **1928** Amelia Earhart was the first woman to fly *over / past* the Atlantic Ocean.
7 **1961** Yuri Gagarin was the first man to go *across / into* space.
8 **1969** Neil Armstrong climbed *around / out of* his spaceship and became the first man on the Moon.

3 Describe your journey from home to school. Use as many prepositions of movement as possible.

I go out of my house and get into my car. I drive along Green Street …

Listening

1 2.50 Listen to a news report about the American adventurer, Steve Fossett. Answer these questions.

1 Why is the reporter talking about Steve Fossett?
2 Which of these activities did Steve Fossett **not** try?

ballooning	dog racing	flying
long-distance swimming		motor racing
space travel	speed sailing	

2 2.50 Listen again and complete the sentences with the correct number.

1 Steve Fossett was ______ when he died.
2 He set ______ records in ______ different sports.
3 He flew ______ kilometres in a balloon around the world.
4 He made ______ attempts to fly around the world in a balloon.
5 He succeeded in swimming between England and France on his ______ attempt.
6 He took part in a ______-kilometre race in Alaska.
7 He set ______ world records for sailing.

3 For some people, Steve Fossett is a hero. Other people think that his achievements are a waste of time and money. What do you think?

Pronunciation: /ɜː/

1 2.51 Listen and repeat these phrases.

first person	third world
journey to work	word search

2 Underline the word in each group that does **not** contain the sound /ɜː/.

1	burn	circle	heart	journey
2	birth	compare	early	nervous
3	earn	girl	heard	record
4	interest	learn	nurse	service

3 2.52 Listen to the recording to check your answers.

Vocabulary: phrasal verbs

1 Replace the words in *italics* with a phrasal verb from the box.

called off	carried on	gave up	put off
sorted out	took off		

1 Steve Fossett's balloon *left the ground* from a town in Western Australia.
2 He almost *cancelled* his attempt to fly around the world.
3 He had to *delay* his departure because of a problem with the wind.
4 He *found a solution to* his difficulties.
5 He *continued* with his journey.
6 He *stopped* ballooning after this journey.

2 In these sentences, one of the words or phrases is **not** possible. Cross out the incorrect words.

1 Unfortunately, the *concert / weather / wedding* was called off.
2 Are you going to carry on *seeing him / the Atlantic Ocean / with your studies*?
3 He has decided to give up *his job / his wife / smoking*.
4 The *decision / meeting / world* was put off until next week.
5 She needs to sort out her *good health / money problems / relationship with her boss*.
6 The *helicopter / plane / ship* took off one hour late.

Speaking

1 Imagine that you have a 'round the world' plane ticket that allows you to make five stop-overs. Decide where you want to make the stop-overs.

2 Work in pairs. Compare your lists and decide on five places you both want to visit. Plan your route and decide what you are going to do in each place.

3 Tell the other students in your class what you are going to do.

Our first stop-over is going to be Sydney. We want to go there to see the koalas and kangaroos and also to visit the Opera House.

Who has planned the most interesting journey?

12B | Let's dance

Speaking

1 Work in pairs. Discuss these questions.

- Which of these festivals have you heard of? What do you know about them?
  Rio de Janeiro Carnival (Brazil)
  Venice Carnival (Italy)
  Las Fallas (Valencia, Spain)
  Notting Hill Carnival (London, England)
  Mardi Gras (New Orleans, US)
- Which of these festivals would you most like to go to? Why?
- What festivals are there in your country? Which is the best?

Vocabulary & reading: festivals

1 Match the words in the box to the parts of the picture A–H.

band	costume	fireworks display	float	mask
parade/procession	speakers	traditional food		

2 Read the email about a carnival in Trinidad. Which of the things in exercise 1 does the writer **not** mention?

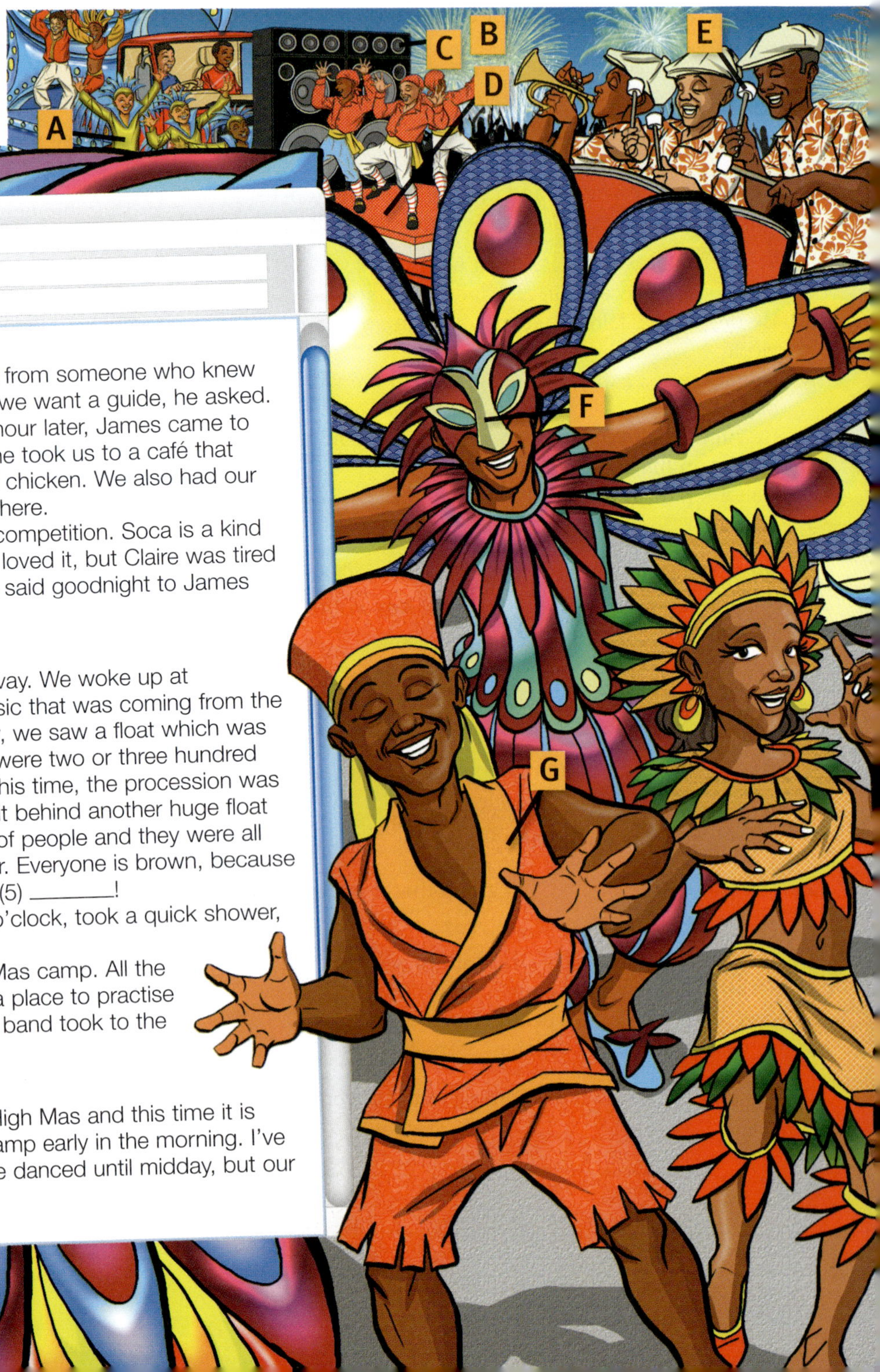

File Edit View Insert Format Tools Table

Send To... Subject... Pam and Claire – Carnival tour

Sunday

Early this morning, we had a telephone call from someone who knew Claire's brother. His name was James. Did we want a guide, he asked. I wasn't too sure, (1) ________ and half an hour later, James came to pick us up at our guest house. For lunch, he took us to a café that serves pelau – a traditional dish of rice and chicken. We also had our first bottle of Carib, the most popular beer here.

Later in the afternoon, we went to a soca competition. Soca is a kind of music which is played at carnival time. I loved it, but Claire was tired (2) ________. Tomorrow is a big day, so we said goodnight to James (3) ________.

Monday

Today is J'Ouvert – they pronounce it joo-vay. We woke up at 3 o'clock this morning because of the music that was coming from the street. Looking out of our upstairs window, we saw a float which was covered in speakers and, behind it, there were two or three hundred people. We got dressed (4) ________. By this time, the procession was a lot bigger and we finally decided to join it behind another huge float with a steel band. There were thousands of people and they were all 'wining' – dancing real close to each other. Everyone is brown, because they cover themselves with dirt, mud, oil, (5) ________!

We got back to Mrs Yorke's at about 10 o'clock, took a quick shower, and changed into our costumes.

At 11, James arrived and took us to his Mas camp. All the bands in the carnival have a Mas camp, a place to practise and meet before the parades. Finally, our band took to the street, (6) ________.

Tuesday

Yesterday was just practice. Today, it is High Mas and this time it is for real. We joined James and his Mas camp early in the morning. I've never seen a bigger parade in my life. We danced until midday, but our feet were really hurting (7) ________.

3 Read the email again and put the phrases a–g into the gaps 1–7.

a and even chocolate sauce
b and for the next four hours, we 'wined' and danced with James and his friends
c and wanted to get an early night
d so we found a place to watch
e and went downstairs to join the parade
f but Claire said yes
g and went back to the guest house

4 Look at the email again and say what these words refer to.

1 he (line 5) *James*
2 it (line 9) ______
3 it (line 13) ______
4 it (line 16) ______
5 us (line 24) ______

GRAMMAR: relative clauses

We can join two sentences with a relative pronoun (*who, that, which*).

He took us to a café. It serves pelau.
*He took us to a café **that** serves pelau.*

We use *who* for people, *which* for things, and *that* for both people and things.

The relative pronoun takes the place of *he, she, it* or *they*.

*We had a phone call from someone **who** ~~he~~ knew Claire's brother.*
*Soca is a kind of music **which** ~~it~~ is played at carnival time.*

SEE LANGUAGE REFERENCE PAGE 124

1 Replace *that* in the following sentences with *who* or *which*.

1 James was a Trinidadian that looked after us.
2 We were woken up by some music that was very loud.
3 They stayed in a guest house that was near the town centre.
4 We joined the people that were 'wining' behind the float.

2 Three of these sentences have a word which should not be there. Cross out the unnecessary words.

1 Pelau is a dish that it is made from rice and chicken.
2 Soca is a kind of music that started in the 1970s.
3 She went to a soca competition which it started in the afternoon.
4 The writer went to Trinidad with a friend who was from college.
5 They bought costumes that cost $250.
6 They stayed with a woman who she was very friendly.

3 Join the pairs of sentences to make one sentence with a relative clause.

1 Venice has a carnival. It is famous for its beautiful masks.
2 Belgium has an important festival. It takes place in Binche.
3 The summer festival in Verona is for music lovers. They like opera.
4 During the Rio carnival, the keys of the city are given to a man. He is called King Momo.
5 At Las Fallas, the people of Valencia make statues of famous people. They are burnt on the last night.
6 At Notting Hill in London, people wear costumes. They cost thousands of pounds.

SPEAKING

1 You are going to talk about a festival that you have been to. Before you speak, prepare your answers to these questions.

- Where and when did the festival take place?
- What does the festival celebrate?
- Does the festival have any special traditions (costumes, food, drink, music, dance, etc)?
- Who did you go to the festival with?
- How long did you stay?
- What did you do there?
- What did you like most and least about the festival?

2 Describe your festival to other students in the class and listen to their descriptions.

12c | Global English

Speaking

1 In your town, where can you find signs that are written in English? What do the signs say?

Where can you hear people speaking English? Why is English used?

Vocabulary: countries & languages

1 Where are these cities?

1 Greece

1 Athens	5 Riyadh	9 Madrid
2 Budapest	6 Tokyo	10 Paris
3 Sao Paolo	7 Beijing	11 Rome
4 Moscow	8 Istanbul	12 Warsaw

Put the countries in order from 1–12 (1= nearest to your country → 12 = furthest from your country).

2 Which languages are spoken in the countries in exercise 1? Write the languages in the correct place in the table.

ending in *-an*	ending in *-ish*	ending in *-ese*	with other endings
Hungarian			

Can you add one more language to each column?

3 In how many different languages can you say *hello*?

4 Which of the languages in exercise 2 are the most widely-spoken in the world? Complete the list with the languages from exercise 2.

The World's Most Widely-Spoken Languages

1 Mandarin Chinese
2 Indian language family (Hindi, Bengali, etc)
3 ________
4 ________
5 ________
6 ________
7 ________
8 ________

5 2.53 Listen to the recording to check your answers.

Reading

1 Work in pairs. Discuss these questions.

- How many different countries can you name where English is the first language?
- What kind of English do you find it easiest to understand?
- Is it better to learn American or British English?

2 Read the article. Does the writer think that it is better to learn American or British English?

English as an International Language – no problem, OK?

'You say to-may-to, I say to-mah-to'

The British and the Americans like to talk about the differences between British and American English. There are a few small differences in the grammar and there are a few words that are different on either side of the Atlantic, but the big difference is the accent. Some British films have subtitles in America because people can't understand what the actors are saying, and some American TV series (*The Sopranos*, for example) are difficult for the British to understand.

However, if you listen to Standard English (the language that TV newsreaders use, for example) in Britain or the US, there are no problems of understanding at all. The problems are with the different kinds of American and British English. These different dialects and accents depend on people's social class and the geographical area where they live. It is possible, for example, that a middle-class speaker from the south of England will find it difficult to understand a working-class speaker from the north. In the same way, a wealthy Californian may not understand a working-class New Yorker. All of these people have accents, but the middle-class accents are usually closer to Standard English.

With so many different Englishes, it is difficult for learners of the language. What sort of English should they learn? Is American English better than British English, or the other way round? The answer depends on their reasons for learning English. If they are learning English for their work, the choice will probably be easy. But for many students, it doesn't matter. What matters is that they understand and are understood.

The world is changing and English is no longer the property of the British, Americans or Australians. Most English that you hear and see around the world is spoken or written by non-native speakers – between, for example, a Greek and a German, or between a Russian and an Italian. English is the main language of business, academic conferences and tourism, of popular music, home computers and video games. English has become the Latin of the modern world.

Because of this, the question of American or British English is becoming less and less important. More and more people now talk about English as an International Language – a language that is not American or British. It has hundreds of different accents, but if people can understand what you are saying, no problem. OK?

3 Read the article again and say if these sentences are true (T) or false (F). Correct the false sentences.

1 There are a lot of important differences between British and American grammar.
2 Some Americans can't understand British films.
3 There is only one British accent.
4 For many students, it doesn't matter if they learn British or American English.
5 Many different nationalities use English to communicate.
6 English as an International Language is a kind of American English.

4 Which accents in your language do you find difficult to understand? What do other people think of your accent?

What is the best accent in your language for a student to learn?

Pronunciation: British & American accents

1 **2.54** You will hear these words said twice. Which speaker is American and which is British?

answer ask banana castle
dance example France glass

2 **2.55** Listen to another group of words. You will hear each word said twice: first by an American speaker, then by a British speaker. Mark the stress on the words.

US	UK
address	address
café	café
cigarette	cigarette
magazine	magazine
weekend	weekend

12D | Global issues

animal and nature conservation
genetic engineering
global warming
education
internet
poverty
health

SPEAKING & VOCABULARY: global issues

1 Match the newspaper headlines A–N to the global issues above.

A LA children who cannot read

B Police need more money to fight online crime

C Protesters destroy fields

D Brazil opens rainforest reserve

E EUROPEAN PARLIAMENT TO VOTE ON MINIMUM WAGE

F New Aids drug

G Temperatures reach record high

H Researchers find new flu virus

I WHO WILL SAVE THE JAVAN RHINOCEROS?

J FOREST FIRES IN SOUTHERN FRANCE

K Computer virus shuts down government websites

L More teachers needed in central city schools

M Scientists clone 12 sheep

N NEW HOSTELS FOR HOMELESS MEN

2 Work in pairs. Discuss these questions.

- Can you think of any other global issues?
- Which three issues are most important to you? Why?
- Which issues are important in your country at the moment?
- Do you know any stories in the news at the moment that are connected to these issues?

LISTENING

1 2.56–2.58 Listen to three dialogues at a party. Which global issues above are discussed?

2 2.56–2.58 Listen to the dialogues again to check your answers. Complete the sentences with a word from the box.

global warming	internet	junk	online
organic	planet	press	

Dialogue 1

1 The woman doesn't want to eat ______ food.
2 The man thinks that ______ food is a waste of money.
3 The woman is worried about the future of our ______.

Dialogue 2

4 The woman knows someone who has had a problem with a (an) ______ virus.
5 The man thinks that the police should do more to stop ______ crime.

Dialogue 3

6 The man doesn't care about ______.
7 The man doesn't believe everything in the ______.

Functional language: agreeing & disagreeing

1 Complete the table with these phrases.

a I see what you mean, but …
b I'm not sure about that.
c Oh, absolutely/definitely.
d That's how I feel, too.
e That's not the way I see it.
f That's what I think, too.
g Well, maybe, but …
h You must be joking!

agree	**partly agree**
I agree with you. (1) ______ (2) ______ (3) ______	I see your point, but … (4) ______ (5) ______
disagree	**strongly disagree**
I'm afraid I disagree. (6) ______ (7) ______	You can't be serious! (8) ______

2 2.59 Listen to the phrases and repeat.

3 Work in pairs. Complete and continue the dialogue. Use as many of the phrases in exercise 1 as possible.

A: Have you heard the news about ______________? It's terrible, isn't it?
B: Yes, I agree with you. I think we should all do something about it.
A: ______________. But what?
B: ______________.

4 Look at these sentences and decide if you agree, partly agree, disagree or strongly disagree.

1 We should find solutions to our own problems before we try to help the rest of the world.
2 Women worry about the world's problems more than men do.
3 Politicians will find solutions to the world's problems.
4 There is nothing that I can do about the world's problems.
5 It is the job of the United Nations (not national governments) to solve the world's problems.

Work in small groups and compare your opinions.

Did you know?

1 Read the information about Oxfam and discuss the questions.

- What charities are there in your country?
- What do these charities do?
- Do you ever give money to charities? Which ones?

Oxfam International

Oxfam International is one of the world's biggest charities. Oxfam's aim is a simple one: to work with others to find lasting solutions to poverty and suffering.

- Oxfam has programmes in more than 70 countries. It works with local people to improve their lives. Oxfam trains health workers and sets up schools, for example.
- Oxfam responds to emergencies, providing food and shelter for people who have lost their homes in floods, hurricanes and war.
- Oxfam speaks to governments and powerful organizations about the problems of poor people. It encourages people to speak for themselves and change their lives for the better.

Oxfam was started in Oxford in 1942. It now has 3,000 partner organizations in 100 countries, including the US, Australia and many countries in Europe.

Self-assessment (tick ✔)

☐ I can understand newspaper headlines.
☐ I can agree and disagree with someone.
☐ I can have a discussion about global issues.

12 Language reference

GRAMMAR
Prepositions of movement

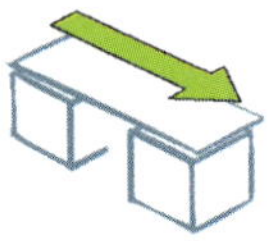

*How long does it take to sail **across** the lake?*

*They walked **along** the street until they found the restaurant.*

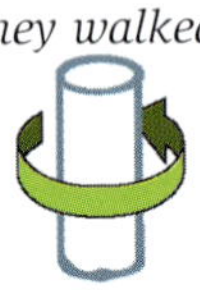

*The tour guide took them **around** the walls of the old city and back to their starting point.*

*The family got **into** the car.*

*She took her lipstick **out of** her handbag.*

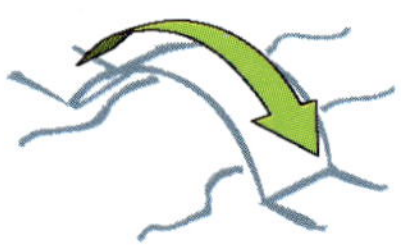

*We are now flying **over** London.*

*He drove **past** my house but he didn't stop.*

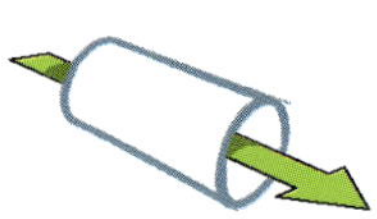

*It took a long time to go **through** passport control.*

Relative clauses

We can join two sentences with a relative pronoun (*who, that, which*).

We often go to a restaurant. It serves Chinese food.
*We often go to a restaurant **that** serves Chinese food.*

We use *who* for people, *which* for things, and *that* for both people and things. The relative pronoun takes the place of *he, she, it* or *they*.

*Yesterday, I met someone **who** went to my old school.*
*Cheddar is a kind of cheese **which** is very popular in England.*

The examples above are defining relative clauses. A defining relative clause identifies the thing that we are talking about. We do not use a comma before the relative pronoun in a defining relative clause.

FUNCTIONAL LANGUAGE
Agreeing & disagreeing

agree

I agree with you.
That's how I feel, too.
That's what I think, too.
Absolutely.
Definitely.

I see your point, but …
I see what you mean, but …

Well, maybe, but …
I'm not sure about that.
I disagree, I'm afraid.
That's not the way I see it.

You can't be serious!
You must be joking!

disagree

Word list

Phrasal verbs

call (sth) off	/kɔːl ɒf/
carry on (+verb + *-ing*)	/ˈkæri ɒn/
give (sth) up	/gɪv ʌp/
pick (sb) up	/pɪk ʌp/
put (sth) off	/pʊt ɒf/
sort (sth) out	/sɔː(r)t aʊt/
take off	/ˈteɪk ɒf/

Festivals

band *n C* ***	/bænd/
carnival *n C*	/ˈkɑː(r)nɪv(ə)l/
costume *n C*	/ˈkɒstjuːm/
display *n C* **	/dɪˈspleɪ/
fireworks *n pl*	/ˈfaɪə(r)ˌwɜː(r)ks/
float *n C*	/fləʊt/
mask *n C*	/mɑːsk/
parade *n C*	/pəˈreɪd/
procession *n C*	/prəˈseʃ(ə)n/
(loud) speaker *n C*	/(laʊd)ˈspiːkə(r)/

Countries & languages

Arabic *n*	/ˈærəbɪk/
Brazil *n*	/brəˈzɪl/
China *n*	/ˈtʃaɪnə/
Chinese *n*	/ˌtʃaɪˈniːz/
France *n*	/frɑːns/
French *n*	/frentʃ/
German *n*	/ˈdʒɜː(r)mən/
Greece *n*	/griːs/
Greek *n*	/griːk/
Hungarian *n*	/hʌŋˈgeəriən/
Hungary *n*	/ˈhʌŋgəri/
Italian *n*	/ɪˈtæljən/
Italy *n*	/ˈɪtəli/
Japan *n*	/dʒəˈpæn/
Japanese *n*	/ˌdʒæpəˈniːz/
Latin *n*	/ˈlætɪn/
Poland *n*	/ˈpəʊlənd/
Polish *n*	/ˈpəʊlɪʃ/
Portuguese *n*	/ˌpɔː(r)tʃʊˈgiːz/
Russia *n*	/ˈrʌʃə/
Russian *n*	/ˈrʌʃ(ə)n/
Saudi Arabia *n*	/ˈsɔːdi əˈreɪbiə/
Spain *n*	/speɪn/
Spanish *n*	/ˈspænɪʃ/
Turkey *n*	/ˈtɜː(r)ki/
Turkish *n*	/ˈtɜː(r)kɪʃ/

Global issues

clone *n C/v*	/kləʊn/
crime *n C/U* ***	/kraɪm/
environment *n C/U* ***	/ɪnˈvaɪrənmənt/
genetic engineering *n U*	/dʒəˈnetɪk ˌendʒɪnɪərɪŋ/
genetically modified *adj*	/dʒəˌnetɪkli ˈmɒdɪfaɪd/
global warming *n U*	/ˈgləʊb(ə)l ˈwɔː(r)mɪŋ/
health *n U* ***	/helθ/
homeless *adj*	/ˈhəʊmləs/
minimum wage *n C*	/ˈmɪnɪməm weɪdʒ/
nature conservation *n C*	/ˈneɪtʃə(r) ˌkɒnsə(r)veɪʃ(ə)n/
organic food *n C*	/ɔː(r)ˈgænɪk fuːd/
poverty *n U*	/ˈpɒvə(r)ti/
protester *n C*	/prəˈtestə(r)/
rainforest *n C/U*	/ˈreɪnˌfɒrɪst/

Other words & phrases

academic *adj* *	/ˌækəˈdemɪk/
achievement *n C* **	/əˈtʃiːvmənt/
adventurer *n C*	/ədˈventʃ(ə)rə(r)/
attempt *n C* **	/əˈtempt/
balloon *n C*	/bəˈluːn/
ballooning *n U*	/bəˈluːnɪŋ/
charity *n C/U* **	/ˈtʃærəti/
coast *n C* **	/kəʊst/
collect *v* ***	/kəˈlekt/
compare *v* ***	/kəmˈpeə(r)/
confirm *v* ***	/kənˈfɜː(r)m/
delay *v* **	/dɪˈleɪ/
departure *n C*	/dɪˈpɑː(r)tʃə(r)/
determination *n U* *	/dɪˌtɜː(r)mɪˈneɪʃ(ə)n/
dialect *n C*	/ˈdaɪəlekt/
dirt *n U*	/dɜː(r)t/
easily *adv* ***	/ˈiːzɪli/
emergency *n C* **	/ɪˈmɜː(r)dʒ(ə)nsi/
endurance *n U*	/ɪnˈdjʊərəns/
epic *adj*	/ˈepɪk/
explorer *n C*	/ɪkˈsplɔːrə(r)/
field *n C* ***	/fiːld/
flood *n C* *	/flʌd/
forest *n C* ***	/ˈfɒrɪst/
geographical *adj*	/ˌdʒiːəˈgræfɪk(ə)l/
guest house *n C*	/ˈgestˌhaʊs/
guide *n C* **	/gaɪd/
helicopter *n C*	/ˈhelɪˌkɒptə(r)/
hero *n C*	/ˈhɪərəʊ/
horse *n C* ***	/hɔː(r)s/
hostel *n C*	/ˈhɒst(ə)l/
hurricane *n C*	/ˈhʌrɪkən/; /ˈhʌrɪkeɪn/
inspiration *n U*	/ˌɪnspəˈreɪʃ(ə)n/
lasting *adj*	/ˈlɑːstɪŋ/
middle-class *adj*	/ˈmɪd(ə)l klɑːs/
mud *n U*	/mʌd/
native speaker *n C*	/ˈneɪtɪv ˌspiːkə(r)/
newsreader *n C*	/ˈnjuːzˌriːdə(r)/
ocean *n C* **	/ˈəʊʃ(ə)n/
onion *n C*	/ˈʌnjən/
opera *n C/U*	/ˈɒp(ə)rə/
politician *n C* **	/ˌpɒləˈtɪʃ(ə)n/
property *n U* ***	/ˈprɒpə(r)ti/
respond *v* **	/rɪˈspɒnd/
rhinoceros *n C*	/raɪˈnɒs(ə)rəs/
sail *v* **	/seɪl/
sailing *n U*	/ˈseɪlɪŋ/
sailor *n C*	/ˈseɪlə(r)/
soca *n U*	/ˈsəʊkə/
social class *n C*	/ˈsəʊʃ(ə)l klɑːs/
solo *adj/adv*	/ˈsəʊləʊ/
solution *n C* **	/səˈluːʃ(ə)n/
solve *v* **	/sɒlv/
speed *n C/U* ***	/spiːd/
steel *n U* *	/stiːl/
suffering *n C/U*	/ˈsʌfərɪŋ/
virus *n C* *	/ˈvaɪrəs/
wage *n C* ***	/weɪdʒ/
wealthy *adj*	/ˈwelθi/
working-class *adj*	/ˈwɜː(r)kɪŋ klɑːs/

Communication activities

4C Functional language exercise 1 page 41

Pair A

Read the story of this film twice and then close your books.

An Education
Jenny, a 16-year-old schoolgirl, lives with her parents and wants to get a place at Oxford University. One day, she meets an older man, David, and they start going out together. David meets Jenny's parents and they like him. Jenny has a lot of fun with David and his friends, but at school she begins to have problems. She leaves school. Jenny finds out that David is a thief, but she continues with the relationship. Jenny and David get engaged, but Jenny then learns that David is already married and has a child. She and David split up. She cannot return to school, but she studies hard and wins her place at Oxford University.

1B Speaking exercise 2 page 9

Student A

Read your information and use the questions in exercise 1 page 9 to find out about Christine's other friends.

File Edit View Favourites Tools Help Links

Click on name to send email

Helga Flint (née Eriksson) (born 1959)
I'm living in Finland with my partner, Chris, and my two children, Sally and Nicole (from my first marriage). I'm a teacher at an English school here. I would love to hear from old friends.

3A Speaking exercise 1 page 27

Student A

Read your rolecard and decide what you want to say to your flatmates.

You share a flat with the other students in your group. There are some problems in the flat and no one is happy.

You are studying for your exams and are very busy. You want to stop smoking but this is not a good time. In the evening, you want to go to bed early, but Student B has always got some friends in his room and they play music all night. You can't sleep.

With your flatmates, make a list of four rules for the flat.
No smoking in the flat.

1D Functional language exercise 3 page 12

Student A

Write two more telephone numbers in column A. Dictate the numbers in column A to your partner. Then listen to your partner and write her/his numbers in column B.

A	B
a 999	a ______
b 015 33 30 00	b ______
c 02 513 23 36	c ______
d 03273 177 711	d ______
e 03865 405700	e ______
f 00 44 207 3641	f ______
g ______	g ______
h ______	h ______

Now check your answers with your partner.

11A Functional language exercise 2 page 107

Take it in turns to choose one of the objects. Describe the object to your partner but do not say what it is. Your partner must guess which object you are describing.

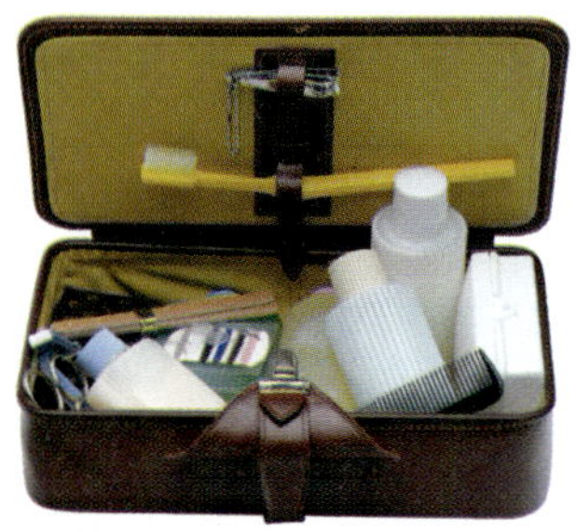

1B Grammar exercise 4 page 9

Student B

Ask and answer questions with your partner to complete the missing information.

Christine Smith left school in 1976. She studied (1 *What?*) ______ at Leeds University and then got a job at (2) *the United Nations in New York*. When she was there, she met (3 *Who?*) ______ at the White House. He worked for (4) *the British Embassy*. They started going out together and they got married (5 *When?*) ______. They now have (6) *seven* children. Christine and her husband now live (7 *Where?*) ______. She works for (8) *the International Red Cross* and he is writing (9 *What?*) ______. Christine wants to get in touch with (10) *old school friends* and promises to reply to all emails.

2C Grammar exercise 2 page 21

Work in pairs. Ask and answer the questions.

Picture A
1 Who was standing at the door?
2 Who was he looking at?
3 What was he wearing?
4 What were the students doing?

Picture B
1 Where was the teacher standing?
2 What was she holding?
3 Where was the boy with blonde hair sitting?
4 How many students were taking the exam?

Picture C
1 What was the man at the door wearing?
2 What were the other people in the room wearing?
3 What was the man with the red tie holding?
4 What was the woman doing?

1B Speaking exercise 2 page 9

Student B

Read your information and use the questions in exercise 1 page 9 to find out about Christine's other friends.

File Edit View Favourites Tools Help Links

Click on name to send email

Nicholas Flint (born 1957)
Working in Orlando, Florida for Disney. I got married for the third time last year, and my wife, Cindy, and I now have a lovely daughter, Verity. We have lots of room and would love to see old friends. Come and stay with us for a holiday.

3C Speaking exercises 1 & 2 page 30

Complete column A with information about a town that you know. Do not choose your home town.

	Town A	Town B
Name of town		
Cheap accommodation		
Restaurants		
Nightlife		
Parks and gardens		
Traffic		
Public transport		
Cinemas and theatres		
Crime		
Pollution		

Ask questions about your partner's town. Write the answers in column B.

3A Grammar exercise 3 page 27

Student A

Look at the picture. Then ask and answer questions with your partner to see how many differences you can find.

9C Grammar exercise 3 page 91

Answers

1 *Titanic*
2 *Toy Story 3*
3 *Moulin Rouge*
4 *ET*
5 *Avatar*
6 *Harry Potter and the Deathly Hallows*
7 *Gladiator*

3A Speaking exercise 1 page 27

Student B

Read your rolecard and decide what you want to say to your flatmates.

You share a flat with the other students in your group. There are some problems in the flat and no one is happy.

There is never any food in the house. You often buy food, but you think that Student C eats it all. Student C never does any shopping! In fact, you spend more money than everybody else in the flat. It is time for others to pay.

With your flatmates, make a list of four rules for the flat.
No smoking in the flat.

2B Grammar exercise 1 page 19

Answer: Jonathan Rhys Meyers

1D Functional language exercise 3 page 12

Student B

Write two more telephone numbers in column A. Listen to your partner and write her/his numbers in column B. Then dictate your numbers (in column A) to your partner.

A		B	
a	911	a	________
b	02790 16 16	b	________
c	02 511 4529	c	________
d	03223 344323	d	________
e	0800 60 800	e	________
f	00 1 245 44 45	f	________
g	________	g	________
h	________	h	________

Now check your answers with your partner.

6B Speaking exercise 2 page 58

Calculate your score.

Are You A Foodie?

1 a) 15 points
b) 10 points
c) 5 points

2 a) 5 points
b) 10 points
c) 15 points

3 5 points for each food item

4 a) 15 points
b) 10 points
c) 5 points

5 a) 15 points
b) 10 points
c) 5 points

6 a) 15 points
b) 10 points
c) 5 points

25–45 points Champion foodie
You certainly like your food! You know what food is fashionable, you know the best food shops and you are happy in a kitchen. Your friends sometimes say that you should open a restaurant – and they are probably right.

50–75 points Part-time foodie
You like the idea of cooking, but it's sometimes easier to get something out of the freezer and put it in the microwave. You like going out to restaurants, especially when someone else pays. Food is important for you, but there are more important things in your life.

80–95 points Fast foodie
You probably like traditional food, but your life is too busy for cooking or shopping for food. After all, what's wrong with hot dogs and ice cream? You eat because you need to eat and you don't care too much what it is.

7D Pronunciation exercise 2 page 73

Student A

Dictate the addresses in column A to your partner and write the addresses your partner dictates in column B.

A	B
www.bbc.co.uk	______
www.google.com	______
www.geocities.com/index	______
ruby.tuesday@hotmail.com	______
marywhitehead@socksareus.net	______

Now check your answers with your partner.

3A Grammar exercise 3 page 27

Student B

Look at the picture. Then ask and answer questions with your partner to see how many differences you can find.

1B Speaking exercise 2 page 9

Student C

Read your information and use the questions in exercise 1 page 9 to find out about Christine's other friends.

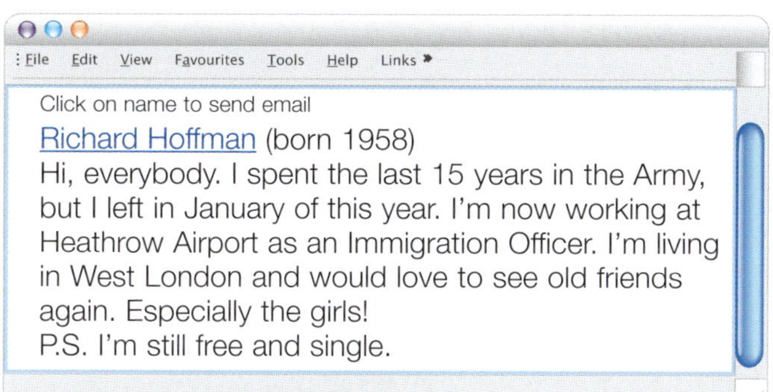
File Edit View Favourites Tools Help Links »

Click on name to send email

Richard Hoffman (born 1958)

Hi, everybody. I spent the last 15 years in the Army, but I left in January of this year. I'm now working at Heathrow Airport as an Immigration Officer. I'm living in West London and would love to see old friends again. Especially the girls!

P.S. I'm still free and single.

3A Speaking exercise 1 page 27

Student C

Read your rolecard and decide what you want to say to your flatmates.

> You share a flat with the other students in your group. There are some problems in the flat and no one is happy.
>
> You stay at home a lot because you do not have a job. The other people in the flat never do any housework. You do it all. There are never any clean glasses when you want a drink. You can't hear the TV in the evening because Student B always listens to loud music.
>
> With your flatmates, make a list of four rules for the flat.
> *No smoking in the flat.*

5D Functional language exercise 7 page 53

Student A

Roleplay 1

> You are a passenger on a long-distance flight. You want to request some things from the flight attendant. Look at the ideas below and decide what you are going to say to the flight attendant.
>
> - You would like: a newspaper/a magazine; a cup of coffee/can of Coke; a sandwich/packet of peanuts.
> - You don't know how to use the headphones.
> - You feel cold.
> - You want to sleep but you can't close the window blind.

Roleplay 2

> You are the passenger. Listen to what the flight attendant asks you to do.

1B Grammar exercise 4 page 9

Student A

Ask and answer questions with your partner to complete the missing information.

Christine Smith left school in 1976. She studied (1) *business management* at Leeds University and then got a job at (2 *Where?*) ______. When she was in America, she met (3) *Adam* at a party at the White House. He worked for (4 *Who?*) ______. They started going out together and they got married (5) *two years later*. They now have (6 *How many?*) ______ children. Christine and her husband now live (7) *in West London*. She works for (8 *Who?*) ______ and he is writing (9) *his second novel*. Christine wants to get in touch with (10 *Who?*) ______ and promises to reply to all emails.

4B Grammar exercise 3 page 39

Prepare five questions with the present continuous about the picture. Then close your books and ask your partner the questions.

3A Speaking exercise 1 page 27

Student D

Read your rolecard and decide what you want to say to your flatmates.

> You share a flat with the other students in your group. There are some problems in the flat and no one is happy.
>
> When you got home yesterday, there was cigarette smoke in your room. You hate smoking! And there were some empty bottles of cola on the table. Who was smoking and drinking in your room? And why in **your** room? Student A is the only smoker in the house.
>
> With your flatmates, make a list of four rules for the flat.
> *No smoking in the flat.*

6B Grammar exercise 3 page 59

Look at pictures A and B. How many differences can you find? Use the adjectives in the box to help you.

> beautiful big cheap clean cold dirty
> early expensive happy late long old
> short small tall young warm

The customers are older in picture A.

5D Functional language exercise 7 page 53

Student B

Roleplay 1

You are a flight attendant. Help the passenger.

Roleplay 2

You are a flight attendant. One of your passengers is very difficult. Look at the ideas below and decide what you are going to say to the passenger. Remember to be polite.

- The passenger is using her/his mobile phone which is not allowed during the flight.
- The passenger is snoring loudly and disturbing other passengers.
- The passenger is listening to very loud music on headphones and disturbing other passengers.
- The passenger has her/his legs stretched out in the aisle so it is difficult for people to pass.

7C Grammar exercise 3 page 70

Student A

Look at the *Things to do* list. Ask your partner questions.

Have you ... yet?

Don't forget!
Check the mailbox
Write to the bank
Call the boss
Get some more paper
Speak to Trevor (in the Personnel dept.)
Do last week's accounts
Arrange a meeting with Sue + David
Read the horoscope!

1B Speaking exercise 2 page 9

Student D

Read your information and use the questions in exercise 1 page 9 to find out about Christine's other friends.

File Edit View Favourites Tools Help Links »

Click on name to send email
Philip Jones (born 1959)
I'm living in London with my wife, Alison. We run a TV production company and we are making a film about old school friends and the internet. Do you want to be in the film? We can pay £500 to everybody we interview. If interested, please send an email as soon as possible.

4C Functional language exercise 1 page 41

Pair B

Read the story of this film twice and then close your books.

Gnomeo & Juliet
Gnomeo is a blue garden gnome and the son of the leader of the blue gnomes. The blue gnomes are enemies of the red gnomes, and Gnomeo is angry with Tybalt, a red gnome, who cheats in a race. Then, Gnomeo falls in love with Juliet, the daughter of the leader of the red gnomes. The families do not want Gnomeo and Juliet to get married. The red gnome, Tybalt, attacks one of Gnomeo's friends, and then dies in the fight that follows. Gnomeo asks a statue of William Shakespeare for advice. In the end, the red and blue gnomes stop fighting and Gnomeo and Juliet get married.

3A Speaking exercise 1 page 27

Student E

Read your rolecard and decide what you want to say to your flatmates.

You share a flat with the other students in your group. There are some problems in the flat and no one is happy.

Two weeks ago you lost some CDs in the house. Now, you can't find your favourite DVD. Is someone borrowing your things? You know that Student C sometimes borrows things without asking.

With your flatmates, make a list of four rules for the flat.
No smoking in the flat.

7D Pronunciation exercise 2 page 73

Student B

Dictate the addresses in column A to your partner and write the addresses your partner dictates in column B.

A	B
www.cnn.com	________
www.onestopenglish.net/	________
kerrphilip@macmillan.com	________
r.dailly@doncaster.ac.uk	________
www.aol.co.uk/msgview.adp	________

Now check your answers with your partner.

7c Grammar exercise 3 page 70

Student B

Look at the *Things to do* list. Answer your partner's questions.

Yes, I have. *No, I haven't.* *No, not yet.*

Don't forget!
Check the mailbox ✔
Write to the bank
Call the boss
Get some more paper ✔ yes
Speak to Trevor (in the Personnel dept.)
Do last week's accounts
Arrange a meeting with Sue + David
Read the horoscope! ✔ done!

2c Grammar exercise 2 page 21

A

B

C

10a Speaking exercise 1 page 97

Take it in turns to choose one of the animals in the picture. Ask and answer *yes/no* questions to find out which animal it is.

Audioscripts

1A Speaking exercise 1 1.1

The Joneses are a typical English family. Mother Sally is 35 and she is a part-time secretary. Father Mike is 37 and works in an office. Sally is very busy with her job and the housework, so she doesn't have time for any hobbies. Mike likes doing things in the garden and repairing things in the house, but he sometimes goes to the pub with his friends.

They have two children: Jason, who is seven and likes football and video games, and his sister, Jane, who is six, and likes playing with her Barbie dolls. They have a cat called Snowy.

There is no work or school on Saturdays and the family usually goes somewhere for the day – a walk in the country or a day at the beach. On Sundays, they visit friends and family. In the summer, they go on holiday to Spain for two weeks. The family has dinner together at half-past six. The children's favourite dinner is chicken and chips, but Sally prefers spaghetti. On Sundays, they always have traditional roast beef or roast lamb. Sally cooks and Mike cuts the meat. After dinner, they watch TV. They enjoy comedy programmes and soap operas and they always watch the Lottery results. One day they will win and move to a bigger house.

1B Vocabulary exercise 2 1.2

David is one of my oldest friends. We were at college together. We didn't get on well at first, but later we became good friends. We come from similar backgrounds and we have a lot in common. He lives in Spain now, so we don't see each other very often, but we keep in touch by phone and email.

1B Listening exercise 3 1.3

C = Christine A = Adam

A: Oh look at those red shoes! Very cool …
C: What are you laughing at? Where did you get that photo, Adam?
A: And that lovely flowery dress. You look love-ly.
C: Give me that photo. Where did you find it?
A: It was in this box.
C: Oh God, I look terrible. And look at Susan, next to me on the floor.
A: Susan who?
C: Susan. My sister, Susan.
A: Susan!? Never! How old were you?
C: Well, it was 1973. I remember it well. It was the year that Pink Floyd made *Dark Side of the Moon*. That's what we were singing. God, 1973, that's so long ago, I was only fifteen, and Susan, she was, what, thirteen, I guess. Maybe twelve.
A: And who's the boy with the guitar and the pink shirt? A boyfriend?
C: No. That's Nicholas, and he wasn't my boyfriend. He was going out with Helga, my best friend at the time. That's Helga there, with the blonde hair, sitting next to Nicholas. You can see how much she was in love with him.
A: So, who was your boyfriend? The boy in the yellow shirt?
C: Why do you want to know?
A: Well, I am your husband.
C: Hmm, I'll tell you later. I wonder where they all are now. You know, I mean, what do they do? Are they married? Do they have children, where do they live, that sort of thing.
A: Maybe you'll find them on Facebook™.
C: Hey, good idea.

1B Pronunciation exercise 1 1.4

1 do not don't
2 did not didn't
3 what is what's

1B Pronunciation exercise 3 1.5

1 doesn't
2 he's
3 that's
4 wasn't
5 weren't
6 who's

1C Pronunciation exercise 2 1.6

1 A H J K
2 B C D E G P T V
3 F L M N S X Z

1C Pronunciation exercise 3 1.7

I O Q R U W Y

1C Pronunciation exercise 4 1.8

1 Jones
2 Smith
3 Williams
4 Brown
5 Taylor
6 Davies

1C Pronunciation exercise 5 1.9

1 Jones J-O-N-E-S
2 Smith S-M-I-T-H
3 Williams W-I-L-L-I-A-M-S
4 Brown B-R-O-W-N
5 Taylor T-A-Y-L-O-R
6 Davies D-A-V-I-E-S

1D Functional language 1 exercise 1 1.10

M = Message K = Kate

M: Thank you for calling Sayers Recruitment and Training. To listen to the menu, please press the star button on your telephone now. Thank you. For general enquiries, press 1 followed by hash. For business callers, press 2 followed by hash. To make an appointment with a careers adviser, press 3 followed by hash. Thank you. You have reached the voicemail of:
K: Kate Woods
Hi, this is Kate Woods. I'm not in the office today, but you can call me at home on 0307 7 double 5 3046 or on my mobile 04 double 7 3201 double 8. That's 0307 7 double 5 3046 at home or 04 double 7 3201 double 8 for the mobile. You can also leave a message after the beep. Thanks.

1D Listening exercises 1 & 2 / Functional language 2 exercise 1 1.11–1.15

1 M = Message D = Davina

M: This is 641480. I'm afraid there's no one to take your call right now. Please leave your name and number after the tone and I'll call you back.

D: Ah, yes, hello. Mr Trotter, my name is Davina and I'm, I'm interested in your, erm, advertisment. Could you call me back, please? Any time before 6 o'clock. The number is 0870 double 4 6091. Ask for Davina. Bye.

2 M = Message B = Bella

M: Stuart here. I'm not home at the moment, so please leave a message after the beep.

B: Hello, good morning. This is Bella Moor, that's Moor, M-double O-R. I'm calling about the Kung Fu classes. You can call me back on my mobile, that's 0 double 47 3958 double 2. But I'll try to call you again later.

3 Re = Receptionist R = Ruby

Re: Sayers Recruitment and Training. Can I help you?

R: Hello, yes, erm, I'm, er, I saw your advert and I'm looking for a job, I mean, I'm interested in a new job, and …

Re: Ah, yes, you need to speak to Mrs Sayers, but I'm afraid she's not in the office right now. Could I take your name and number and I'll ask her to call you back?

R: Er, yes, yes. Er, the name's Ruby, Ruby Tuesday and my number is 0308 double 5 71919.

Re: Thank you, Miss Tuesday. I'll pass on your message.

R: Thanks. Bye.

Re: Goodbye.

4 M = Message S = Sara

M: This is 727 23 double 7. I'm afraid there is no one to take your call right now. Please leave your name and number after the beep and I'll call you back.

S: Oh, hello. This is a message for Mary Sharp. I'm interested in having English lessons because I need to prepare for an exam in Spain. Can you call me back? Some time this afternoon before six? My name is Sara and my number is 0308 3 double 4 7031.

2A Listening exercises 1 & 2 1.16–1.18

1 Mr Miller taught biology and everybody, well, all the girls anyway, we all loved him. I was afraid of lots of the teachers, but with Mr Miller, I was really fond of him, maybe more than a little fond, actually. You know, he really cared about his students; he was really interested in us, in us as people, I mean. I never missed his lessons. And I always got good grades in his classes. Some of the boys, though, some of the boys weren't very keen on him. Jealous, probably.

2 I didn't like my school at all. I was terrible at most subjects, but I was good at art. The teachers thought I was stupid, and they put me in a class with all the difficult pupils. The teachers weren't interested in us and we didn't worry about them. I never worked in class, I never did my homework, and nobody was surprised when, at sixteen, I failed my exams. I failed all of them except art. I'm a painter now, and people don't care if I have any exams.

3 I didn't really like school very much, but Fridays were OK. Friday was music day and I was really keen on music. Still am. I played the guitar and I sang well, quite well, and the music teachers were always cool. We made a CD with one of them and another organized a gig at the end of term. I had such fun that I didn't want to leave that school.

2A Pronunciation exercise 1 1.19

open – opened love – loved try – tried want – wanted decide – decided

2A Pronunciation exercise 3 1.20

No extra syllable (NS): helped, worked
Extra syllable (ES): ended, hated, needed, studied, waited

2B Vocabulary exercise 2 1.21

1 Some schools in England are for boys and girls and some are single sex.
2 In the English education system there are private schools and state schools.
3 Some subjects, like English and maths, are compulsory until the age of sixteen in England.
4 English children must sometimes stay in class at break as a punishment.
5 The minimum leaving age in England is sixteen, but most students continue for another two years.
6 There is no leaving certificate in England, but many students take 'A level' exams when they are eighteen.
7 School students in England get their exam results in the summer holidays after they leave school.

2B Pronunciation exercise 2 1.22

1 bought, caught, found, thought
2 came, gave, made, said
3 broke, drove, lost, spoke
4 felt, knew, met, went

2D Listening exercises 1 & 3 1.23

R = Receptionist P = Patrick

R: Good afternoon. Bonjour. Can I help you?

P: Er, yes. Bonjour. Please could I have some information about your school?

R: Certainly, sir. What would you like to know?

P: Well, could you tell me about your courses? I mean, for example, how many students are in a class?

R: There are fifteen students in a class. We have day-time classes and evening classes. And all our teachers are native French teachers. Do you speak any French?

P: Er, oui. Un petit peu.

R: Pardon?

P: Yes, sorry, my accent isn't very good. I think that I'm probably a beginner. Do you have classes for beginners in the evenings?

R: Yes, we do. On Tuesdays and Thursdays.

P: And what time are the classes?

R: Between eight o'clock and half past nine.
P: Eight to nine thirty. I see. And how long does the course last?
R: It's a ten-week course. It starts next Tuesday, actually.
P: Oh, right. Excellent. And, er, are there any social activities?
R: Oh yes, we have our French club on Friday evenings.
P: Sounds fun. Oh, I almost forgot. How much are the course fees?
R: It's one hundred and eighty pounds for the ten weeks. Would you like a registration form?

3A Pronunciation exercise 2 1.24

happy holiday honest hotel who hospital home house what whole

3A Pronunciation exercise 4 1.25

In Hertford, Hereford and Hampshire hurricanes hardly every happen.

3A Listening exercises 1 & 2 1.26

A = **Ali** **C** = **Charlie**

A: Hey, Charlie, do you have any time this week when I can come and look at your flat?
C: Yeah, what about this afternoon? There's nothing to eat in the flat, so I'm going to the shops on the way home to get some food.
A: Pizzas again?
C: No, I want to get some bread and cheese, actually. Anyway, why don't you come with me and look at the flat after that?
A: Yeah, all right. Good idea.
C: So, things are still difficult at home? Still the same problems?
A: Things are worse. We've got twin cousins from London staying with us at the moment. They're sleeping in the room with me and my brothers. Fourteen-year-old twins!
C: Tough, eh?
A: Yeah, and I've got some exams in a week or two. I get no peace and I can't do any work. It's driving me mad.
C: Can't the cousins sleep in another room?
A: No, there's no space in the house. We only have two bedrooms. And my mum's always in the living room watching TV. I can't do my homework in there with the TV on.
C: Well, you know my flat's not very big either, and there are five of us already. No peace there, I'm afraid. We don't go to bed early and, well, I don't want to put you off …
A: No, it's not just that. I can't have any friends in the house. I get no independence. I mean, I love my parents, but I think it's time to move.
C: And you really want to move in with us? I mean, it's only a sofa in the living room. Oh, by the way, the kitchen's a bit dirty. I think it's my turn to do the housework. Haven't you got any better ideas for a place to stay?
A: No. Anyway, let's get that food.
C: Yeah, OK. Oh, have you got any cash on you? Money is a bit of a problem at the moment.

3D Listening & functional language exercises 1 & 2 1.27–1.29

K = **Kate** **A** = **Ali** **M** = **Man** **M2** = **Man 2**

1

K: Come on, Ali. Let's get out of here and find the station.
A: I've no idea of the way. Hang on, I'll ask this guy. 'Scuse me, could you tell us the way to the station, please?
M: Aye. The station you want? Well, turn right when you come out of the stadium, OK. Go straight on. And then, take the first street on the right. Take the first street on the right, OK?
K / A: OK, got that.
M: It's called Strawberry Place, all right. Cross the road, cross onto the other side, and walk a bit, it's not far. Go past the Metro station, on your left. And go to the end of the road. Turn left and you come to a roundabout, all right? And on the other side, you'll see the bus station. It's not hard to find, but you'd better ask for more directions from there.
A: So we go past the Metro, then turn left and look for the bus station? OK, thanks.
M: Aye, that's right. Ta-ra.

2

K: I wonder where the Metro is. He said it was near.
A: Yeah. And he didn't say anything about that church in front of us. And, look, there's a roundabout, but I can't see a bus station.
K: We're lost, aren't we? Come on, let's ask someone. Excuse me, how do I get to the train station, please?
M2: The train station. Just go down this street, keep going, keep going, and it's sort of down there. Not far, you know. You'll see the cathedral, and then the train station is very near after that.
A: Oh, right. Thanks a lot.

3

A: I think we're really lost this time. That man never said anything about a shopping centre.
K: And the shopping centre was ages ago.
A: And he didn't mention that castle we walked past either.
K: No, he talked about a cathedral.
A: Ah well, it's nice here, anyway, isn't it? You see the bridge over there?
K: Yeah, that's the famous bridge, isn't it?
A: Why don't we go into one of these bars? Or we could have a pizza in that restaurant.
K: Good idea. We can always look for the station later.

3D Pronunciation exercise 1 1.30

interesting place to visit difficult to give directions next to the castle

3D Pronunciation exercise 3 1.31

1 Could you tell us the way to the station, please?
2 And go to the end of the road.
3 Turn left and you come to a roundabout, all right?
4 It's not hard to find.

4A Pronunciation exercise 1 1.32

/z/ goes, lives, days, friends
/s/ likes, wants, books, streets

4A Pronunciation exercise 4 1.33

/z/ knows learns spends parties problems questions things
/s/ maps talks writes facts states

4B Vocabulary & speaking exercise 3 1.34

The ceremony usually takes place in a church or registry office. After the ceremony, the couple and their guests go to the reception, where they drink champagne and eat the wedding cake. Later on, at the wedding meal, the best friend of the groom makes a speech. The married couple often leave the party early to go on their honeymoon.

4C Listening exercises 1 & 2 1.35

OK, so there are these two women: Amanda, who lives in America, and Iris, who lives in England, and they're both very unhappy. Amanda has split up with her boyfriend, and Iris is unhappy because there's a man she is in love with, Jasper, but he is going to get married to someone else. So, yes, anyway, the two women, they want to change their lives and they decide to swap homes, to go and live in the other woman's house. Amanda arrives in England and she meets Graham, who is the brother of Iris. Amanda and Graham have a lot in common, they talk a lot about their families and so on, and they start going out together. And then, Amanda has to go back to America, but she doesn't go because she realizes that she's in love with Graham, and so she stays in England for a bit.

At the same time, Iris is in America, and she's still crazy about a guy in England, the one who is getting married to someone else. Iris meets Miles; he's Amanda's best friend, and they get on very well, but Miles is also crazy about someone else, his girlfriend, but he doesn't know that she is cheating on him. So, Iris and Miles become friends, but they both have someone else in their lives. Then, one day, Iris goes home and she finds Jasper at the front door, the one that she was crazy about. But she realizes that she's not in love with him any more, and she sends him away. And Miles splits up with his girlfriend because he finds out that she's cheating on him, and then, yes, then Miles asks Iris out, he asks if she wants to go on a date with him, and she has fallen in love with him, so she says yes. And then they go to England together, and they meet up with Amanda and Graham, and everyone is happy, and, er, that's it, really.

4C Pronunciation exercise 1 1.36

/ɪ/ live think still rich hit
/iː/ leave teeth street feel meet

4C Pronunciation exercise 3 1.37

Beauty and the Beast The Big Sleep Mission Impossible
Pretty Woman ET Robin Hood: Prince of Thieves
The Prince of Egypt

4D Listening exercises 1 & 2 1.38–1.39

1 N = Nancy S = Sebastian

S: Yeah, hi.
N: Oh, hi. Erm, Sebastian, hi, it's Nancy. Nancy. We met at Melanie's place last Friday.
S: Oh, right. Yes, hi.
N: I was just ringing to, well, the thing is, some friends are coming to my place for dinner on Saturday, and, erm, well, would you like to come?
S: Oh, that's very kind of you. Saturday, you say?
N: Yep. This Saturday.
S: Sorry, Nancy, I'd love to, but I'm afraid I'm busy on Saturday. It's my parents' wedding anniversary.
N: That's a shame.
S: I tell you what, though. I'm meeting up with some friends for lunch on Sunday. Why don't you come along?
N: All right. Yes, why not?
S: You know the little café on the river. By the bridge. We're meeting there.
N: Yeah, I know. Great.
S: Well, I don't know. Shall we say one o'clock? No, let's say half past one, OK?
N: OK, cool. I'll see you there. Thanks.
S: OK, see you on Sunday, Nancy.

2 S = Sebastian J = Jason

J: Hello.
S: Jason, hi, it's Seb. Sebastian.
J: Hi, Seb. What's up?
S: Hey, listen, a whole group of us are meeting for lunch on Sunday at the river café. Do you fancy joining us?
J: Thanks, Seb, but I'd rather not. You know, I always go running on Sundays.
S: Yeah, I know, but how about doing something different for a change? Just once?
J: I guess I could come along later, maybe. What about joining you for coffee after you've eaten? At about half-past two, something like that?
S: Yeah, OK, great. Good idea. But if you change your mind about the meal …
J: You never know! Let's see what the weather's like, OK?
S: OK. Let's wait and see. But the weather forecast says it's going to rain. See you at the weekend, then. Take care.
J: You take care, too. See you.

5B Listening exercises 2 & 3 1.40

P = Presenter N = Nicki M = Manager
G = Gavin

P: Welcome to *The Holiday Programme*. Today, we continue our search for the worst hotel in Britain. We sent our reporters, Nicki and Gavin Becks, to the Cumberland Hotel in Brighton for a weekend by the sea.
N: When we arrived at the hotel, a sign in the window said 'Vacancies'. We rang the bell, but we had to wait five minutes before the manager finally appeared.
M: Yes?
G: Hello. We'd like a double room for two nights, please.

M: It's ninety pounds a night. No credit cards and you need to pay in advance.
G: That's fine, fine. I'll pay now. Here.
M: Room 51. Fifth floor. On the right. Oh, and the lift's not working. The stairs are over there.
G: Never mind. We'll walk.
N: The room itself was not too bad. There was a good view of the sea from the window, the bathroom was small but clean and the bed looked clean and comfortable.
G: We had a quick (cold) shower, got changed and went back downstairs where we handed in the key.
M: Everything all right?
G: Yes, the room's fine, but the shower's very cold.
M: I know, I know. I'll fix it this evening, OK.
G: That's kind of you. Thanks.
M: What time are you going to come back this evening?
N: I'm not sure. We're going to see a film at the cinema and maybe have a meal afterwards. Why?
M: Well, just remember I close the doors at eleven.
N: Eleven?
M: Eleven.
N: We had a good evening, and when we got back to the hotel, it was two minutes past eleven. The door was locked; we rang and rang, but after fifteen minutes, there was still no answer. We finally decided to give up and look for another hotel. Fortunately, there were vacancies at the Grand Hotel, only a few minutes away.
G: The next morning, after a hot shower, we went back to the Cumberland Hotel to get our bags. When we got there, the manager was standing outside the front door. 'Who do you think you are,' she shouted. 'Waking up all the guests in the middle of the night! Next time you do that, I'll call the police.'
N: 'It won't happen again,' I said. 'We won't be back. We're going to stay at another hotel, thank you very much.' The manager went back into the hotel, came outside with our bags and threw them at us.
G: Britain's worst hotel? This one gets my vote.

5B Grammar exercise 4 1.41

G = Guest M = Manager

G: Excuse me, I'm going to visit the old part of town this afternoon. Can you tell me the way?
M: Yes, no problem. I'll give you a map.
G: Is it far?
M: No, not far. Do you want to walk or take a bus? It's a nice walk.
G: Oh, well, I'll walk, I think.
M: Or, if you like, I'll take you in my car. I'm going to do some shopping this afternoon.
G: That's kind of you. Thanks. When are you going to leave?
M: About four o'clock.
G: Great. I'll see you here at four o'clock.
M: OK. I'll see you later.

5C Pronunciation exercise 2 1.42

1	castle	4	hour	7	ghost	10	wreck
2	climb	5	knife	8	Wednesday		
3	foreign	6	receipt	9	whole		

5D Listening exercises 2 & 3 1.43–1.45

1 C = Check-in assistant P = Passenger

C: Good afternoon, sir.
P: Oh, hello. I'm, er, sorry, but I can't find my ticket. It's here somewhere. Ah, here it is. Sorry about that.
C: That's all right. Could I see your passport, please?
P: Yes, sure. Here.
C: Thank you. That's fine. Do you have any bags to check in?
P: No, no, just this. Er, excuse me, but I wonder if I could have a window seat, please.
C: Certainly, yes. 23A. That's a window seat.
P: Great. Thanks.
C: You're welcome. Your plane is boarding in fifteen minutes at twelve-thirty. So, you'd better hurry, I think. It's departure gate 41, boarding at twelve-thirty.
P: OK, right, thanks. Bye.
C: Have a nice flight.

2 S = Security guard P = Passenger

S: Can you put any metal objects, money, keys and so on, here, please, sir, and walk through the gate?
P: And the phone?
S: Yup, that too.
S: Can you stand over here and put your arms like that, please?
P: Yes, yes, all right, but I'm in a hurry. I've only got five minutes.
S: It's the Dublin flight, is it?
P: Yeah, Dublin. Please. Could you hurry up a bit?
S: Now, could you just empty your pockets, please, sir?
S: Ah, it's a metal comb. I'm afraid you can't take that on the plane, sir. It's a dangerous object.
P: OK, OK. You keep it. Now, can I go?

3 F = Flight attendant P = Passenger
P2 = Second passenger

F: Would you like anything to drink?
P: Yes, I'd like a coffee, please. Strong. No sugar, no milk.
F: Certainly, sir. And for you, madam?
P2: Just a glass of water for me, please.
F: Certainly, madam. That will be four euros fifty, please, for you sir.
P: It's not free? Oh, right, well, here you are. I'd like to have a receipt, please.
F: I'm afraid we don't do receipts, sir. Here's your water, madam.
P2: Many thanks.
P: I'm sorry, but can I get past? I need to go to the, er, the, you know …
P2: The toilet? Yes, sorry, of course.
P: Sorry.
P2: Mind out! Watch your coffee!
P: Aaagh! That's hot!

5D Pronunciation exercises 3 & 4 1.46

Polite: Excuse me, could I have a coffee, please?
Rude: Excuse me, could I have a coffee, please?
Polite: Can you stand over here, please?
Rude: Can you stand over here, please?

5D Pronunciation exercise 5 1.47

1 Excuse me, can I have a window seat, please?
2 Could I get past?
3 I wonder if I could have another glass of water, please.
4 Can you sit down?
5 I'd like a black coffee.
6 Could you put your bag up there, please?
7 Can I see your passport, please?

6B Listening exercises 1 & 2 1.48

J = Jilly M = Maura

J: Today, we are in the market in Bologna, perhaps the food capital of Italy, but if you come to Bologna hoping to eat Spaghetti Bolognese, traditional, authentic Spaghetti Bolognese, you will be disappointed. No Spaghetti Bolognese in Bologna? I asked Maura Giuliani, an expert on Italian food to tell me more. Maura, why is there no Spaghetti Bolognese in Bologna?

M: Well, we have a dish called Tagliatelle al Ragu, and the sauce is very similar to the sauce you call Bolognese. But we use tagliatelle, not spaghetti. Spaghetti comes from the south of Italy and we do not use it here.

J: How strange!

M: Well, the sauce called 'Bolognese' that you buy in a bottle from a supermarket is even stranger.

J: In what way?

M: Well, it has a very complicated recipe, tomatoes, of course, salt and sugar, but lots of other things and most of them are completely artificial; chemical tomato flavour, artifical colours, and so on. When we make Ragu sauce at home, we use local, fresh ingredients. We make a simpler, more traditional recipe. It's healthier for you, and it tastes better. But, and there is a but, it's a lot slower to prepare. Good food is slow food.

J: Yes, absolutely. I understand that you call yourself a 'slow foodie'. What exactly does that mean?

M: Slow food is a movement that started in Italy back in 1986, but now has members in over one hundred countries. Who are we? Well, it's quite difficult to say because all sorts of people are slow foodies. It's easier to say who we are not …

J: And you are not fast food!

M: Right. We're not pasta sauce in a bottle, we're not a quick hamburger and chips for dinner. We think food is more important and more interesting than that. We're interested in making food more enjoyable, more traditional, slower, better.

J: Maura, thanks. After the market, Maura took us to a demonstration of pasta making.

6B Pronunciation exercises 1 & 3 1.49

1	healthy	4	modern	7	simple
2	difficult	5	important	8	artificial
3	enjoyable	6	complicated	9	traditional

6C Grammar exercise 4 1.50

1 The most expensive meal in the world was in Bangkok in 2007. For their food and drink, the 15 diners paid £150,000.
2 The best caviar in the world comes from the Caspian Sea.
3 The largest restaurant in the world is in Syria. It seats 6,000 people.
4 The biggest donut in the world was made in 2007. It was 6 metres in diameter.
5 The longest hot dog in the world was made in Japan. It measured 600 metres.
6 The most popular fast food in Britain is sandwiches.
7 The heaviest tomato in the world weighed 3.5 kilograms.
8 Scientists think that the oldest soup in the world was made from hippopotamuses.

6D Listening & functional language 1 exercises 1 & 2 1.51

S = Student W = Waiter

W: Hello. *La Vie en Rose*. Can I help you?

S: Er, yes, good afternoon. I'd like to book a table for Friday, please.

W: Certainly, madam. For how many people?

S: There'll be ten of us.

W: Yes, that's fine. What time would you like? We open at seven.

S: Oh, no, not seven. Nine. Nine o'clock, if that's possible, please.

W: Yes, certainly, we can do that for you. So, that's a large table for ten at nine o'clock on Friday. Could I take your name, please?

S: Yes, the name's Mayer. M-A-Y-E-R. Betty Mayer.

W: OK, I've got that, Ms Mayer. We look forward to seeing you on Friday evening.

S: Great. So, er, yes, we'll see you on Friday. Bye.

6D Pronunciation exercise 1 1.52

Not seven. Nine.

6D Pronunciation exercise 3 1.53

1 Friday evening. Not Thursday evening.
2 It's Ms. Not Mrs.
3 Good? It was excellent!
4 No dessert, thanks. Just coffee.

6D Listening & functional language 2 exercises 1 & 2 1.54

W = Waiter B = Betty S1 = Student 1
S2 = Student 2 S3 = Student 3 S4 = Student 4

W: Good evening, madam. Welcome to *La Vie en Rose*.

B: Good evening. The name is Mayer. I have a reservation for ten people. Two of them aren't here yet, but they'll be here soon.

W: Certainly, madam. Let me show you to your table. It's this way.

B: Thank you.
W: Can I take your coats?
S1/S2/S3: Yes, thanks. / Thanks. / No, that's all right.
W: Would you like something to drink? Or would you like to see the menu first?
...
W: Are you ready to order?
B: Yes, I think so.
S1: Yes, for starters, I'll have a mixed salad, please.
S2: And I'll have the soup, I think.
S3: No starters for me, thanks.
S4: Mixed salad for me, too, please.
W: OK, so that's two mixed salads, one soup ...
B: Oh, and could we have a bottle of mineral water, please? In fact, make that two. One sparkling, one still.
...
S1: Mmm, that was delicious.
B: Yeah, really good. Marvellous.
S2/S3/S4: Hmm, yes. / Excellent. / Fantastic soup!
S3: And the service was good, too. He was ever so friendly.
B: Well, shall we get the bill?
S1/S2: Yes, let's./Yes, let's do that.
B: Excuse me. Could you bring us the bill, please?
W: Certainly, madam. I'll get it right away.

7A Listening exercises 1 & 2 2.1

J = Jerry V = Valerio M = Michelle
T = Tony

J: Welcome back to *Tell Jerry*. Today we're taking calls from people who've met famous people in their work. Our first caller is Valerio from New Jersey. Valerio, hello. I understand you work as a chauffeur in New York.
V: Yeah, that's right. It's my own company, man. I'm in charge.
J: Valerio, have you ever met anyone famous in your work? I mean, have you ever driven any stars in your car?
V: Yeah, I've had a few. Like, erm, I've had, like, Madonna, recently, Leonardo DiCaprio, yeah, I've had some.
J: Have you ever spoken to any of them?
V: No, I've never had, like, a real conversation. Just 'Good day, sir', 'Good day, ma'am', that kind of thing.
J: OK, thank you, Valerio. And over to our next caller. On the line is Michelle from Santa Monica. Michelle, hi, what do you do for a living?
M: Hi, Jerry. I'm a customer service assistant in a restaurant. You know, a waitress?
J: Michelle, who have you met at work?
M: Brad Pitt and Angelina Jolie. I've served Brad and Angelina.
J: Hey, what were they like?
M: I guess, they were, you know, kind of cute.
J: Michelle, have you ever had any difficult customers? Difficult stars?
M: I can't tell you that! I'll lose my job, I mean, I'll get fired if I tell you that!
J: OK, Michelle, thanks. To our next caller. Hi, this is Jerry, who is on the line?
T: Hello, Jerry. My name's Tony Lewington, calling from Manhattan.
J: Good afternoon, Tony. Tony, that's not an American accent.
T: No, I'm from Perth in Australia. I'm working for an ice cream shop in downtown Manhattan. Um, I've met a few stars in the shop. Tom Cruise, for example. And that other Tom, I can't remember his name, the one who was in *The Da Vinci Code*, Tom ...
J: Tom Hanks?
T: Yeah, that's the one. Nice guy. He paid with a ten-dollar bill and told me to keep the change. Nice guy.
J: OK. Thank you, Tony, from Perth in Australia.

7A Pronunciation exercise 1 2.2

drunk sang began run drank swam ran
begun sung swum

7B Vocabulary & speaking exercise 3 2.3

When Pat Side's children finished their studies and left home, Pat wanted to find a job. She had no qualifications, so she went on a training course to become an assistant in a home for retired people. After the course, she applied for many different jobs. She went for a few interviews, but it was six months before she got a job. She was good at her work and, two years later, she was promoted to 'senior assistant'. She also got a small pay rise. Unfortunately, the home closed a year after that and Pat lost her job.

7D Listening exercises 1 & 2 2.4

C = Consultant R = Ruby

C: Come in.
R: Oh, hello. Good morning. I have an appointment.
C: Yes, come in. It's Miss Tuesday, isn't it?
R: Erm, yes, it's Ms, actually. Not Miss.
C: I'm sorry. Come in, have a seat. Why don't you take your coat off?
R: Thanks. And sorry I'm a bit late. I was making a copy of my CV.
C: That's OK. Could I see it? Thanks.
R: I know it's a little short, but I didn't know what else to write. Should I make it a little longer?
C: Well perhaps a little more information would be a good idea. I mean, for example, do you have any qualifications?
R: Not yet, no. But I'm thinking of going to evening classes. It's just, I haven't decided what to study.
C: Well, all in good time. But getting a qualification is definitely something you should think about. And perhaps you could include your personal interests on your CV?
R: Mmm. I could put down computers, perhaps. I'm quite interested in computers and the internet and things like that.
C: What about doing a course in computer skills? Anyway, I see that you're working in a fast food restaurant ...
R: Yes, and I hate it. That's why I'm here. I'm looking for something else. I don't know what. But anything is better than serving hamburgers all day.
C: Well, we'll see what we can do. But first, I think you should think about getting a qualification.
R: You mean you can't do anything for me now?

C: Not really, no, I'm sorry. But I could give you a bit more advice, if you like.
R: Oh, yes, please. Thanks.
C: Well, the first thing is, I mean, if I were you, I'd arrive for interviews on time. It gives a good impression.
R: Yes, I'm sorry about that ...
C: And, erm, what about wearing something smarter next time? I don't think jeans are a terribly good idea for an interview.
R: Oh, right ... Anything else?
C: Well ...

7D Pronunciation exercise 1 2.5

davina at sayers dot co dot uk
www dot sayers hyphen rt dot com
www dot sayers hyphen rt dot org slash index slash html
davinasayers (all one word) at srt dot net

8A Pronunciation exercise 1 2.6

I'll it'll there'll we'll what'll you'll

8A Pronunciation exercise 3 2.7

1 Aren't you ready yet? Hurry up! / I won't be long.
2 Be careful – it's very dangerous. / I'll be OK.
3 I wonder where they are. / They'll be here soon.
4 Let's have a drink before the film starts. / We'll be late.
5 What's this? I've never eaten that before. / You'll like it.

8A Speaking exercise 1 2.8–2.10

1 Right, er, well, there'll be more and more supermarkets ... Um, you see more and more of the same kinds of shops everywhere, you know. Everywhere you go you see the same things, the same chains – so more supermarkets on the outside of the town. Er, the town centres will get quieter and quieter, no – there'll, there'll be less, um, less shops in the town centres and there'll be more bars and cafés and things like that, um, so people will ... er, use their cars, I guess, more. Is that thirty seconds yet?
2 Everybody says that, er, you know, everybody will need English in the future, but I ... I don't think this is true because, um, you know, you need, um, English for computers and the internet and that, but with ... with, um ... There's more and more Chinese people in the world, so, you know, we'll, maybe, we'll speak Chinese, we'll all need to speak Chinese because, um, 'cos ... 'cos we will, and, er, um ...
3 If you think about medicine now and you think about medicine, say one hundred years ago, the differences, um, are ... are incredible because we can ... we can do so many things now that we couldn't do then, like, you know, we've got a cure for polio, we've got a cure for lots of diseases, and ... and transplants and things, so I guess in the future we'll, you know, carry on and we'll find cures for more and more things and we'll, um ... That must be thirty seconds.

8B Listening exercises 2 & 3 2.11

Back in 2001, American millionaire Dennis Tito became the world's first space tourist. He wrote a 20-million dollar cheque for the privilege. Since then, there have been another six space tourists, and they have all paid millions for the experience. Others will probably follow soon, but who will they be? One thing is for sure: it certainly won't be you, unless you have a few million dollars. Or perhaps it will be!

A European television consortium, Eurorbit, has announced plans for a new TV game show. The show, which will probably be called *Star Quest*, will have contestants from all the countries in the European Union. It will test the contestants' general knowledge, their skills and their ability to work in a team. Contestants will need to be fit and to speak English, but men and women of all ages are welcome to apply. The programme's organizers hope to film the thirteen-part show at different science museums around Europe – in London, Florence, Paris and at the New Metropolis Science and Technology Center in Amsterdam. And the prize? The winner of the show will take his, or her, seat in a space ship some time next year. After training at the European Space Academy, the winner will blast off for an eight-day trip to the stars and a visit to the International Space Station. Or perhaps not. Not everyone is happy with the idea. Will scientists in America at NASA refuse permission for the winner to visit the space station? They were unhappy with Dennis Tito's trip and say that this kind of space tourism is too dangerous. 'This idea is so stupid,' said one expert at New York University. However, a spokesman for Eurorbit said that the Americans will probably agree some kind of deal. Whatever happens, he said, the winner of the competition will definitely go into space. But it's possible that they won't be able to visit the space station. The organizers of the programme are taking applications now. So if you want to be the next space tourist, send your request to contestant@eurorbit.com. That's contestant@eurorbit.com. And good luck!

8B Pronunciation exercise 2 2.12

1 certainly energy probably unhappy
2 businessman engineer president scientist
3 dangerous internet invention satellite
4 advantage computer conference contestant
5 equipment exciting possible remember

8C Listening & speaking exercise 1 2.13

1 Looking for a laugh? Get one of these gooey balls and throw it at a window. Just watch your colleagues' faces as it slides down the window making strange shapes.
2 Now you can write secret messages with our invisible ink. With a special ultraviolet light reader, you can read them, too!
3 You can't find your keys? Again! Just whistle and it will flash and beep. You'll find your keys in an instant ... and losing them will be fun!
4 Feeling thirsty? Well, here's your own personal water machine for your desk in the office. It holds eight cups. With this in front of you, you can be sure you'll drink all the water you need.

5 Did you know that colours can change the way you feel? Do you sometimes wake up in the morning feeling (and looking!) grey? With one of these, you can wake up in the morning to a bright, colourful tomorrow.

8D Listening exercises 1 & 2 2.14

G = Grandfather K = Karen

G: Karen, could you give me a hand with this?
K: Sure. What are you trying to do?
G: I want to send an email.
K: Yes, OK. Are you online?
G: Erm, not sure.
K: Here, look, first of all, click on that button there. That connects you to the internet.
G: Oh, right. Like this?
K: Yes, that's right. But do it twice, a double click. OK, now you're online. Right, now click on that email icon. There.
G: OK, got it.
K: OK, then click on 'Write Mail', OK?
G: Yes, OK. There's a lot to remember, isn't there?
K: You'll soon pick it up. Oh, you see the little picture of an address book? You type the address there next to the icon. You're writing to Dad! What are you writing to Dad for?
G: Just to surprise him. And I want to send him one of those pictures you took.
K: Oh, OK.
G: Anyway, what next?
K: Well, next you write your message. In the big space there.
G: It's a short message! S-U-R-P-R-I-S-E. That's it. And the photo?
K: OK, first of all, click there on 'attach'. OK, good, and then we have to find the photo. Here, I'll do it for you. OK, that's it.
G: That's it. So, I just click on 'send'?
K: Yes. And don't forget to log off.
G: OK. Wonderful. Thanks. When will he get it? Does it take long to arrive?

9A Speaking & listening exercises 2 & 3 2.15

N = Nick S = Sarah

N: Now for our weekly look at what's on. Sarah, what have you got for us this week?
S: Well, probably the most exciting concert of the summer is happening on Sunday and Monday this week at half-past seven. Lady Gaga, the incredible Lady Gaga is in town for two nights at the Wembley Arena. If you haven't got tickets, you'll be disappointed, but we've got two tickets to give away in this week's competition. Stay tuned. Also, this week, at the Sound Barrier in Oxford Street, there's a special Brazilian night with top DJs playing the latest sounds from Brazil's coolest clubs. Doors open at ten o'clock and you can dance until four in the morning. The place to be for a really cool night out.
N: Erm, yes, a little past my bedtime, I think. Sorry to be boring and old-fashioned. What else have you got for us?
S: Well, there's a fascinating afternoon of dance at Canary Wharf. It's part of a festival and they've got groups from Switzerland, France and Spain. It all sounds very interesting and it's free. That's Saturday between one and five, and let's hope the weather stays fine.
N: Yes, indeed. Sounds very interesting.
S: And if you're interested in dance, don't forget that you can still see *Mamma Mia*, London's most popular and enjoyable musical, at the Prince of Wales Theatre. Performances are on at half-past seven Monday to Saturday, with an afternoon show on Saturdays at half-past three. No shows on Sunday.
N: Right.
S: The next thing I've got is something for you. This Friday, there's a performance of Verdi's *Requiem* at the Royal Festival Hall. That's half-past seven Friday.
N: Ah, yes, a beautiful piece of music!
S: Isn't it a bit depressing going to listen to a requiem?
N: Pardon?
S: Right, what next? Yes, there's an absolutely fantastic exhibition at the National Gallery. Paintings by the Spanish impressionist, Camille Pissarro.
N: Pissarro.
S: Yes. You'll be surprised – these paintings are really amazing. Every day from nine in the morning to six o'clock. Ooh, and one last idea. A fun idea for all the family. The Moscow State Circus is in Alexandra Park this week from Tuesday to Sunday. Not to be missed.
N: Thank you, Sarah. Time now to go over to the news room, but stay tuned for details of our competition with two tickets for Lady Gaga ...

9A Vocabulary exercise 3 2.16

1

A: I'm so excited. I've got tickets for the Lady Gaga concert.
B: Lady Gaga? I think her music is boring.

2

A: I'm really tired. I didn't get home until three o'clock this morning.
B: I know. And it was extremely annoying that you came home singing.

3

A: I think this music is really relaxing.
B: Really? It makes me feel depressed.

4

A: The concert was a bit disappointing, wasn't it?
B: Yes, I was surprised. Celine Dion is usually so good.

9A Pronunciation exercise 2 2.17

night /aɪ/ find, kind, quite, time, twice
know /əʊ/ go, home, most, show
now /aʊ/ down, house, out, sound, town
name /eɪ/ fame, place, Spain, state, stay

9B Grammar exercise 3 2.18

Star Academy

Thousands of young people apply to take part in this programme. They send video tapes to the producers and a group of them are chosen to take part. During the series, they live in a castle, where they are taught to sing and dance. They are not allowed to speak to their friends or family and every moment of their life in the castle is filmed. Their lives are shown on TV every evening, and on Saturday, there is a special show. A famous TV star is invited on the show and one of the contestants sings a song with him or her. At the end of the programme, there is a vote and one person is sent home. At the end of the series, the winner is given a contract to make an album.

9D Pronunciation exercise 1 2.19

first second third fourth fifth sixth eleventh twelfth thirteenth fifteenth sixteenth twentieth twenty-first twenty-second twenty-third twenty-fourth thirty-first

9D Pronunciation exercise 2 2.20

1 September the twentieth.
2 The twentieth of September.

9D Pronunciation exercise 3 2.21

On the seventh of August, we have the Cuban salsa band, Los Van Van. Then, for two nights, on the twelfth and thirteenth of August, we have Justin Timberlake. Coldplay are coming on the twenty-second of August, and we have the Red Hot Chili Peppers on September the third and fourth. For lovers of classical music, there is an evening with Cecilia Bartoli on September the twenty-first. Also, beginning on October the thirty-first, you can see Tchaikovsky's *Swan Lake*. Shakira is coming on the third of November, and on the fifth of November we have Handel's *Messiah*. The sixteenth of November is *A Night with Mr Bean* and on November the twenty-second, the Wynton Marsalis Septet are in town. Justin Bieber is coming on the second of December, and on the fourth of December there is a special tribute to the Beatles. From December the seventeenth to the twenty-fourth, we have our children's show, *Beauty and the Beast*, and finally on the thirty-first of December, there is the Johann Strauss New Year concert.

9D Listening exercises 3 & 4 2.22–2.25

1 BO = Box office M = Mary

BO: Metropolitan Box Office. This is Trevor speaking. Can I help you?
M: Yes, hello. I'd like to book three tickets for *Beauty and the Beast*, please.
BO: Certainly, madam. How many tickets do you want?
M: Three, please.
BO: Yes. And what date would you like?
M: The Tuesday before Christmas. December the twenty-third.
BO: And would you like the matinee or the evening performance?
M: Oh, the matinee, the matinee. It's for a young child, you see.
BO: OK. Well, we've got all tickets available for that performance. what sort of seats would you like?
M: The front of the stalls if you have them.
BO: We do indeed. Those seats cost eighty pounds each, so that'll be three times eighty, that's two hundred and forty.
M: Two hundred and forty.
BO: Right. Can I have your name, please?

2 BO = Box office B = Becky

BO: Metropolitan Box Office. This is Trevor speaking. Can I help you?
B: Hello, good afternoon. I'd like two tickets for Wynton Marsalis, please.
BO: Yes, the Wynton Marsalis Septet. Saturday the twenty-second of November. Half-past seven.
B: Have you got anything in the circle?
BO: Front or rear?
B: How much are the seats at the front?
BO: I've got two right in the middle at the front for thirty-eight pounds.
B: Oh, great. Fine.
BO: So, that's seventy-six pounds altogether. Could I take your details, please?
B: Yes, the name's …

3 BO = Box office S = Stephen

BO: Metropolitan Box Office. This is Trevor speaking. Can I help you?
S: Yeah, I want a ticket for the Red Hot Chilis on the fourth of September.
BO: The Red Hot Chili Peppers? I'll just check for you. September the fourth … No, I'm sorry, sir, we're sold out.
S: What about the other day? The third of September.
BO: Yes, we've got a few tickets left in the rear stalls.
S: Oh, great. How much are they?
BO: Er, they're forty-six pounds, including a booking fee of two pounds.
S: How much?
BO: Forty-six pounds altogether.
S: Forty-six pounds!? Forget it.

4 BO = Box office P = Pablo

BO: Metropolitan Box Office. This is Trevor speaking. Can I help you?
P: Good afternoon. I'd like two tickets for the evening with Cecilia Bartoli, please.
BO: Certainly, sir.
P: The best seats you've got, please.
BO: I'll see what seats we've got available. We've got a couple of seats at the front of the circle at eighty pounds each.
P: Oh, fantastic.
BO: And there's a booking fee of five pounds, so that'll be one hundred and seventy pounds altogether.
P: Fine.
Could I take your details, please …

10A Grammar exercise 2 2.26

Oscar Werbeniuk, who is 61, has lived all his life in the same New Jersey house. He has loved animals, especially cats, since he was a child. He found his first cat, Tabatha, in the street in 1981, and he has found another 43 cats since then. But Tabatha – who died in 1990 – had babies and Oscar soon had more than a hundred cats. For the last fifteen years, there have been more than two hundred cats in his house. Oscar is lucky because his parents were very rich, so he has never worried about money. In fact, since 1999, Oscar has been so busy that he hasn't left his house.

10C Listening exercises 2 & 3 2.27

P = **Presenter** **S** = **Sunil**

P: ... and now it's over to Sunil Gupta in New York to bring us up to date with news of this weekend's big event, the New York Marathon.

S: Yes, it's all over here. This year's winner of the men's race was the Kenyan, Martin Lel, in an official time of 2 hours 10 minutes and 30 seconds. In an exciting finish, Lel pushed last year's winner, Rodgers Rop into second place. Another Kenyan, Margaret Okayo, took the women's race in a time of 2 hours 22 minutes and 31 seconds. But the big event of the afternoon for many of the spectators in Central Park was the arrival of two Britons, Ranulph Fiennes and Mike Stroud. Despite their slow time of almost five and a half hours, they will surely be in the *Guinness Book of Records*.
For Fiennes and Stroud, this was an incredible seventh marathon in seven days in seven different continents. Their marathon began last week in Patagonia in the deep south of South America. In the last week, they have been to the Antarctic, Sydney, Singapore, London and Cairo, completing a marathon at each stopover. Incredibly, Ranulph Fiennes suffered a heart attack earlier this year and had a heart operation just three months ago. Fiennes and Stroud have raised millions of pounds for the British Heart Foundation by completing the marathon in New York today. On previous expeditions, they have raised more than four million pounds for a multiple sclerosis research centre and two million pounds for a breast cancer clinic. They have been to the North and South Poles, and they have walked across the Andes. The two runners, however, did not celebrate at the party in Central Park after the race. A spokesman for the British Heart Foundation said, 'Both runners have gone home. They caught a plane to London earlier this evening. Dr Fiennes has gone to join his wife before going into hospital for a check-up on his heart next week. Dr Stroud has gone to London for a day of rest before returning to work on Tuesday morning.' This is Sunil Gupta reporting from New York's Central Park.

10C Grammar exercise 3 2.28

J = **Jane** **M** = **Mark**

J: Hello.
M: Hi, it's Mark here. Is Rick there, please?
J: Hi, Mark. No, I'm sorry. He's gone away for the week.
M: Oh? Work? Holiday?
J: Both. He's gone to Patagonia – for a walk.
M: Oh, I've been there. Twice. It's really nice. Why didn't you go with him?
J: Because my boss has gone to Nepal on business so I'm in charge of the office.
M: Nepal? Nice!
J: Have you been there, too?
M: Yes, I've been a few times, actually.
J: Really? I've only been there once. I liked it.
M: Yes, it's an excellent place for walking.
J: Yes. Well, I'll tell him you called.
M: OK. Thanks. Bye, Jane.
J: Bye, Mark.

10C Pronunciation exercise 3 2.29

1 awful /ˈɔːfəl/
2 caught /kɔːt/
3 cause /kɔːz/
4 daughter /ˈdɔːtə/
5 important /ɪmˈpɔːtənt/
6 morning /ˈmɔːnɪŋ/
7 squash /skwɒʃ/
8 thought /θɔːt/
9 walk /wɔːk/
10 would /wʊd/

10D Listening exercises 1 & 2 2.30–2.31

1 **D** = **Doctor** **S** = **Sarah**

S: Hello.
D: Come in, come in, take a seat.
S: Thanks.
D: Now, how can I help you? What seems to be the matter?
S: Well, lots of things, actually.
D: Mmm?
S: I've got a headache all the time. And a cold.
D: And a cough.
S: Yes. And it hurts everywhere. I mean, I've got pains in my back, my chest, my neck, everywhere. I just feel awful.
D: OK, well, let's start by taking your temperature, OK? Hmm, let's see. 39° – that's quite high.
S: Nothing serious, is it? Is it flu?
D: Yes, it's probably flu. But it's nothing to worry about. Now. Anything else? Any other symptoms?
S: Well, I suppose I'm feeling a bit depressed. But maybe that's normal. There are lots of problems at work at the moment.
D: Well, that's understandable. I hope everything works out. Anyway, you've got flu and you'll need to take four or five days off work. Rest as much as possible; stay in bed. Take some aspirin or paracetamol for the pain.

S: OK.
D: I'll give you a prescription for some strong paracetamol, and I'll give you a letter for work. Four or five days and you feel much better. OK?
S: Oh, right, thanks. I was worried that it was something much more serious. And a few days off work is always good – even when you're ill!
D: But make sure you rest, eh?

2 D = Doctor R = Roger

D: Ah, Mr Hunter, good morning.
R: Morning.
D: Nice to see you again. What seems to be the matter?
R: I've, er, I've had a stomach ache for a few days. It really hurts. Very bad, you know, I don't even want to think about food.
D: So, you're not eating anything?
R: Not really, no. I mean, coffee, I'm drinking coffee, that's about the only thing I can take at the moment.
D: Just coffee?
R: Yes, I mean, the thing is I've got a meeting in New York later in the week, and I hate flying, and every time I think about getting in the plane, my stomach hurts, and sometimes I get a headache, sometimes I feel cold, sometimes I feel hot, or hot and cold, you know, and I'm not hungry, and I think of that plane, and I think, no, I can't, I mean, you know, what if the plane crashes or something, and then I get this really, really big, big headache, and my eyes hurt, here, my eyes, behind the eyes, you know, it's really painful.
D: Calm down, calm down. Now, I think that it's probably not a very good idea for you to go to New York. Not this week, anyway.
R: What?
D: Well, it seems to me that you are not well enough to travel. Your symptoms point to stress, extreme stress. I'll write a letter for your work, OK? But I think you should see a specialist. Someone who can help you with your fear of flying. But first of all, you need to eat.
R: You mean, I won't have to fly to New York?
D: Here, I'll write the letter, but you must promise that you will eat something, all right?
R: I'm feeling better already!

10D Functional language exercise 3 2.32

D = Doctor P = Patient

D: Come in. Take a seat.
P: Thank you.
D: Now, what's the matter?
P: I feel awful. It's my back.
D: Where does it hurt?
P: Here and here.
D: OK. I'll have a look at you. Take off your shirt. Does this hurt?
P: Yes, it does. It's very painful. Is it serious?
D: No, it's nothing to worry about.
P: What's wrong with me? Do you know?
D: I think you've pulled a muscle.
P: Is there anything I can take for it?
D: Yes, I'll give you a prescription.
P: Thank you. And what about work? Is it OK to work?
D: No, not at the moment. I think you should take a few days off work. And come back and see me in ten days.
P: OK. I'll make an appointment with the receptionist. Thank you. Bye.

10D Pronunciation exercise 1 2.33

P: Doctor, doctor, what did the X-ray of my head show?
D: Absolutely nothing!

10D Pronunciation exercise 3 2.34–2.36

P = Patient D = Doctor

1

P: Doctor, doctor, I'm seeing double.
D: Take a seat, please.
P: Which one?

2

P: Doctor, doctor, I've got a memory problem.
D: How long have you had this problem?
P: What problem?

3

P: Doctor, doctor, I feel very nervous. This is the first operation I've ever had.
D: Don't worry. It's my first time, too.

11A Listening exercises 2 & 3 2.37–2.38

S = Susan K = Katy

S: I was just starting in business, a small advertising business with my sister, and in those days it was hard for women to run a business. Most of our clients were men, and we took them out to restaurants and ball games, you know, we took them out to make them feel good, to impress them, too, of course, and we wanted them to take us seriously. Then, one evening, I was in a restaurant and the woman at the table next to mine, when the check came, she held up this little card to pay. American Express, I think it was. I really, really wanted a card like her. So, I spoke to my sister, and she agreed it was a good idea, and we filled in a form to apply for a card. The first time I used it, you know, to pay for a meal with a client, he was really impressed. He signed the contract right there in the restaurant! Best investment we ever made!
K: What did I really want when I was younger? Independence, really. I was living with my parents and it took me ages to get into town to go out for the evening. And I needed some way to get home because the last train was really early. So, anyway, I was saving up to buy a Mini, but when I saw my first Ford Capri, I took one look at it and knew that was what I wanted. It took me two years to get enough money, but, in the end, there I was, the owner of my very own sexy Capri Mark I 1600, metallic yellow and sexy sports wheels. It was the biggest change in my life. I've done hundreds of thousands of miles in it. And I've still got it, actually.

11A Functional language exercise 1 2.39–2.40

1 Good afternoon, I'm looking for a – I'm sorry I don't know the right word. It's a kind of computer, a little one that you can put in your pocket. You know, it's a thing you send emails with, I think. In fact, I'm not really sure what you do with it. But you know what I mean. A little computer. It's a present for my grandson.

2 Good morning. I'm looking for some, erm, what do you call them? You know, they're a sort of shoe. Well, not really a shoe, but, erm, well, yes they're a sort of shoe, really. You use them to go to the beach. In the summer. You see all the young people wearing them. Do you know what I mean?

11A Pronunciation exercise 1 2.41

/θ/ thanks thing thousand
/ð/ than this those

11A Pronunciation exercise 3 2.42

What do you think of their theory?
Do they think the same thing as the others?
Let's meet on Thursday the thirteenth at three o'clock.
They thought the theatre was over there.

11C Grammar exercise 3 2.43

My twin brother and I are the oldest in a family of seven. When I was a teenager, I had to look after my brothers and sisters until my parents came home from work. My brother was really lucky – because he was a boy, he didn't have to do anything. I couldn't see my friends or go out because I had to do my homework when my parents got home. I wanted to go to college, but I couldn't get a place because I did badly in my exams. I got a job where I didn't have to work in the evenings, so I could go to evening school. For ten years, I had to work and study really hard, but I finally got the qualification that I wanted and I became a teacher.

11D Listening exercises 2 & 4 2.44–2.47

1

A: Ooh, that looks nice! What do you think?
B: For you maybe, not for me.
A: Do you think so?
B: Yeah. That kind of thing really suits you.
A: All right, come on. Let's go in.
B: You know you can't afford shops like that!
A: You never know. Let's see if they have my size.
B: Come on, let's go and have a look.

2

A: Hey, look. This one would go well with my new trousers.
B: I don't think black goes with brown at all.
A: It's not black. It's grey. Anyway, who says that black doesn't go with brown?
B: I dunno, I just, I don't think they go together. Why don't you try it on? You'll see what I mean.
A: All right. I believe you.
B: Anyway, the shirt you're wearing suits you just fine.

3

A: How do I look?
B: You look great.
A: You really think so?
B: Yes. Really. Although it's a bit tight perhaps. Perhaps one size bigger would fit you better.
A: But I couldn't find the next size.
B: Well, just wear a thin top under it, and then it'll be OK.
A: That's a thought. It's a summer jacket anyway, isn't it? I'm not exactly going to wear a heavy sweater or anything, am I?

4

A: Do they fit at the back?
B: Yes, the length looks about right. But they don't really go with the boots you're wearing.
A: They feel comfortable. But perhaps I'll try on the next size.
B: No, they're fine. Take them. They look really good on you. Seriously.
A: You're just saying that because you want to get out of here.
B: No, I'm not. You look almost smart. Get them.
A: No, I'm going to think about it. I can always come back tomorrow.

11D Pronunciation exercise 1 2.48

What do you think?
Let's go and have a look.
Why don't you try it on?
That's a thought.
I'm going to think about it.

11D Functional language exercise 2 2.49

1

A: Good morning, sir. Can I help you?
B: No, thanks. I'm just looking.

2

A: Excuse me.
B: Yes, madam. How can I help you?
A: I'm looking for a black jacket.
B: Certainly. What size are you?
A: Medium.

3

A: Can I try this on, please?
B: Of course, the changing room is over there.

4

A: How does it fit?
B: Fine, fine. Have you got it in green?
A: I'm afraid not, sir.

5

A: I'll take this, please.
B: Certainly, madam. How would you like to pay?
A: Credit card.

12A Listening exercises 1 & 2 2.50

More than a year after Steve Fossett disappeared, while flying over the Sierra Nevada Mountains, police have confirmed that they have found the remains of his body. Fossett was 63 and one of the world's most extraordinary people. With 116 world records in five different sports, Steve Fossett was a hero and an inspiration to thousands.

Perhaps his greatest achievement was to become the first person to fly solo in a balloon around the world. During the journey of more than 33,000 kilometres, Fossett had a number of serious problems and he almost called the attempt off. At the start, he had to put off his departure for three hours because of a problem with wind, but finally managed to take off, flying past Sydney and New Zealand and over the Pacific Ocean. At one point, his burner stopped working; later, there was a fire in the balloon, but Fossett was not a man who gave up easily. This was, after all, his sixth attempt! The difficulties were sorted out and he carried on with his epic journey. He arrived back in Australia after just under fifteen days.

Fossett had both determination and endurance. As a young man, he enjoyed mountain climbing and cross-country skiing, but one of his great early achievements was, on his fourth attempt, to swim across the Channel between England and France. He twice took part in a 2,000-kilometre dog race in Alaska, he twice drove in the 24-hour motor-racing Classic at Le Mans in France, and he also drove in the Paris to Dakar Rally. As a sailor, he set world records for sailing around the world and across the Atlantic, along with records for speed sailing. In total, he set 32 world records in a boat. It seemed that Fossett was a man who could do anything. Sadly, he is with us no more.

12A Pronunciation exercise 1 2.51

first person /fɜ:st ˈpɜ:sən/
third world /θɜ:d wɜ:ld/
journey to work /ˈdʒɜ:nɪ tə wɜ:k/
word search /wɜ:d sɜ:tʃ/

12A Pronunciation exercise 3 2.52

1 burn /bɜ:n/; circle /ˈsɜ:kəl/; heart /hɑ:t/; journey /ˈdʒɜ:ni/
2 birth /bɜ:θ/; compare /kəmˈpeə/; early /ˈɜ:li/; nervous /ˈnɜ:vəs/
3 earn /ɜ:n/; girl /gɜ:l/; heard /hɜ:d/; record /ˈrekɔ:d/
4 interest /ˈɪntrəst/; learn /lɜ:n/; nurse /nɜ:(r)s/; service /ˈsɜ:vɪs/

12C Vocabulary exercise 5 2.53

The most widely-spoken language in the world is Mandarin Chinese with approximately 1 billion speakers. Next comes the Indian language family of Hindi, Bengali, Punjabi and so on. More than half a billion people speak one or more of these languages. After that, we have English which also has more than 500 million speakers (including speakers of English as a second or third language). The next language on our list is Spanish, with speakers in Spain, Central and South America. Next is Russian, followed by Arabic. At number seven on our list is Portuguese with about 200 million speakers and finally, at number eight, is French with about 130 million.

12C Pronunciation exercise 1 2.54

1 answer ask banana castle dance example France glass
2 answer ask banana castle dance example France glass

12C Pronunciation exercise 2 2.55

address, address
café, café
cigarette, cigarette
magazine, magazine
weekend, weekend

12D Listening exercises 1 & 2 2.56–2.58

M = Man **W** = Woman

1

M: Hiya.
W: Hi.
M: Can I get you a drink? Do you want some crisps?
W: A juice, please. But crisps, no. I try to avoid junk food.
M: Oh, I think they're quite tasty myself.
W: They taste of chemicals, and genetically modified potatoes. I prefer to eat natural, organic food, if I can.
M: I see what you mean, but I still think they're quite tasty. Nothing wrong with a crisp or two, surely?
W: Well, I'm sorry, but that's not the way I see it. I think we should all eat organic.
M: Yes, yes, I agree with you, but not all the time, maybe. And some of that organic food is a real waste of money.
W: I'm afraid I disagree. It's not just about taste. It's about saving our planet. I'm worried about it, even if you're not. Now, sorry, will you excuse me?
M: So you don't want me to get the juice for you, then?

2

M: Have you heard about this new internet virus that's going around?
W: Yeah, a friend of mine got it on her laptop, and she's lost everything.
M: That's terrible. God knows why people spend their time inventing viruses.

W: But I don't know what anyone can do about it. Maybe the United Nations could do something.
M: The United Nations? You must be joking! They never do anything about anything.
W: Well, I don't know. I'm sure the Americans could do something about it. I mean, if they wanted to.
M: Oh, definitely. But, well, I don't know ... but the police could do something more about online crime. It can't be that difficult.
W: Yeah, you're probably right. Anyway, let's get a drink.

3

M: 'Scuse me. Have we met before?
W: I don't think so. No.
M: Oh, well. Nice weather, innit? Nice and warm, eh?
W: Well, it's definitely very warm, but 'nice', no, I wouldn't say that.
M: You prefer it cold, then?
W: Definitely not. I just mean that there's nothing very nice about global warming.
M: Oh, you don't believe all that stuff about global warming? I don't care about that! You can't believe everything you read in the press.
W: Well, maybe, but it's not just the journalists. It's the politicians and it's the scientists, too.
M: Not all of them! And you can't believe everything the scientists say, either.
W: Perhaps not. But most scientists are very sure about global warming.
M: Well, you may be right. I don't really know a lot about it to be honest. My name's Ben, by the way.

12D Functional language exercise 2 2.59

Agree: I agree with you. Oh, absolutely ... (definitely)
That's how I feel, too. That's what I think, too.
Partly agree: I see your point, but ...
I see what you mean, but ... Well, maybe, but ...
Disagree: I'm afraid I disagree. I'm not sure about that.
That's not the way I see it.
Strongly disagree: You can't be serious. You must be joking.

1 | Review

1 Complete the questions with a word from the box.

how (x2)	what (x3)	when	who	why

1 _______ is her name?
2 _______ was she born?
3 _______ many brothers and sisters does she have?
4 _______ colour is her hair?
5 _______ languages does she speak?
6 _______ is she famous?
7 _______ rich is she?
8 _______ was her grandfather?

2 Match the answers below to the questions in exercise 1.

1 because she is very rich
2 in 1985
3 reddish brown
4 Athina Roussel
5 she has more than $2 billion
6 Swedish, French and English
7 the Greek businessman, Aristotle Onassis
8 three

3 Write questions for the sentences below.

1 *What did Athina's mother give her for her second birthday?*

1 Athina's mother gave her a zoo for her second birthday.
2 Her mother died in 1988.
3 Athina lived in Switzerland.
4 Her father and step-mother have a house in Lausanne.
5 Athina's first boyfriend was Alvaro Alfonso de Miranda Neta.
6 He comes from Brazil.
7 Athina calls him Doda.
8 Athina is very popular in Greece.

4 Rearrange the words to make questions.

1 a common do have him in lot with you ?
2 are best friend his you ?
3 go he school to did with you ?
4 at friends good school were you ?
5 married he is ?
6 live you near he does ?
7 did him see yesterday you ?
8 English speak can he ?

5 Match the short answers below to the questions in exercise 4.

a No, he doesn't.
b No, I didn't.
c No, I'm not.
d No, we weren't.
e Yes, he can.
f Yes, he did.
g Yes, he is.
h Yes, I do.

6 Think of a (male) friend. Work in pairs. Ask and answer the questions in exercise 4.

7 Each of the telephone messages below has two words missing. Insert the missing words.

1 I'm afraid ^ *there* is no one to take your call right now. Please leave ^ *your* name and I'll call you back.

2 Hello, this 2470362. There's no one at home the moment. Please leave a message after the beep.

3 Hello, my name is Sayers and I'm calling your advertisement in the newspaper. My number is 446091. Could call me back later, please?

4 This Ruby here. I'm not at home right now. Please leave your message and I'll try call you later. Many thanks.

5 Ruby, are you there? Ruby? It's Stuart. Can you give me a call at work some time afternoon? Or you can call me my mobile. It's urgent, OK?

8 Look at Sean Connery's family tree and decide if the sentences are true (T) or false (F). Correct the false sentences.

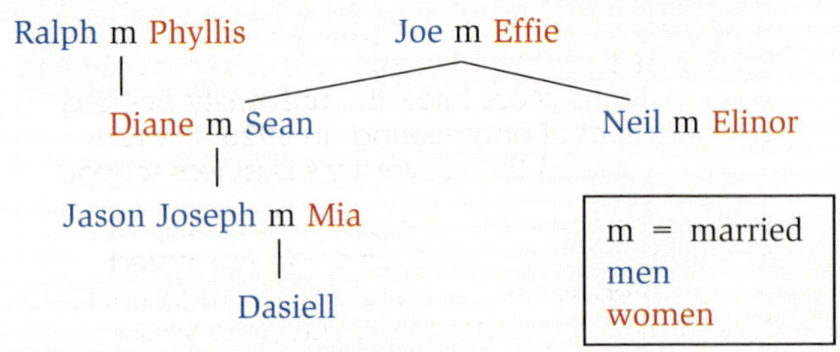

1 Diane is Mia's mother-in-law.
2 Effie is Jason Joseph's grandmother.
3 Elinor and Diane are cousins.
4 Elinor is Effie's aunt.
5 Jason Joseph is Neil's nephew.
6 Mia is Sean's niece.
7 Phyllis is Diane's mother.
8 Sean is Ralph's son-in-law.

2 | Review

1 Complete the text. Put the verbs in brackets into the past simple or the past continuous.

A few years ago, a student (1) ________ (*work*) for a telephone pizza company in the evenings after college. One day, she took a pizza to the richest man in town. The man (2) ________ (*pay*) the money, took the pizza and (3) ________ (*go*) into his house. He (4) ________ (*open*) the pizza box when the doorbell (5) ________ (*ring*) again. He went to the door and saw that the student was still there. Clearly, she (6) ________ (*wait*) for something. 'What do you want? A tip?' the man (7) ________ (*ask*). 'No, sir,' replied the student. 'When I (8) ________ (*put*) the pizza on my bike, I spoke to the boy who brought your pizza yesterday. He said you didn't give tips.' 'That's not true,' the man (9) ________ (*reply*). 'In fact, I'm very generous. Here, take five dollars.' 'That's very kind of you, sir,' said the student. 'I needed the money to buy a book for my course at college.' 'What are you studying?' asked the man. 'Psychology, sir.

2 Read the information about Trinity College in Dublin. Write six questions about the text in the past simple. Begin your questions with:

When
What did ...?
Where
When did Trinity College open?

Trinity College, Dublin, became the first Irish university when it opened in 1594. All the students studied the same subjects - Latin, Greek, mathematics, science and philosophy. In 1834, the university allowed students to study specialized subjects. Eight years later, the university opened a department of engineering. In 1925, the first students entered the university's business school.

At the beginning, Trinity College was only for Protestants. The first Catholic students arrived two hundred years later. Many famous writers studied at Trinity. Jonathan Swift (who wrote *Gulliver's Travels*) and Bram Stoker (who wrote *Dracula*) both went there. The first women did not enter Trinity College until 1904. Mary Robinson, who became the first woman Irish president in 1990, studied law at Trinity in the 1960s.

3 Work in pairs. Close your books. Ask and answer the questions in exercise 2.

4 Change the sentences below so that they are true for you. Use *used to* or *didn't use to* with the correct form of the verb in *italics*.

1 I used to go to a school near home when I was young.

1 I *went* to a school near home when I was young.
2 I *sat* at the front of the class.
3 I *was* the teacher's favourite pupil.
4 I *did* extra homework every day.
5 We *had* sport every Wednesday afternoon.
6 I *enjoyed* sport.
7 I *got* very good grades in all my subjects.
8 I *liked* English lessons.

5 Complete the first word of the questions below.

1 ________ I have some information about your English courses, please?
2 ________ there any examinations I can take?
3 ________ you have a school in the centre of town?
4 ________ long do the courses last?
5 ________ you tell me anything about the teachers?
6 ________ much do the courses cost?
7 ________ there a library that students can use?
8 ________ time is the class for beginners?

6 Match the sentences below to the questions in exercise 5.

1 The tuition fees are all on this piece of paper.
2 They're all very experienced and qualified.
3 Usually about ten weeks. We have the same terms as state schools.
4 We're very flexible and we have many different timetables.
5 Yes, certainly. And we usually get very good results.
6 Yes, certainly. There's a meeting for new pupils this afternoon, if you're interested.
7 Yes. We also have a language laboratory and multi-media centre.
8 Yes. We have eight different locations. You can choose.

3 | Review

1 In the newspaper article below there are eight mistakes. Correct the mistakes.

Melbourne
is the world's best city

The Australian city of Melbourne is the best place in the worlds to live.

THE AUSTRALIAN city of Melbourne is the best place in the worlds to live, says a report from the Economist Intelligence Unit. The EIU looked at more than one hundred city around the world. Melbourne got high grades for educations, entertainments and culture, housing, healths and weather. Because of this, more and more visitor are coming to Melbourne.

Other Australian cities also did well, but the report showed that there was more crimes in Sydney.

The best European cities were Vienna and Geneva, but Paris (28), Madrid (45=) and London (45=) were much lower in the list because of problems with crime, the weathers and the prices in the shops. New York and Washington had similar difficulties, but were lower in the list. ■

2 Complete the dialogue with *some*, *any* or *no*.

A: I'm phoning you about the flat you advertised in the newspaper. Are there (1) ______ rules I should know about?

B: Er, yes. You can't have (2) ______ pets. (3) ______ dogs, (4) ______ cats. We've had (5) ______ problems with animals in the past.

A: Oh, fine. I've got (6) ______ friends coming to visit me at the weekend. Is that OK?

B: That's (7) ______ problem. Visitors are very welcome until ten o'clock.

A: And after ten?

B: No. You can't have (8) ______ guests in your room after ten. House rules, I'm afraid.

A: Do you have (9) ______ other rules like that?

B: There are (10) ______ other little things, but nothing important.

A: OK, well, I'm going to look at (11) ______ other flats this afternoon. I'll give you a call this evening.

B: OK, speak to you later.

3 In three of the sentences below, *of* is not necessary. Cross out *of* where it is incorrect.

1 Did you know that there are many of places in the world called London?
2 Most of them are in North America.
3 Many of them are very small towns.
4 However, some of them, like London, Ontario, are big.
5 There are also some of places called London in Africa.
6 Most of people in London, England, have never heard of these other places.

4 Choose the best quantifier to complete the sentences.

1 My flat's really nice but the neighbours make *a lot of* / *not enough* / *too many* noise.
2 There's *a few* / *not many* / *too much* traffic in my street.
3 My flat's quite small and there's *a lot of* / *not enough* / *too many* space when we have visitors.
4 I often invite *a few* / *not much* / *too much* friends for dinner in the evenings.
5 I'm looking for a new flat because this one costs *a little* / *not enough* / *too much* money.
6 I like going out so I only spend *a few* / *a little* / *a lot of* time at home.
7 I've lived in *many* / *not much* / *too much* different places, but this is my favourite.
8 There's *a few* / *not much* / *too many* nightlife in this part of town.

5 Look at the map on page 32 and complete the directions from the train station to the bars and restaurants near the river.

of	bridge	to (x2)	out	go	take	on

When you come (1) ______ of the train station, turn right. Walk along this road and then (2) ______ the first street (3) ______ your right. You go under a (4) ______ and then you come to the castle. (5) ______ left and follow this road. Keep to the right and you'll come (6) ______ the river. The bars and restaurants are on the other side (7) ______ the Tyne Bridge next (8) ______ the river.

6 Work with a partner. Choose one of the places in the box. Give directions to this place from your school, but do not say the name of the place. Your partner must guess which place you are talking about.

art gallery	bus station	cinema	museum
nightclub	park	shopping centre	theatre

4 | Review

1 Each of the advertisements below contains three mistakes. Correct the mistakes.

File Edit View Favourites Tools Help Links

Muriel
Why do so many pen pals wants a romantic relationship? It doesn't interest me! I am happily married and has two childen. I just want to find out more about life in other countries. The world is a big place. Are you want to know more about life in New Zealand? Write!
Click here.

File Edit View Favourites Tools Help Links

Steffi
Hi, everyone! Does you want to write to me once or twice a week? My ideal pen pal lives in South America, studies English and (like me) don't find it easy to make friends in their home town. He (or she) likes books and movies and want a friend in a different country.
Click here.

File Edit View Favourites Tools Help Links

Jamal
Do you study at university or college? Do you want to improves your English? I likes talking about sport and music and travel. Do you share my interests? I am live in Sweden, but I come from Tunisia. Get in touch!
Click here.

2 Put the words in brackets in the correct place in the sentences.

1 We don't go out on our own. (*often*)
2 We have arguments about little things. (*sometimes*)
3 We share all the housework. (*usually*)
4 We speak on the phone. (*six times a day*)
5 We talk about our day at work. (*every evening*)
6 We tell each other all our secrets. (*always*)
7 We want to have children. (*never*)
8 We wear the same colour clothes. (*often*)

3 Complete the phrases with *in*, *on* or *at*.

1 ______ 1917
2 ______ Friday afternoon
3 ______ lunchtime
4 ______ October
5 ______ the start of the lesson
6 ______ the weekend
7 ______ February 29
8 ______ half past two
9 ______ New Year's Day
10 ______ Sunday
11 ______ the summer holidays
12 ______ the winter

4 Put the verbs in brackets into the present simple or the present continuous.

A: ______ (*you / have*) a boyfriend at the moment?
B: Yes, I ______ (*go*) out with a guy called Paul.
A: Paul? Paul what? ______ (*I / know*) him?
B: No, I ______ (*not / think*) so. He's a journalist.
A: Really? Who ______ (*he / work*) for?
B: The BBC. He ______ (*make*) a TV programme about English churches.
A: That's interesting! I ______ (*see*) a guy who is interested in old churches.
B: Really? ______ (*you / want*) to meet Paul? He'd love to meet you two.

5 Rearrange the words to make questions.

1 also are English friends studying your ?
2 come does from Scotland teacher your ?
3 do go often restaurants to you ?
4 are jeans today wearing you ?
5 do like your parents travelling ?
6 at is it moment raining the ?

6 Match the short answers to the questions in exercise 5.

a No, I'm not.
b No, they don't.
c No, they're not.
d Yes, I do.
e Yes, it is.
f Yes, she does.

7 Now give answers that are true for you to the questions in exercise 5.

8 In each suggestion/response below, there is one word missing. Insert the missing word.

1 How tomorrow? Dinner at my place tomorrow?
2 I'd rather. I'm always tired afterwards.
3 It's kind you, but I have an evening class this evening.
4 Well, why don't meet after your class?
5 Would you like come to dinner this evening?
6 Yes, why not? I'd love.

9 Rearrange the lines in exercise 8 to make a dialogue. Practise the dialogue with a partner.

5 | Review

1 Philip has planned a weekend in Poland. Continue the description of his plans using *going to* + infinitive or present continuous.

He is arriving in Krakow on Friday evening and then he is going to look for a hotel. On Saturday morning, he …

2 Make questions/sentences from the prompts. Use *going to* + infinitive or the present continuous.

1 **A:** how / he / get / to Krakow ?
  B: he / catch / a plane / from Heathrow
2 **A:** he / buy / a guide book ?
  B: no / his friends / show him around
3 **A:** he / visit / other Polish cities ?
  B: no / he / not have / enough time
4 **A:** why / he / stay / only two days ?
  B: he / go back / to Poland / next year

3 Choose the correct form to complete the dialogues.

1 **A:** Have you got a single room for two nights?
  B: I think so. *I'll just check / I'm just going to check.*
2 **A:** Would you like a room with a view? It's a bit more expensive.
  B: No thanks. *I'll have / I'm going to have* the cheaper room.
3 **A:** Do you want to book a table for dinner?
  B: No thanks. *I'll have / I'm going to have* dinner with some friends.
4 **A:** Could you give me a wake-up call in the morning?
  B: Yes, sir. *We'll do / We're going to do* that for you.
5 **A:** Do you need a taxi?
  B: No thanks. A friend *will come / is coming* to pick me up.

4 Complete the sentences. Put the verbs in brackets into the correct form.

1 I'm interested in ________ (*hear*) more about your special offers.
2 I would like ________ (*spend*) a couple of weeks in the Swiss Alps.
3 I want ________ (*climb*) a few mountains.
4 I hope ________ (*do*) some sky diving as well.
5 I intend ________ (*take*) my own equipment.
6 I'm planning ________ (*go*) there in the late spring.
7 I'm looking forward to ________ (*hear*) from you.

5 In the dialogue below there are six mistakes. Correct the mistakes.

A: Good morning, sir. How can I help you?

B: Yes, I've got a ticket to London for tomorrow morning and I wonder if could I change it for a flight in the evening.

A: I'll see what I can do. Could I to see your ticket and passport, please?

B: Yes, of course. Here you are.

A: No problem. About what time do you want to leave?

B: I'd like take the last flight, please.

A: I'm afraid but the last flight is fully booked, but we have a seat on the 19.35.

B: That's fine. Can I having a window seat, please?

A: I sorry, but I can't do that for you now. Ask when you get to check-in.

B: OK.

A: Could you just sign here, please?

6 Complete the sentences with a word from the box.

air conditioning	facilities	lift	location
room service	shower	twin	

1 The hotel has excellent ________ with a fantastic gym and sauna.
2 It has an incredible ________ near the cable car station.
3 We asked for a room with a ________ and toilet.
4 We wanted a double room but they only had one with ________ beds.
5 The ________ didn't work and, unfortunately, our room was on the sixth floor.
6 It's very hot here, but all the rooms have ________.
7 In the mornings, we telephoned ________ and had breakfast in bed.

6 | Review

1 Replace the adjectives in the sentences below with their opposites. Choose from the adjectives in the box.

artificial	authentic	boring	delicious	empty
expensive	traditional	slow	unhealthy	weak

1 We had an extremely cheap meal last night.
2 The food was quite interesting, especially the dessert.
3 It was a very healthy menu, too.
4 Everything was really modern.
5 The service was a bit fast.
6 I'm not surprised that the restaurant was fairly full.

2 Put the adjectives in brackets into the comparative form. Then complete the sentences with your own ideas.

1 It's often ______ (*cheap*) to do your shopping at the market than …
2 Pizza is usually ______ (*popular*) with children than …
3 For breakfast, it's ______ (*good*) to eat fruit and yoghurt than …
4 Fruit and vegetables are ______ (*healthy*) for you than …
5 I often have a ______ (*big*) lunch on Sundays than …
6 I think that Chinese food is ______ (*interesting*) than …
7 Having a healthy diet is ______ (*important*) than …
8 It's ______ (*easy*) to cook pasta than …

3 Complete the questions. Put the adjectives into the superlative form.

1 What is ______ (*good*) night to go out in your town?
2 Who is ______ (*strong*) student in your class?
3 What is ______ (*bad*) time of day for you?
4 Which is ______ (*busy*) street in your town?
5 Which is ______ (*expensive*) shop in your town?
6 Which is ______ (*hot*) month of the year?
7 Who is ______ (*calm*) person you know?
8 Who is ______ (*famous*) person in your country?

4 Work in pairs. Ask and answer the questions in exercise 3.

5 Some of the meals below are very strange. Put a cross (✗) next to the strange meals.

1 bacon and eggs
2 caviar doughnuts
3 chicken and rice
4 chocolate cookies
5 coffee noodles
6 ham and yoghurt
7 lemon sorbet
8 pasta and tomato sauce
9 peanut butter crisps
10 potato salad
11 steak and chips
12 strawberry ice cream

6 Put the adjectives in brackets into the correct form.

Ristorante Palio

For a good, honest meal, you won't find (1) ______ (*good*) than this. It serves traditional Italian food and it's (2) ______ (*authentic*) than other Italian restaurants in town. The service is (3) ______ (*slow*) than we would like, but it's a lot (4) ______ (*friendly*).

★★★

The Cut

The Cut is probably (5) ______ (*fashionable*) restaurant in the centre of town. It's got (6) ______ (*loud*) music and (7) ______ (*uncomfortable*) chairs, but it seems that everyone wants to go there. The prices are (8) ______ (*high*) than the other restaurants in the area, but for (9) ______ (*unforgettable*) night out, this is the place to go.

★★★★

7 Put the sentences into two groups:

1 making a reservation for a restaurant
2 in a restaurant

a Certainly, madam. For how many people?
b Have you got anything for nine o'clock?
c Hello. We have a reservation for two people. The name is Wilson.
d I'd like to book a table for this evening, please.
e It's just for two people.
f Lovely. It is a non-smoking table, isn't it?
g No, thanks. Just the menu, please.
h This is the Taj Mahal. How can I help you?
i What time would you like?
j Yes, madam. A table for two at nine. We look forward to seeing you.
k Yes, madam. Let me show you your table. It's over there, by the window.
l Yes, madam. Would you like something to drink now?

8 Now put the sentences in exercise 7 in the correct order to make two dialogues.

Dialogue 1 ___ ___ ___ ___ ___ ___ ___
Dialogue 2 ___ ___ ___ ___ ___

7 Review

1 Complete the sentences. Put the verbs in brackets into the present perfect simple.

1 She ___ (*apply*) for the senior manager's job, but she doesn't have much experience.
2 She ___ (*be*) very stressed at work and she gets angry very quickly.
3 She ___ (*already / leave*) – she hates waiting.
4 She ___ (*do*) lots of different training courses, so she can do almost anything in the office now.
5 She ___ (*never / need*) to ask for help from the boss.
6 She ___ (*think*) of some unusual new ways to recruit staff.

2 Choose the correct word to complete the sentences.

a She hasn't got a lot of *patience / patient*.
b She's extremely *skilled / skills*.
c She's got a lot of *imagination / imaginative*.
d She's probably too *ambition / ambitious*.
e She's very *emotion / emotional* at the moment.
f She's very *independence / independent* at work.

3 Match the sentences in exercise 2 to the sentences in exercise 1.

4 Complete the sentences. Put the verbs in brackets into the present perfect simple or the past simple.

1 I ___ (*drive*) the president to the airport yesterday.
2 I ___ (*not / give*) him his medicine yet.
3 I ___ (*be*) on the cover of three different women's magazines.
4 I ___ (*make*) six films but I usually work in the theatre.
5 I ___ (*never / have*) a customer who was so hungry.
6 In my last job, I ___ (*work*) for the company that is building a bridge over the river.
7 Last week, I ___ (*write*) an article about the salaries of top businessmen.
8 You are the best student that I ___ (*ever / have*)!

5 Match the sentences in exercise 4 to one of the jobs in the box.

actor	chauffeur	engineer	journalist	model
nurse	teacher	waitress		

6 Work in pairs. Choose four more jobs and write a sentence (as in exercise 4) for each one. Your partner must guess the job.

7 Complete the sentences with a word from the box.

apply	career	company	course	fired	leave
living	salary	unemployment			

1 Why did you ___ for this job?
  a) Because I've got no money and the ___ is good.
  b) I've always wanted to work for this ___.
2 Why did you ___ your last job?
  a) My boss hated me and I was ___.
  b) Because I wanted a more interesting ___.
3 What do you do for a ___ at the moment?
  a) I'm between jobs, but I'm doing a training ___ in personnel management.
  b) I get ___ benefit.

horoscope	manager	experience
charge	responsible	get

4 Have you ever been in ___ of other people?
  a) Yes, I was ___ for a team of five people in my last job.
  b) No, I haven't. I've never been a ___.
5 Why do you think you should ___ this job?
  a) My ___ said this was my lucky day.
  b) I think I have the right ___ and personal qualities.

8 Choose the best answers to the questions in exercise 7. Then work in pairs and practise the interview with your partner.

9 Complete the dialogue with a phrase from the box.

do you think I should	how about	if I were you
what should I	why don't you	you should

A: I hate this job. (1) ___ leave?
B: Not yet. (2) ___ wait until you find another one.
A: I haven't got the time at the moment.
B: (3) ___ taking a day off so you can look for something else?
A: (4) ___ tell the boss?
B: (5) ___ ring and say you're not well.
A: I can't do that!
B: Why not? I'd take a few days off (6) ___.

8 | Review

1 Rearrange the words to complete the (unsuccessful) predictions.

1 a be not popular way will
The telephone ________________ of communicating. (1876)
2 able be machines never will
Heavy ________________ to fly. (1895)
3 actors hear to want won't
People ________________ talking in films. (1927)
4 be four might possible sell to
It ________________ or five computers. (1943)
5 future may more no the weigh
Computers in ________________ than 1.5 tons. (1949)
6 never television the use will
We ________________ for entertainment. (1955)
7 a computer people that want will
I don't think ________________ in their homes. (1977)

2 In four of the sentences below there are grammatical mistakes. Correct the mistakes.

1 Computers will definitely get smaller and smaller.
2 English definitely won't be an important language fifty years from now.
3 It won't be possibly necessary to find new sources of energy.
4 Military engineers will probably develop more powerful lasers.
5 Scientists maybe will find a way to travel in time.
6 The world's population will possibly double before the end of the century.
7 There won't be probably another world war.
8 We perhaps will make contact with aliens in the next few years.

3 Decide if the sentences describe predictions or plans. Then choose the correct verb form to complete the sentences.

1 *Are you going to / Will you* watch the football on TV this evening?
2 Do you think the talk *is going to / will* be interesting?
3 *I'm going to / I'll* check my email when I get home.
4 *It's going to / It will* be more difficult for young people to find a job.
5 New kinds of medicine *are going to / will* make us all live longer.
6 *We're going to / We'll* buy a new car next month.
7 Why *is she going to / will she* live in Japan?
8 *You're never going to / You'll never* see a more frightening film.

4 Put *if* in the correct place in the sentences below.

1 He won't like it you do that.
2 I have time, I'll come and see you.
3 I need some money, I'll ask the bank.
4 I'll help you you like.
5 They'll be very sad you go away.
6 We don't leave soon, we'll be late.
7 We'll miss the plane we don't hurry.
8 You'll be ill you eat that.

5 Choose the correct verb form to complete the text.

If the world's population (1) *continues / will continue* to rise, it (2) *becomes / will become* more and more difficult to feed everyone. Some scientists think that genetically modified (GM) food is the answer. But not everyone agrees. We will need more research before we (3) *know / will know* if GM food is really safe, they say. For example, what (4) *happens / will happen* to ordinary plants and animals if we (5) *grow / will grow* GM food on our farms? The GM companies say there is no danger. They say that when farmers (6) *use / will use* GM crops, they (7) *need / will need* fewer chemicals on their farms. And if we (8) *use / will use* fewer chemicals, our food (9) *is / will be* healthier to eat.

6 Put the instructions below in the correct order.

☐ all, click on 'Tools' on the main toolbar. Next,
☐ that says 'current selection'. After that, choose the dictionary that
☐ the word that you want to translate and click on the button
☐ select 'Language' and click on 'Translate'. You
☐ you will see the translation in the box.
☐ You can probably use your computer to translate words into English. First of
☐ you want to use. Finally, click on the 'Go' button and
☐ will then see a 'Translate' window on your screen. Highlight

7 Choose the best adjective to complete the questions about your town.

1 What is *important / impossible* for a visitor to know?
2 Where is it *unhealthy / unusual* to see tourists?
3 Where is it *easy / healthy* to park in the centre of town?
4 When is it *legal / usual* for people to eat?
5 Where is it *illegal / possible* to buy English books?
6 When is it *difficult / safe* to find a taxi in your town?
7 At what age is it *healthy / legal* to go to a nightclub?
8 When is it *dangerous / important* to walk in the park?

8 Work in pairs. Ask and answer the questions.

9 | Review

1 Choose the correct word to complete the sentences.

1 At what time in the evening do you usually get *tired* / *tiring*?
2 Do you ever get *annoyed* / *annoying* with your best friend? Why?
3 What do you do when you are *bored* / *boring*?
4 What's the most *excited* / *exciting* thing you've ever done?
5 When was the last time you felt really *frightened* / *frightening*?
6 Where was your most *disappointed* / *disappointing* holiday?
7 Who is the most *interested* / *interesting* person you've ever met?

2 Work in pairs. Ask and answer the questions in exercise 1.

3 Complete the text. Put the verbs in brackets into the present simple passive.

China Central Television (CCTV) (1) _______ (*own*) by the Chinese government. It receives some money from the government but programmes (2) _______ (*pay*) for with advertising money. It has thirteen different channels and these are called CCTV-1, CCTV-2, CCTV-3, etc. Programmes (3) _______ (*make*) in three different languages: Mandarin, Fujian dialect and English.
The most popular programme is the news, which (4) _______ (*watch*) by more than 300 million people every day. Soap operas are also very popular and the stars of the shows (5) _______ (*know*) to millions of people.
The English language programmes (6) _______ (*show*) on CCTV-9. It has a variety of programmes, including news, business news, documentaries and sport. For foreigners it is interesting because current affairs (7) _______ (*look*) at from a Chinese point of view. CCTV (8) _______ (*see*) by many viewers in the US.

4 Complete the questions with a verb from the box. Use the past simple passive.

call direct hit play receive save win build

1 When and where _______ the *Titanic* _______?
2 What _______ the captain of the ship _______?
3 How many warnings about icebergs _______ _______ by the ship?
4 When _______ the ship finally _______ by an iceberg?
5 How many people _______ _______ from the ship?
6 Who _______ the film _______ by?
7 Who _______ the main roles in the film _______ by?
8 How many Oscars® _______ _______ by the movie?

5 The information below gives you the answers to the questions in exercise 4. Use the information to make sentences about the *Titanic*.

1 *The Titanic was built in 1911 in Belfast.*

1 in 1911 in Belfast
2 Edward Smith
3 six, or possibly seven
4 at 11.40 pm on April 14th 1912
5 about 700
6 James Cameron
7 Kate Winslet and Leonardo DiCaprio
8 eleven

6 Complete the text. Put the verbs in brackets into the correct present simple form: active or passive.

The Simpsons is probably the most popular TV show in the world. It (1) _______ (*watch*) in more than 70 countries around the world. It's also expensive to buy. In the UK, Channel 4 (2) _______ (*pay*) £700,000 for every episode.
The show's creator, Matt Groening, (3) _______ (*write*) other cartoons for TV and newspapers. In one episode of *The Simpsons*, we (4) _______ (*see*) Groening signing books. He (5) _______ (*introduce*) as the creator of the TV show, *Futurama*.
The characters in *The Simpsons* (6) _______ (*base*) on Groening's own family. Groening's father, for example, (7) _______ (*call*) Homer and his mother Margaret. The main characters (8) _______ (*play*) by a team of actors. It (9) _______ (*think*) that these actors (10) _______ (*earn*) more than $250,000 for every episode. From time to time, famous Hollywood actors like Mel Gibson or Danny DeVito (11) _______ (*star*) in the show.

7 Rearrange the lines to make a dialogue at a box office.

☐ Certainly, I'll see what we've got available. Which show do you want – the Friday or the Saturday?
☐ Could you hold on and I'll check for you? No, I'm afraid that's sold out, but we've got seats in the stalls for the Saturday.
☐ Fine. Can I pay by credit card?
☐ Hi. I'd like ten tickets for the Beenie Man concert, please.
☐ OK, that's ten tickets for Beenie Man on the Saturday. That will be £180 altogether, sir.
☐ That's fine. Ten, please.
☐ The Friday. Downstairs in the stalls if that's possible.
☐ Yes, of course. Could I take your details, please?

10 Review

1 Complete the sentences with *for* or *since*.

1 She's seen many different specialists ________ the illness started.
2 She hasn't had a cough ________ she was a child.
3 She's had high blood pressure ________ the last few days.
4 She's lost a lot of weight ________ the beginning of the year.
5 She's felt exhausted ________ a week or two.
6 Her back has been painful ________ about ten days.
7 She's taken five days off work ________ the problems began.
8 She hasn't taken antibiotics ________ a long time.

2 Complete the text. Put the verbs in brackets into the past simple or the present perfect simple.

When Valerie Brasseur (1) ________ (*finish*) nursing school, there was only thing that she (2) ________ (*want*) to do. For the last six months, Valerie (3) ________ (*be*) in the Sudan where she is working as a nurse for the organization Médecins Sans Frontières (Doctors Without Borders).
A group of French doctors (4) ________ (*begin*) the organization in 1971. Since then, MSF (5) ________ (*provide*) medical help in more than 80 countries around the world. Because the staff work in countries at war, MSF (6) ________ (*never / be*) out of the news and, in 1999, it (7) ________ (*win*) the Nobel Peace Prize.
Valerie (8) ________ (*know*) about MSF since she was 18 – the year that she (9) ________ (*leave*) home and (10) ________ (*go*) to nursing school. It was also the year that her parents (11) ________ (*begin*) to work for the organization. Because Valerie is in the Sudan and her parents in Central America, she (12) ________ (*not / see*) them for over eighteen months.

3 In the dialogue below there are six grammatical mistakes. Correct the mistakes.

A: Good morning, Mr Riley. I didn't see you for at least two weeks. What's wrong with you?

B: It's my chest, doctor. It's been really painful.

A: How long do you have the pain?

B: Since I stopped smoking.

A: When exactly have you stopped smoking?

B: Oh, I stopped the day before yesterday.

A: So you haven't had a cigarette since two days?

B: Yes, I've found it very difficult.

A: Where exactly does it hurt?

B: Here and here and here. I feel awful.

A: Anything else?

B: Well, I am under a lot of stress in the last few days.

A: I see. Take off your shirt. I'll have a look at you. Yes, it's as I thought. It's normal, I'm afraid, when people stop smoking.

B: Can you give me a prescription for it?

A: No, but come back and see me if the pain hasn't been away in the next few days, OK?

4 Choose the best way to continue the mini-dialogues below.

1 She's been to see the doctor.
a) What did the doctor say?
b) What time did she leave?
2 I went to the station this morning to say goodbye to my parents.
a) Where have they been?
b) Where have they gone?
3 Where has your boss gone?
a) I don't know. He didn't want to say.
b) He's just had a week's holiday in Tunisia.
4 I played golf at the new club near the river at the weekend.
a) Oh, I've been there, too.
b) Oh, I've gone there, too.
5 So, is this the first time you've seen the new hospital?
a) Yes, I've been away a long time.
b) Yes, I've gone away a long time.

5 Complete the questions with a word from the box.

check-up	operation	pressure	specialist
suffer	symptoms	treatment	weight

1 Do you ever ________ from stress?
2 Have you ever been to hospital for an ________?
3 How long do you have to wait for an appointment with a ________?
4 How often should you see a doctor for a ________?
5 What are the ________ of flu?
6 What is the best ________ for a hangover?
7 What is the best way to lose ________?
8 What should you do if you have high blood ________?

6 Work with a partner. Ask and answer the questions in exercise 1.

11 Review

1 Combine the pairs of sentences with an infinitive of purpose and make any necessary changes.

1 He needs a new suit to wear for his interview.

1 He needs a new suit. He'll wear it for his interview.
2 He bought a new car. He wanted to impress his girlfriend.
3 She called the restaurant. She booked a table for this evening.
4 He spoke to his boss. He asked for a pay rise.
5 She went to the changing room. She tried on the jeans.
6 She's started swimming. She's hoping to get fit.
7 He used a thesaurus. He found a better word.
8 She always reads the newspaper. She looks at her horoscope.

2 Choose the best explanation for the signs.

1 **Credit Cards welcome**

a) You can't pay by credit card.
b) You don't have to pay by cash.
c) You have to pay by cash.

2 **WE DO NOT ACCEPT CHEQUES UNDER £20**

a) You can pay by cheque if it's more than £20.
b) You can't pay by cheque if it's more than £20.
c) You have to pay by cheque if it's more than £20.

3 **Buy 2 packets – Get 1 free**

a) You can't buy more than two packets.
b) You don't have to pay for the third packet.
c) You have to buy three packets.

4 **NO DOGS ALLOWED**

a) You can't bring dogs in here.
b) You don't have to bring dogs in here.
c) You must have a dog.

5 **STAFF TOILET ONLY**

a) Customers can use this toilet.
b) Customers have to find another toilet.
c) Staff can't use this toilet.

6 **BUY NOW, PAY LATER (12 MONTHS FREE CREDIT)**

a) You can't pay later.
b) You don't have to spend anything now.
c) You must pay now.

3 Match the sentences 1–5 to the sentences a–e.

1 At my primary school, all the boys had to wear a uniform.
2 When it was cold in winter, we didn't have to wear shorts.
3 The girls couldn't wear trousers.
4 We couldn't wear trainers.
5 The teachers had to wear black gowns.

a Some of them also wore a funny hat, but they didn't have to.
b The school rules said we could only have black shoes.
c It was grey shorts, a grey jacket and tie.
d They had grey skirts or a grey dress in the summer.
e We could wear trousers instead.

4 Rewrite the sentences with the present or past form of *can/can't, have to/don't have to.*

1 A few years ago, it was possible to smoke almost anywhere.
You ________________________.
2 Was it necessary for you to wait a long time?
Did ________________________.
3 It isn't necessary to say 'Sorry' all the time.
You ________________________.
4 It was impossible to find anywhere to park my car.
I ________________________.
5 It was necessary to get a new car after the accident.
We ________________________.
6 It's necessary for me to work overtime this evening.
I ________________________.
7 Hats are not allowed in many churches.
You ________________________.

5 Correct the mistakes in the sentences below.

1 Can you tell me where the change room is, please?
2 Do you like shopping for clothe?
3 Excuse me, have you got this suit on a darker colour?
4 I like this top. Can I try on it?
5 I really like your jeans. Where did you get it?
6 I'm sorry, this doesn't suit. Can I try another size?
7 She's gone to the department store to buy some underwears.
8 What size trouser do you take?

12 Review

1 Complete the sentences with a preposition from the box.

across	along	around	out of	over	past	through	into

1 How long does it take a supersonic jet to fly _______ the world?
2 Schumacher got _______ his car and waited for the race to begin.
3 She plans to swim _______ the Straits of Gibraltar between Spain and Morocco.
4 The bus drove _______ the bus stop without stopping.
5 The prisoners climbed _______ the wall and escaped from the prison.
6 There was a lot of traffic in the city centre and it was difficult to get _______.
7 What time do you get _______ class after your lesson?
8 You need to drive _______ this road for about five miles.

2 Complete the phrasal verbs in the sentences below.

1 Marco Polo's family called _______ their plan to travel to China by sea and decided to go by land instead.
2 Columbus had many problems crossing the Atlantic, but he decided to carry _______.
3 Roald Amundsen gave _______ his attempt to go to the North Pole because of the start of the First World War in 1914.
4 Amelia Earhart often had to put _______ her flights for a few days because of the weather.
5 Humboldt often needed to sort _______ diplomatic problems before he could travel.
6 Neil Armstrong's Apollo 11 mission took _______ from the Kennedy Space Centre in Florida.

3 Choose the correct form to complete the sentences.

1 Do you know anyone *which is* / *who is* / *who are* homeless?
2 Hungary is a country *that has* / *that have* / *who have* no sea coast.
3 I never eat food *that is* / *which are* / *who is* genetically modified.
4 I was surprised that there were some people *that has* / *who has* / *who have* never heard of Marco Polo.
5 It's a journey *that take* / *which takes* / *who takes* more than five days.
6 The newspaper showed pictures of protesters *that was* / *which were* / *who were* in the trees.
7 There are many mysteries *that has* / *which has* / *which have* never been solved.
8 There are some English accents *that is* / *that are* / *which is* very difficult to understand.

4 Read the newspaper article below. Put the relative clauses a–h in the gaps 1–8.

a that led to Jaschan's arrest
b that protects them from the Sasser worm
c that were found in his home
d who were responsible for another virus, Netsky
e who has admitted creating the Sasser computer virus
f who have problems with their computers
g who knew the identity of the virus creator
h which closed down their machines

Police arrest virus writer

GERMAN POLICE have arrested Sven Jaschan, a teenager (1) _______. They have also taken a number of computers and disks (2) _______.

The virus first appeared on the internet on May 1 of this year. Millions of computer-users around the world were hit by the virus (3) _______. Some businesses had to close temporarily so that they could install software (4) _______.

It is understood that the police received a phone call from someone (5) _______. Microsoft® said that they would pay for information (6) _______.

Jaschan, an 18-year old high school student from Rotenburg, wrote the virus alone. However, police believe that he was also part of a group of people (7) _______.

Jaschan's mother runs a company from the family home. The company provides help to people (8) _______.

5 Complete the sentences with a word from the box.

conservation	engineering	global	homeless	organic	poverty	viruses	wage

1 The government should increase the minimum _______.
2 We shouldn't worry too much about _______ warming.
3 People who design computer _______ must be crazy.
4 I think _______ food is a waste of money.
5 There's always a strong connection between _______ and crime.
6 Animal _______ is not a very important issue.
7 Genetic _______ is the solution to the world's food problems.
8 There will probably be more and more _______ people on the streets.

6 Work in pairs. Discuss your responses to the opinions in exercise 5.

Macmillan Education
4 Crinan Street
London N1 9XW
A division of Macmillan Publishers Limited

Companies and representatives throughout the world

ISBN 978-0-230-41400-6 Student's Book
ISBN 978-0-230-42446-3 Student's Book & website access

This edition published 2012
First edition published 2005

Designed by eMC Design Ltd.
Original design by Oliver Design
Illustrated Rowan Barnes-Murphy: pp52, 53, 102-103, 112; Russ Cook: pp127, 129; Stephen Dew: p33; Mark Duffin: pp80, 81; Tony Forbes: pp118-119; Martin Sanders: p29
Cover design by eMC Design Ltd.
Cover photograph by Corbis/Roger Tidman, Getty Images/Doug Chinnery, Alamy/Robert Harding Picture Library Ltd, Corbis/Lois Ellen Frank, Corbis/Gerolf Kalt, Alamy/Images & Stories.
Picture research by Sally Cole

Author's acknowledgements
The author would like to thank Nicola Gardner for her sterling work as Content Editor. He would also like to express his debt of gratitude to Louise Fonceca, editor for the Pre-intermediate level, the designers at eMc Design Limited, Sally Cole for picture research and James Richardson for the sound recording, who all played vital roles in the development of this new edition. Finally, he would like to thank Katy Wright and the late David Riley, the driving forces behind the first edition of Straightforward.

The publishers would like to thank all the teachers from around the world who provided invaluable comments, suggestions and feedback on the first edition. The publishers would also like to thank the following people for their help and contribution to the second edition:
Tatiana Baytimerova (Russia), Lenka Boehmová (Czech Republic), Dr. Manuel Padilla Cruz (Spain), Svetlana Elchaninova (Russia), Jennifer Diaz Green (Dublin), Elena Mokeeva (Romania), Lynn Thomson (freelance editor), Amany Shawkey (Macmillan Egypt), Maria Teresa Rius Villaplana (Spain), Natalia Vorobyeva (Russia).

The author and publishers are grateful for permission to reprint the following copyright material:
Page 6: Material about '*The Boehmer Family*', reproduced with kind permission of Judy & Larry Boehmer.

The authors and publishers would like to thank the following for permission to reproduce their photographs:
Alamy/G.Allison p100(D), Alamy/G.Andrushko p51(H), Alamy/Artostock p107(tr), Alamy/R.Bamber p109(tm), Alamy/A.Bramwell p42(ml), Alamy/J. Collins p106(A), Alamy/T.Cordoza p106(E), Alamy/M.Dembinsky Photo Associates p79(tr), Alamy/Denkou Images p113(tl), Alamy/C.Ehlers p6-7(b),Alamy/Fancy p110(tl), Alamy/I.Miles-Flashpoint Pictures p153(tr), Alamy/A. Fox p23(mr), Alamy/C.Franklin p6(br), Alamy/J.Greenberg p31(bl), Alamy/J. Henshall p38(tm), Alamy/D.Hurst p106(J), Alamy/ICP p106(H), Alamy/Imagebroker p106(I), Alamy/mediablitzimages (uk) Ltd p47(L), Alamy/O. Maksymenko p106(G),106(B), Alamy/Motoring Picture Library p106(b), Alamy/N.Rains p150(tr), Alamy/I.Nolan p107(mr), Alamy/NSP p6(tr), Alamy/D. Red p126(ml), Alamy/G.Roebuck p38(tr), Alamy/A.Segre p110(tr), Alamy/P. Springett 01 p51(G), Alamy/Studiomode p47(G), Alamy/S.Toren p126(bl), Alamy/The Photolibrary Wales p18(mr), Alamy/Wildscape p96(C), Alamy/WoodyStock p126(br); **Apple Inc** p126(bml); **Bananastock** p22(br); **Blend Images** p12(b); **BrandX** p56(burger); **Bridgeman Art Library**/Shepherdess, Montfoucault,1875(oil on canvas),Pissarro Camille(1831-1903)/Private Collection/Photo(c)Christies Images p86, Bridgeman Art Library/Christopher Columbus (colour litho)/Private Collection p116(tl); **Judy Boehmer** p7(ml); **Comstock Images** p56(crisps); **Corbis** pp38(tml),39(br), 38(tl), 38(tmr), 47(C), 116(m), Corbis/Beathan p101(bl), Corbis/H.Berggren p106(F), Corbis/Bettmann Archive p116(tm), 116(tr), 116(mr), Corbis/G.Breloer p86(musical), Corbis/L. Chamberlain p22(ml), Corbis/J.Chillingworth p18(bl), Corbis/Chip East p100(A), Corbis/Encyclopedia p50(D), Corbis/C.Farina p86(Lady Gaga), Corbis/S.Hammid p113(bml), Corbis/R.Hellestad p10(mr), Corbis/R.Hutchings p86(club), Corbis/B. Krist p86(clown), Corbis/P.Libera p22(mr), Corbis/L.Manning p101(bm), Corbis/Food Passionates p62(bml), Corbis/A.Peisl p113(tml), Corbis/J.Gress/Reuters p90(b), Corbis/R.Ressmeyer p106(bl), Corbis/Sygma p86(dance), Corbis/P. Turnley 50-51(t), Corbis/Yellow p72(b); **Digital Stock**/Corbis p50(C), **Getty** pp12(br), 56(pizza), (eggs), 106(D),Getty/AFP pp60(E),Getty/ M.Ochs Archives pp6(br), 66(bm), Getty/DEA/G.Cigolini/Veneranda Biblioteca Ambrosiana/De Agostini Picture Library p71, Getty/Lambert/Archive Photos p8(tr), Getty/Archive Photos p66(bl), Getty/Britain on View p153(mr), Getty/A.Dragulin p58(tr), 40(tm), Getty Images Entertainment pp19(bl), 92(mr), Getty/D.Evans p56(doughnut), Getty/R.Glenn p69(tl), Getty/Moviepix p40(tr), Getty/Redferns p92(br), Getty/Getty Images Sport p101(mr), Getty/Stockbyte p126(bmr), Getty/StockImage p42-43(b); **Glow Images**/L.Bobbe p97(t), Glow Images/Designpics p48(tr), Glow Images/B.Merle p31(br), Glow Images/Zoomphotographics p63(tr); **Hard Rock cafe** logo, by permission of The Hard Rock Cafe. p57(mr); Permission granted to reproduce front cover of Angela's Ashes, **Harper Collins/Harper Perennial**;(reissue)edition (3rd Oct 2005) p19tr; **Hulton Archive** p40(tl); **Robert Harding**/Age fotostock p31(t); **Ronald Grant Archive**/Paramount Pictures/Cruise Wagner Productions p67(b); **Iconica** pp20(mr), 96(D); **Image Bank** pp17(b), 61(br), 78, 96(A); **Imagesource** pp56(tl), 100(E); **Kobal**/BBC Films p41(mr), Kobal/Touchstone Pictures p41(br); **Macmillan Publishers Ltd** p47(J), Macmillan Publishers Ltd/P.Bricknell p47(D), Macmillan Publishers Ltd/Haddon Davies pp26(tr), 108(tr), Macmillan Publishers Ltd/R.Judges/D.Dubber p47(A), Macmillan Publishers Ltd/D.Tolley/D.Ryan pp 47(K),106(C); **Magnum Photos**/S. McCurry pp120(tl),120(m), 120(tr); **Mayhem UK Ltd** p80(A), 80(B),80(C),80(E); **Mixa co Ltd** p58(bm), **Oxfam**/G.Sayer p123(tr),Oxfam Logo p123; **Photolibrary** pp60(A), 80(D), Photolibrary/P.Adams p28(b), Photolibrary/Bilderlounge p99(br), Photolibrary/C.Bluntzer p109(tr), Photolibrary/M.Brigdale p62(tr), Photolibrary/S.Brown p62(bl), Photolibrary/P.Desnerck p62(br), Photolibrary Photolibrary/R.Dirscherl p50(B), Photolibrary/S.Dunwell p22(t),Photolibrary/J. Greim/The Medical File p100(B), Photolibrary/R.Tidman/FLPA p100(F), Photolibrary/Foodcollection p56(icecream), Photolibrary/J.Frechet p100(C), Photolibrary/F.Frei p56(hotdog), Photolibrary/M&A Gibson p49(mr), Photolibrary/R.Giling p60(D), Photolibrary/M.Hamblin p98, Photolibrary/Imagebroker RF p56(fries), Photolibrary/J.Lee p62(bmr), Photolibrary/I. Lishman p16(bl), Photolibrary/RomRom p47(I), Photolibrary/S.Shamsudin p50(A), Photolibrary/C Squared Studios p126(mr), Photolibrary/Britain on View p32(ml), Photolibrary/S.Vidler p111(tr), Photolibrary/W.Whitehurst p122(tr); **Photographers Choice** pp43(bm), 56(cookies), 60(B),109(tl),113(bl); **Photonica** p80(ml); **Razzie Award**/ TM & ©2011, G.R.A.F; **Rex Features** pp10(br), 106(br), Rex/G.Allen p19(bm), Rex/P.Brooker p96(br), Rex/D.Sicolo/Design Pics p47(E),Rex/Paramount/Everett p17(bl), Rex/Columbia Everett p17(br), Rex/Universal/Everett p40(br), Rex/Excel Media p88(br), Rex/20th century Fox/Everett p90(ml), Rex/J.Hannah p106(bm), Rex/Imagesource p47(B), Rex/A.Muir p92-93(b), Rex/Offside p33(t), Rex/J.Pepler p47(H), Rex/Voisin/Phanie p12(m), Rex/Startraks Photo p19(br), Rex/Roger-Voillet p60(c), Rex/E.Welch p101(bm); **Riser** pp21(tr), 80(mr), 110(b); **Science Photo Library**/J-P. Metsavainio p76; **Stockbyte** p47(F); **Stone** pp37(bmr), 82(tr), 96(B); **Taxi** pp68(b), 83(mr); **Topfoto**/D. Porges/ArenaPal p86(orchestra), Topfoto/Image Works p12(mr), Topfoto/Topham Picturepoint pp51(E), 56(br).

Printed and bound in Great Britain by Ashford Colour Press Ltd

2018
17